George Melhuish
1916–1985

ARTIST · PHILOSOPHER

GEORGE MELHUISH
1916–1985

ARTIST · PHILOSOPHER

Michael de Cossart

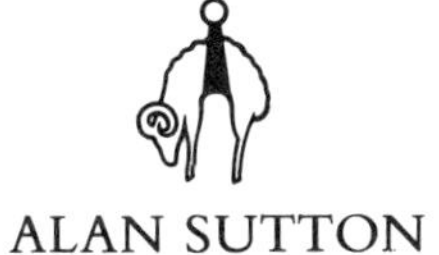

ALAN SUTTON

First published in the United Kingdom in 1990 by
Alan Sutton Publishing Ltd · Brunswick Road · Gloucester

First published in the United States of America in 1990 by
Alan Sutton Publishing Inc · Wolfeboro Falls · NH 03896–0848

British Library Cataloguing in Publication Data

De Cossart, Michael *1944– 1989*
George Melhuish : artist, philosopher.
1. English paintings. Melhuish, George 1916
I. Title
759.2

ISBN 0-86299-588-4

Library of Congress Cataloging in Publication Data applied for

Typeset in Bembo 10/12,
Typesetting and origination by
Alan Sutton Publishing Limited,
Printed in Great Britain by
Dotesios Printers Limited

CONTENTS

ACKNOWLEDGEMENTS

I undertook the work for this present volume at the invitation of the Trustees of George Melhuish's estate, the National Westminster Bank, Trustee Branch in Bristol. I should like to acknowledge their help and general forbearance. In particular I must thank Mr Colin Rickard and Mr Colin Clubb.

Otherwise so many people helped me with their memories of George Melhuish that I feel that I must simply list their names by way of thanks: Mrs Victoria Ayling, Miss Kathleen Beer, Mrs Kay Burnett, Dr Stefan Cembrovitz, Miss Elizabeth Clough, Mrs Margaret Carl Hibbs, Mrs Marjorie Comfort, Mr David Cross, Miss Effie Damoglou, Mrs Charmian Deckers, Mr Percy Edgell, Mrs Helen Gleadow, Miss Jean Glen, Mrs Anne Hewer, the late Mrs Dorothy Irving-Bell, Mr John James, Mr Brian Jenkins, Miss Deborah Jones, Mrs Rosemary King, Mr John and Lady Elisabeth Livingstone, Mrs Edna Macdonald, Miss Rita McKerrow, Mr Dennis Mickleburgh, the late Mrs Dorian Mogg, Mr Bernard Perrin, Dr Kenneth Smith and Mrs Vera Apter Smith, Mrs Christine Jones-Territo, Dr Peter Tiley, Mr Eric Toms, Mrs Muriel Ward-Jackson, the Viscount Weymouth, Mr Arthur White, Mr Jack White, Mr Michael Wishart and Professor Richard Wollheim.

For their material help as well as their sustained interest in my project Mrs Patricia Brennan, Mr Andrew Rogers and Mrs Barbara Thorne deserve a very special word of thanks.

Among the individuals invited by the Melhuish Trustees to advise on my suitability as a biographer were Mr Anthony Hill, Dom Sylvester Houédard OSB and Mr Patrick Hughes. Their help was invaluable and I should like to think that their friendship might be enduring.

It goes without saying that responsibility for material and opinions contained in this book rests entirely with myself.

Michael de Cossart
Liverpool, January 1989

After Dr de Cossart's death in May 1989, I was asked by his wife Linda to act as his literary executor, having been a close friend of the author for many years, and having had some experience in publishing books of my own. As Michael de Cossart had courageously managed to complete his study of George Melhuish in the short time that he knew remained to him, my task has been purely editorial, and it has been a pleasure to assist in a small way in bringing this perspicacious and engaging book before the public.

Robert Orledge
Liverpool, December 1989

ACKNOWLEDGEMENTS

I undertook the work for this present volume at the invitation of the Trustees of George Melhuish's estate, the National Westminster Bank, Trustee Branch in Bristol. I should like to acknowledge their help and general forbearance. In particular I must thank Mr Colin Rickard and Mr Colin Clubb.

Otherwise so many people helped me with their memories of George Melhuish that I feel that I must simply list their names by way of thanks: Mrs Victoria Ayling, Miss Kathleen Beer, Mrs Kay Burnett, Dr Stefan Cembrovitz, Miss Elizabeth Clough, Mrs Margaret Carl Hibbs, Mrs Marjorie Comfort, Mr David Cross, Miss Effie Damoglou, Mrs Charmian Deckers, Mr Percy Edgell, Mrs Helen Gleadow, Miss Jean Glen, Mrs Anne Hewer, the late Mrs Dorothy Irving-Bell, Mr John James, Mr Brian Jenkins, Miss Deborah Jones, Mrs Rosemary King, Mr John and Lady Elisabeth Livingstone, Mrs Edna Macdonald, Miss Rita McKerrow, Mr Dennis Mickleburgh, the late Mrs Dorian Mogg, Mr Bernard Perrin, Dr Kenneth Smith and Mrs Vera Apter Smith, Mrs Christine Jones-Territo, Dr Peter Tiley, Mr Eric Toms, Mrs Muriel Ward-Jackson, the Viscount Weymouth, Mr Arthur White, Mr Jack White, Mr Michael Wishart and Professor Richard Wollheim.

For their material help as well as their sustained interest in my project Mrs Leila Gilmore, Mrs Patricia Brennan, Mr Andrew Rogers and Mrs Barbara Thorne deserve a very special word of thanks.

Among the individuals invited by the Melhuish Trustees to advise on my suitability as a biographer were Mr Anthony Hill, Dom Sylvester Houédard OSB and Mr Patrick Hughes. Their help was invaluable and I should like to think that their friendship might be enduring.

It goes without saying that responsibility for material and opinions contained in this book rests entirely with myself.

Michael de Cossart
Liverpool, January 1989

PART ONE

1916–1939

CHAPTER ONE

MELHUISHES AND SEYMOURS

In 1929, when George Melhuish was around the age of thirteen, he stood in his school playground and made three vows to himself. He resolved never to smoke, never to marry and never to work for anybody in the capacity of an employee. For vows that were couched in such negative terms, they were remarkably positive in their objective. He kept to them and, when he died almost fifty-six years later, he could proudly claim to have observed to the letter his self-imposed rules. In many ways the vows were the necessary foundation upon which he built and developed a remarkable dual career as an artist and as a philosopher of great talent and originality.

George's resolutions were the result of an acute early perception of the realities of life and particularly of the domestic circumstance in which he grew up. His parents had an enormous influence upon his developing mentality, but were blessed with the wisdom to encourage their son's individualism. They recognized that there was something unique about George and allowed their adored child to develop in his own peculiar way. Both his father and mother came from relatively ordinary backgrounds and, in terms of material achievement, did little to leave their mark on the world. But in their son their own aspirations came to fruition.

George's father (and namesake) George Barnett Melhuish was born at 36 Wilson Street in the St Paul's district of Bristol on Christmas Eve 1877, the son of yet another George Melhuish and his wife Emma Barnett. The first George Melhuish was born in 1852 and he and his wife saw the birth of their only son when they were respectively twenty-five and twenty-six years old. By that time George Melhuish was a fairly well-established builder. A self-employed man with a practical bent of mind, he prospered in the mid-Victorian period when the city of Bristol, as a thriving commercial and increasingly industrial centre, expanded in terms of its physical dimensions and population. Almost coincidental was the fact that at the moment of his birth the ratio of town dwellers to country dwellers in England and Wales reached and passed the 50 per cent mark. Houses were in demand, and rented property at prices which the urban proletariat and lower middle class could afford had to be constructed. George Melhuish, the grandfather, was technically a carpenter by trade, but he made a respectable living building and decorating dwellings at the modest end of the market. Photographs of him around the time of his marriage to Emma show him as a tall, strikingly handsome man with an impressive spade-beard and expressive eyes. He is well dressed and has the air of a man who would be quite capable of maintaining in some degree of comfort his wife and the three children that she was to bear him.

The surname Melhuish is not common. Most Melhuishes originally came from the south-west of England, from Devon and particularly from Somerset. Some branches of the family were well-connected. They were landowners and had their seat at Bantow Manor at Tedburn St Mary, a few miles to the west of Exeter. The family may have touched the lower ranks of the country gentry, a fact given social credibility by the existence of several Melhuish coats of arms. The precise lineage back beyond the three Georges, however, is slightly vague, but, to his dying day, George the grandson kept prominently displayed on his wall a lithograph of one of his direct ancestors, Joseph Melhuish. The miniature was engraved by Galpin in 1837 and Joseph is described as being 108 years old. For his age and background he looks extremely lively and self-contained. He must have been born around 1729 when George II (king and elector of Hanover) had just acceded to an uneasily united realm.

George Barnett Melhuish, in contrast, first saw the light of day during the heyday of Victorian imperial confidence. For a boy of his background a career in the armed forces or overseas in the colonies held out the allure of the exotic. After a school career in which he appears to have excelled in mathematics and science subjects, he joined the Royal Navy and was trained as a dispensing pharmacist. In January 1897, at the age of nineteen, he found himself on dry land as a member of the sick-berth staff at the Royal Naval Hospital, Haslar, at Gosport in Hampshire, overlooking the entrance to Portsmouth harbour. A year later, in January 1898, he was transferred to the Royal Naval Hospital at Stonehouse in Plymouth. During this period he apparently enjoyed some popularity with staff and patients alike. A letter, dated 11 October 1898, from a barrister called Frank Evans to Melhuish indicates that he could be trusted to work above and beyond the call of duty. Mr Evans's son had been one of the patients at the hospital and, still not fully recovered, had departed for his home in London's St John's Wood, leaving behind his keys. On his son's behalf Frank Evans sent Melhuish a postal order for five shillings and sixpence: 'He wants you to keep five shillings of this for yourself. The remaining six pence is to cover the postage of the keys.' He then added details of his son's condition and passed on a message from him: 'My son wishes me to say that he was sorry he was obliged to go away without saying good-bye to you, and that he wished to thank you for your attention to him during his illness.'[1] George Melhuish's patient had been Edward Evans, RN, later Captain Evans of the destroyer *Broke* and a member of Captain Robert Falcon Scott's ill-fated expedition to the South Pole in 1911–12. He survived Antarctic conditions, severe scurvy and Scott's disagreeable temperament to become Admiral the Lord Mountevans.

George Melhuish was finally posted to a 'real' naval job when he joined the sick-bay staff of the HMS *Hussar* in 1900. The *Hussar* was an elegant ship of the line whose tours of duty during Melhuish's attachment to its crew included visits to British Mediterranean ports in Malta, Cyprus and Gibraltar, and to non-British ones such as Rapallo and Patras. The only exciting thing that happened was when companion ships the *Dragon* and *Dryad* collided off Argostoli and the *Hussar* had to take the crippled *Dragon* in tow. More intriguing was the port of Alexandria. Here the Bristol boy first met the exotic Orient and caught a hint of the undercurrent of political unease that would soon irrupt and bedevil life in the Middle East. George senior often used to talk about this to his son, how even the ostentatious might of the great British navy guaranteed no immunity from the inroads of determined subversive groups.

But, at the time, world attention was focused upon the war in South Africa and the *Hussar* sailed down through the Suez Canal in order to maintain a conspicuous presence in the Indian Ocean and the western Pacific. There Melhuish seems to have been transferred to the HMS *Dart* as it docked in Sydney and then headed for Tasmania and the Solomon Islands. A keen amateur photographer, he left behind a fascinating pictorial record of a strange new world, climbing mountains at Port Davey, receiving on board the scantily-clad King Sogar of Isabel Island and celebrating Coronation Day under palm trees with the natives of Florida Island. (That was in August 1902 and one wonders if, communications being what they were, this might not have been the second such celebration that they enjoyed, since plans for Edward VII's coronation in June were cancelled without notice as the king was rushed to the operating theatre for an emergency appendectomy.)

Melhuish rejoined the *Hussar* and was with it when it complemented the combined fleet at Lagos. But his sailing days were numbered. His skills were more useful to the on-shore medical world and by 1906 he was back at Haslar Naval Hospital in Gosport. A few years later, as his father's health deteriorated, Melhuish resolved to leave behind naval and pharmaceutical life. One suspects that his own health was not the best. He always looked gaunt and drawn as if suffering from weak lungs. This was not helped by the fact that he smoked heavily. It is difficult to discover a photograph or even a portrait of him in adult life without the ubiquitous cigarette. His retirement from the navy did mean that he avoided an even greater hazard to health, the First World War, but this did not mean that his life was problem-free. His father, old George Melhuish, still as handsome as ever and not very advanced in years, died at the age of only sixty-one on 23 July 1913. His son did not consider returning to the family business in construction, but instead took a job in Stokescroft as a dental mechanic with a dentist by the name of Morgan-Fletcher. There were certain advantages in work of this kind. It was steady employment, since the days of prophylactic dentistry had not yet arrived and all levels of society required dental prosthesis to compensate for the inroads made on their teeth by the ravages of time or self-indulgence. The job appealed because, without being routinely mechanical, it stimulated his natural interest in the science of mechanics. Melhuish had not abandoned education with the formal end of his schooling. He adored mathematics and would kneel on the floor with big sheets of paper as he tackled enormously complicated algebraic and mathematical problems. He did this until well-advanced in years, despite the fact that family and friends thought his interests (not to mention his physical position) mildly eccentric. The only problem about the job with Morgan-Fletcher was that he was the only member of his family not to be his own master. He always insisted to his son that working for somebody else was undesirable because it bred insensitivity in a human being. However, nobody could accuse Melhuish himself of being insensitive. Rather the contrary: he was an avid reader; he loved music and had a good singing voice. But his early work and his introspective interests perhaps isolated him from human society and it came as something of a surprise when, at the age of thirty-nine, he decided to marry.

Living at 20 Picton Street, just round the corner from his lodgings at 166 Cheltenham Road, was an intriguing 25-year-old schoolmistress,

Elsie Caroline Seymour. She came from a family background roughly similar to his own. The Seymours had established themselves as builders and decorators in 1862, and Elsie's father, William Samuel, and her two brothers, William and Stanley, successfully carried on the business. Elsie's ancestry was in no way extraordinary, although her son later liked to hint that they shared the same name and blood as the Dukes of Somerset. She herself was a remarkable woman. She was highly intelligent and had followed what was a normal course for bright girls of her generation (indeed, almost the only respectable one open to them). She trained as a schoolteacher at St Matthias's College and was apparently very successful with her junior school pupils. It is a rare thing to come across a photograph or a picture of Elsie with a smile on her face. She wore (and continued to wear) her hair severely close to her head with two braided bangs at either side. She had a fine-set square jaw and always seemed to peer critically at the world through round steel-rimmed spectacles. Appearances were deceptive because anybody who ever came to know her soon realized that she was a kind and intellectually lively individual. She loved children and instinctively they seemed to adore her – as good an indication as any of a sunny and selfless personality.

George Barnett Melhuish and Elsie Caroline Seymour were married on St Michael's Day, 29 September 1915, in the parish church of St Andrew in the Montpellier district. The vicar, the Reverend (later Canon) George Havard-Perkins, officiated. The Seymour family concealed their mild disapproval of the marriage, which was surely not because of his social background, which, if anything, was more impressive than their own. Melhuish's sisters had not disgraced the family: they had married into money and comfortable respectability (with one interesting fly in the ointment in the form of an alliance with the Leach family). More likely, the Seymours thought that Melhuish lacked drive and ambition, and certainly they thought him too old for Elsie, even though at twenty-five, if she had delayed much longer, she too might have been considered on the shelf. None the less, the wedding was successful. The two families attended in force. The marriage that it created was also one of the greatest success and happiness.

Nine days before his marriage Melhuish had bought a distinctive, three-storeyed late Georgian house at 75 Springfield Road in nearby Cotham and he and Elsie settled in soon after their brief honeymoon.

For over half a century the Springfield Road house was to be the Melhuish family's only real domestic base as well as the centre of some remarkable social activities. It was a vibrant and lively place, but the building itself never seemed to change. Its external appearance and interior decor survived more or less untouched, except by a badly-aimed bomb during the blitz. Only the closest of friends were ever permitted to penetrate the inner domestic recesses of the household. The privileged few remarked upon the simplicity of the tiny kitchen and, as the years went by, its fixtures gradually joined the same category as the antiques that adorned the rest of the house. Hot water was supplied by an early form of gas heater, which always gave a loud bang when it was switched on. Just as timeless were the two ground-floor rooms that gave off the hall. One was always known as the Gold Room because of its wallpaper in Georgian patterned gold that tarnished in time. This was a kind of living and working room which George Melhuish, the son, was later to use as his studio and study. The other public room, again deriving its name from its decor, was the Red Room, a spacious drawing-room in which chunky Victorian furniture, an impressive marble fireplace and a piano fitted in comfortably without overwhelming the place. The Red Room could (and did) accommodate large numbers of guests.

Upstairs there were bedrooms, one of them affording a spectacular, if unbeautiful, view over the rooftops of Montpellier towards Jamaica Street. On the top floor was a virtually self-contained flat that was always rented out to another family. In the early days a tailor by the name of Slocombe, with his wife and daughter Barbara, were long-term tenants, thereby helping to supplement the Melhuishes' income. Visitors, however, knew nothing of these domestic arrangements. The most they ever saw was the stair leading up from the hall. That was enough to stop anybody in his tracks: in time it was hung with marble-patterned wallpaper that may have looked impressively artistic, but it was so overpowering that it would have looked out of place even in an Italian *palazzo*. The whole house, including the bedrooms, was furnished with a number of solid pieces of furniture, some of them fine antiques. But there was no consistency of style from one piece to the next and guests thought that everything looked 'higgledy-piggledy', if homely. There was no front garden to speak of, but at the back a spacious walled garden sloped downwards away from the house and provided an ideal and safe playground for children and a haven for the aged.

Such was the setting for the Melhuishes' domestic and social life for the foreseeable future.

CHAPTER TWO

SCHOOLBOY IMPRESSIONS

On 26 August 1916, eleven months after George and Elsie Melhuish's marriage, their only child was born in their house in Springfield Road. The labour was difficult and the child was clearly sickly from birth. But he was the last in the direct male line of Melhuishes and so he was given the name of George, to which William was added (conveniently the name of both his maternal grandfather and uncle and of his father's brother-in-law, a successful dentist called William Lennox). His third given name, Seymour, perpetuated something of a family tradition of incorporating the mother's maiden name into those of the new offspring. Little Georgie, as he was called, was baptized soon after his birth in case he did not survive. But he did. 'We never thought that George would make old bones', is a recurring comment that one hears, but he confounded the Jeremiahs. However, there was every reason for pessimism in the early days because he was a delicate little baby. Among his cousins the news that Georgie was having one of his sick attacks was too familiar and always provoked a hushed silence. Infant mortality was a spectre that still haunted the lives of rich and poor alike. Awareness of death and mortality did not end with the coming of peace in 1918: the great influenza epidemics which followed presented even more of a threat to life than German armed might. That he survived through the early years of childhood was little short of a miracle. The fact that he was a very pale, blond child who was always small for his age and spent his time peering out from under the wide brim of a hat, designed to shield his fair skin from the sun, made it seem as though he existed in a world apart from everybody except his most immediate family.

Elsie Melhuish often used to tell him: 'I should never have had you.'

She felt guilty that, by giving birth to him, she had imposed on her beloved child a burden of suffering. She certainly never contemplated having any more children. Quite apart from the fact that she herself was promised a difficult and pain-racked future by the early signs of a developing arthritic condition (inherited from her mother, Caroline Griffiths Seymour), she felt that there was something so special about her son that nothing should be allowed to detract from his uniqueness. Both George's parents treated him like a little god – quite literally. From an early point Elsie used to refer to him as the second Messiah, a rather blasphemous suggestion which George himself took quite seriously to indicate, not only that he was not quite the same as other human beings, but also that he had a special 'mission' in life and a special message for mankind. Years later, when George had just done something high-handed to a lesser mortal, his best friend Barbara Lloyd exclaimed in indignation: 'Whom do you think you are, George? Jesus Christ?' George answered very simply: 'I may be.'[1] His mother Elsie took her reverence for her son to unusual lengths. Once he was old enough to have a separate bedroom of his own, she would never go into the room without first knocking and asking her son's permission to enter.

What gave the young George an additional sense of his 'uniqueness' was the fact that in early days he had virtually no male companions of his own age. His closest associates were his Seymour cousins, who were roughly his contemporaries, but they were all girls. His uncle William was the father of Dorothy, Betty and Pamela, and his younger uncle Stanley was the father of Kay and Winifred. Kay was just two years older than George and took a special protective interest in him. In turn, George developed a special interest in Winifred, who was two years his junior. This little girl was a source of anxiety. Whereas Kay had been a placid baby, Winifred was very fractious. She was always crying. At the time there was a popular jazz song with the title 'My Tennessee, I hear you calling me'. Whenever the child started crying, her sister used to say that that was Tennessee calling. Baby Winifred soon found that she was called Tennessee and, just as soon, her new soubriquet had been shortened to Tenny – and Tenny she remained for the rest of her life. Even her nearest and dearest were hard put to it to remember that she had been christened Winifred.

Surrounded by his girl cousins and his doting parents, George had a happy, indulged childhood. His mother needed no special excuse to have parties for the children. Despite her devotion to her son, she made a fuss over them all and they loved her for it. Party games and party food, cakes and jellies, all added to the excitement in the big drawing room in Springfield Road or, in good weather, spilled out into the big back garden. And every November the Melhuishes had a bonfire for George. His cousins would arrive with their simple fireworks, squibs and sparklers. His cousin Kay remembers her acute disappointment when one Guy Fawkes night came round and she was too ill to attend Georgie's bonfire party.

The Melhuishes and Seymours often used to go on holiday together. One can imagine the organization that it took to transport the whole clan by train to Teignmouth on the south Devon coast, or to Paignton or Chesil Beach near Weymouth in Dorset. Surviving holiday snaps show scenes of evident, if rather overdressed, enjoyment. The image of a widowed grandmother, dressed in a high-necked, floor-length black taffeta dress and hat, sitting on a deckchair on the beach seems to belong to a distant historical past. Back in Bristol another source of intense pleasure was Uncle Stanley Seymour's open-topped motor car. The Melhuishes could not afford such a luxury, and it was a real treat for George to go for a ride in his uncle's car. He always adored motors, the more ostentatious and luxurious the better, and he resolved to own (if not to drive) one as soon as he had enough money.

Life during George's childhood seems to have consisted of much innocent fun. Even his occasional naughtinesses were relatively harmless. He had one favourite trick whereby he would attach a packet of tea to a string and, at the appearance of some old local dame, would hide around a corner. As she espied the precious packet and stooped down to pick it up, he would pull it away with the string and the good woman would invariably shriek with fright (or disappointment) as the mischievous boy ran laughing away.

One of George's Bristol kinsmen, a cousin by marriage, was, meanwhile, not enjoying such a carefree childhood. One of George's paternal aunts had made a respectable marriage to a member of the Leach family. However, it turned out that her husband's brother was something of a black sheep. He was hopelessly alcoholic and, as for his wife, after giving birth to a son Archibald Alexander in 1904, she became steadily more and more deranged. She was committed to a mental asylum in 1913. As much of this 'scandal' as possible was concealed from the rest of the family and young Archibald Leach long believed that his mother had abandoned him. The boy had to live off his wits and, having joined a troupe of acrobats, he sailed off to the United States with them in 1920. When they returned, he stayed behind, determined to make his name in show business. Gradually he succeeded and in 1932, on signing a contract with Paramount Studios (for 450 dollars a week), Archie Leach was transmogrified into the film star Cary Grant. The unmentionable Leaches of George's childhood became a source of pride at the very point at which the 'talkies' became the epitome of glamour and fantasy in ordinary people's lives.

But, as yet, the world of films and film stars was still distant. Entertainments were invariably home-made, round the drawing-room piano. The wireless was still waiting for its breakthrough in the mid-1920s and so the Melhuishes with their own gramophone, complete with its enormous horn, attracted the admiration (and envy) of George's less fortunate contemporaries.

In 1921, when he was just five years old, his parents decided that it would be better for a delicate child like him to go to a small private school rather than subject him to the rough and tumble of a local school. They sent him to Tellisford House School, a semi-boarding, all-boys establishment situated at 66 Redland Road, within easy walking distance of the family home. It accommodated about 180 boys of all ages and there were eight or nine masters and mistresses under the command of the headmaster Thomas Crawshaw, all pledged to uphold the school motto *Labore et honore*. One gains the impression that the regime at Tellisford was less severe than in ordinary schools. Corporal punishment was not unknown, but there is only one recorded occasion when George came near to being beaten. When the headmaster was in the classroom, he inadvertently dropped his pencil-case on the floor, but one glance at the fragile child convinced the head that this was an accident and no punishment should be administered. George generally made a favourable impression on his tutors and at the end of his first year, in July 1922, he was awarded a prize 'for merit' – a book by Enos B. Comstock entitled *Tuck-Me-In Stories*. A rather charmingly-illustrated collection of anthropomorphic tales about animals, it was devoid of the oppressive moralizing of the 'improving' literature usually chosen as prizes in more sectarian, less humanistic institutions.

There was nothing extraordinary about the curriculum followed by the boys of Tellisford House. Basic reading, writing and arithmetic expanded in later years to include a modicum of science, mathematics and languages. In George's case Latin was the only foreign language in his formal repertoire. He knew no Greek and always regretted that he came to French only after his schooldays, when it was too late to make up for lost time. Whether he realized it or not, Greek would have been invaluable in his career as a philosopher. His lack of it is painfully obvious at times. But, traditionally, schoolboys who studied Greek were destined for the church – and George certainly had no calling for that. He was generally very happy at school, enjoying learning and finding it easy. However, his health was so precarious that he was frequently absent. This meant that he missed a deal of his formal training – and to the end of his days ingrained flaws in, for example, his spelling and syntax, showed only too clearly. But, in a more general sense, George was self-taught. He was seldom without a book in his hands. His days on his sick bed were not wasted. He had an insatiable appetite for knowledge and his parents gently encouraged him. His father's interest in the theory of mechanics and electricity fascinated him and in later years George applied his knowledge in an amusing and practical fashion. As a former schoolteacher, his mother was well qualified to help her son with his basic studies. His parents never made a fuss about his education. They trusted him. They would never have dreamt of waiting at the school gates to pick up their son at the end of the day and, when the termly report arrived, there were none of the hysterics which might characterize the reactions of some parents.

George was remarkably well-directed in his autodidactic approach. He was something of a romantic, a dreamer who from an early point was convinced that he was destined to achieve something remarkable, and so he tended to trim away anything from his intellectual life that was not strictly relevant to his purpose. Such an approach can (and did) have its drawbacks, but George, in his quest for knowledge, developed the ability to know where to go for information to fill in the gaps. He was seldom out of the local public library and, to the end of his life, he employed the technique of button-holing knowledgeable individuals on a face-to-face basis as an intellectual exercise to tease out arguments in the form of a dialectic. Born into a different age and social background, the chances are that he would have gone to university, but there was no suggestion that this was ever a serious consideration for him. He would certainly have benefited from the rigours of formal self-disciplining. On the other hand, it might well have stilted his natural intellectual flair. But the question did not arise because he was bent on an artistic career from an early stage.

Music was an enduring love for George. His father did much to enthuse him with an interest in practical musicianship. Melhuish had an eccentric habit of lying flat out on the floor after the evening meal, (he thought that this facilitated the digestive process), but after he got on his feet again, he would sing for George at the piano. George himself was not much of a singer, although to the end, when he was happy, he used to hum gruntingly to himself as he went about his household chores. He was much more of an instrumentalist. He played the piano with a surprising vigour and expertise and he owned a violin – although he tended to avoid playing it in public. Then there was the famous Melhuish gramophone with its large collection of records ranging from popular songs to serious classics. He developed a general, if faintly elliptical, appreciation of the great composers. Beethoven, Wagner and Puccini he loved, but Mozart was low down on his list of favourites. When he was still young, his mother used to take him to concerts and, whenever there was an opera, they would go to see it together. One's initial response is to wonder just what kind of light entertainment Bristol of the 1920s could rise to – Sullivan or perhaps the latest Franz Lehár. The truth, however, is much more impressive. A vibrant musical life, encouraged by a lively university music department and rich but discerning local impresarios, meant that Bristolians were musically almost as well catered for as London audiences, and at times even more so: it was at the Victoria Rooms that the British première of that rare gem of an opera, Manuel de Falla's *Master Peter's Puppet Show*, took place in 1924.

The result of this was that George decided to become a composer, and he quickly picked up the basic techniques of counterpoint and harmony. One suspects that his father was more of a mentor than his music master at school, whose duties would not have extended beyond singing classes. None of George's compositions from this period have survived. But a late recurrence of the composing impulse in the 1960s indicates a certain rough-hewn skill. However, as a schoolboy, George the potential composer received an unusually serious but sensible piece of advice from his father: keep music and composition as a leisure activity; it is almost impossible to make a living out of it as a professional, even if one has outstanding talent. One feels that this advice, though initially unpalatable, was good for George. If he had tried and failed to make headway on such a precarious road to fame and fulfilment, this might have frustrated all other creative impulses in him.

One has some doubts about George's attitude towards the composer's art. He had a habit of saying:[2]

A piece of music by Beethoven could have been written by an unmusical child fifty years before Beethoven wrote it – merely by the child being given some manuscript paper and having an acquaintance with the symbols for the musical notes and intervals with which to decorate the page, thus, in a suitable case, arriving at the same notes and intervals present as in the Beethoven composition.

As an artist and a philosopher, George could not have been serious. But he loved to provoke his friends by making outrageous statements. The only problem was that some of them did take him seriously. He clearly knew that composition was much more than a mindless game of chance and it was the unfortunately predictable aspects of the musical world that he decided to avoid.

Art soon emerged as the real focus of his interest and as the vehicle for the expression of his talent. He was taught painting and drawing at school. Although this involved only the barest technical training, it did inspire him to study technique on his own and to read as much as possible about the great artistic movements of the past, as well as of the contemporary world. With his conviction that his future lay in art came the realization that it could only achieve its full expression if everything else in life was pared away or kept under strict control. The only thing that ever took precedence over his artistic vocation was when, latterly, philosophy gained something of an upper hand. But by that time he regarded art and philosophy as two complementary aspects of his creative existence, and there was no conflict between them. More than anything it was this vision of his purpose in life which convinced him that everything else must be transcended or controlled. Hence he made his three vows as a budding adolescent.

The no-smoking resolution seems an obvious decision to make. But in an age when smoking was synonymous with manliness (and for the working classes it was the cheapest form of pleasure available), tobacco was an accepted part of life. Little was ever said about any connection between it and lung cancer or coronary and arterial diseases, but George could see well enough the effect that smoking had on his father's bronchitic lungs.

His resolution never to work for anybody as an employee was again inspired by his father, who was too much of an individualist to be happy as anything other than his own master. He was, however, lucky to have as genial an employer as Morgan-Fletcher and, unlike many in his position, he did not allow his work to breed the insensitivity that he so despised in his fellow men. George learned the lesson well. Nothing would come of his talents if he allowed the material considerations of a bread-and-butter type of occupation to relegate his creative life to the level of a hobby.

George's vow never to marry was inspired by the same conviction. One began at a disadvantage as an artist if life were encumbered with the material and emotional burdens and responsibilities of marriage and, inevitably, parenthood. Perhaps this vow is the most surprising of the three, since he was lucky enough to have the example of his own parents' exceptionally happy union. But then, the rest of society convinced him that this was the exception to a general rule. George kept to his resolution, although one cannot say that this allowed him to avoid the emotional clutter of life. This was a problem that he never solved. From the sexual point of view, his non-marriage vow may seem strange, especially in the moral climate of the inter-war period. Around the age of thirteen, when he made his resolutions, he was certainly aware of his own sexual impulses as well as those of others. A weak and rather pretty youth, he was once pinned down in the school playground by an older boy, who proceeded to masturbate himself over his helpless body. The experience was at one and the same time both alarming and horribly fascinating. Equally fascinating was another incident in which he was less directly involved. One summer day in his back garden he observed two women in an adjoining garden making love to each other. He clearly realized what was going on and was afforded a sharp lesson in the fact that some relationships were exclusive, as well as being capable of an infinitely wider range of variations than his youthful mind had imagined. It also told him that much about life for an artist consisted of observation rather than participation.

For the literary enthusiast, the incident of the Cotham lesbians is intriguing because, with an odd refinement, it is remarkably similar to the one described by Proust in *Du côté de chez Swann*, when the boy Marcel witnesses the antics of Mlle Vinteuil and her girlfriend through her garden window.[3] However, George almost certainly never read Proust at any time in his life and could not have known of the literary connotations of the incident, unless some friend described it to him. The simple fact was that, about the same time as the vow-making took place, he also resolved not to read any more works of fiction. He had outgrown schoolboy adventure novels, but he made no attempt to go on to a systematic examination of either the classics of English literature or contemporary fiction. Drama held no interest for him and poetry claimed only the occasional moment of his attention – if it had a polemical purpose that appealed to him. The reason for his indifference to literature was not simply that he found it a distracting consumer of valuable time; he found it genuinely difficult to sustain his interest through hundreds of pages of straight prose. When one looks at his complete *oeuvre* as an artist, one is struck by how totally devoid it is of all literary illusions. And, apart from his portraits, it often lacks any direct reference to human activity. His later career as a philosopher, in which he stressed the validity of the world of the imagination, of fantasy and of dreams, might have tempted him to see the merits of fiction, but even the mild salacity of a novel by Molly Parkin (the wife of his close friend Patrick Hughes) was not sufficient to claim his attention for more than just a few pages. 'What happens to the characters when the book is finished?' he would always say to his friend, fellow artist and philosopher, Anthony Hill.[4]

Otherwise, George was remarkably well-read. The local library saw a rapid turnover in its books on art and history. He particularly loved biographies and, inspired by his father's stories of his navy days, he had a passion for maritime history and for Britain's military and imperial greatness. Nelson and Wellington always remained his heroes. This is surprising because he was not a happy sailor himself (a cross-Channel ferry was strictly the limit of his experience) and because of his strong inclination towards pacifism. Gradually he evolved an interest in books on political and social ideas that led him ultimately to the abstractions of metaphysical thought.

His rejection of the possibility of artistic cross-fertilization may seem dangerously eccentric at first sight, but it certainly enabled him to see more clearly the vision of what his future must be.

CHAPTER THREE

THE ROAD TO WAR

When George Melhuish left Tellisford House School in the summer of 1932, within weeks of his sixteenth birthday, he already had the intention of pursuing a career as an artist. His parents knew perfectly well that their son was unlikely to earn enough money from painting to support himself, but this does not seem to have worried them unduly. They owned the house in Springfield Road; they had an adequate income in the form of Mr Melhuish's salary and rent from lodgers; and George's needs were simple: art materials were his only major item of expenditure and even there he made ingenious economies. He used to rise early each day and make his own canvases, stretching them on frames of his own construction.

George received support from an unexpected source. The local vicar, Canon Havard-Perkins, was impressed by his work and asked him to paint his portrait. The success of the enterprise encouraged George and for the first decade of his career portraits and life-studies figured prominently in his output. As his reputation spread, it became a fairly profitable exercise, although it always required an amount of sales-talk on his part. But he was never shy about self-advertisement. His portrait painting certainly brought him initial success. He was good at it. He gained a deserved reputation for being able to capture the exact likeness of his sitters but, on the other hand, he did not hesitate to cut corners. Taking after his father, he was a keen amateur photographer and possessed a massive, old-fashioned camera complete with tripod and black serge drape. He invariably took snapshots of his sitters and used them as an *aide-mémoire* after giving his subject a number of live sittings. Adults found the sight of George bobbing out from under the black cloth faintly comical; children tended to be alarmed.

Whatever the subject, George always painted quickly and with a remarkable amount of vigour and inventiveness. He had a keen sense of colour and used it to set the mood of his compositions. Women sitters would express surprise at a finished portrait in which their prized green evening-dress had changed into a striking red velvet creation. But that was how he wanted it. He was also inventive about the settings for his portraits. A sitter painted perched on a chair in his chilly studio might find herself transported to the plush luxury of a box at the opera, as the lovely Edna Orchard discovered a few years later. And then, in a second version of the same portrait, he set her against a striking surreal landscape with a completely different set of colour tones.

George often claimed to be self-taught as an artist. This was only partly true and the impression that he himself conveyed to friends was not always accurate. When a collection of George's paintings was published as a book in 1946, Richard Hutton in a biographical introduction claimed that[1]

he had no course of study at any school or atelier, but began to paint in 1933, his first attempts being copies of colour plates in magazines. This idle painting, in hours of leisure, created in him a desire to study the subject, and as he pursued this study he became more and more involved in it. This intense singleness of purpose and sincerity saw him through much hard labour and study.

Hutton's picture is much more relaxed than hard fact suggests. George started painting well before 1933 and it was never an idle occupation pursued in hours of leisure. When Raymond Sawkins, the editor of *The Artist*, published an article on George in the magazine's issue of May 1948, he revealed that he[2]

spent four to five years in general study: he was for a time a student at the School of Visual Arts. During this period he drew and painted in a naturalistic, academic manner, mostly in oils. Some students are confused in their early days by feeling that they must decide *what* they want to paint before they learn *how* to paint: this conflict of ideas sometimes leads them to ape the work of a favourite master. Melhuish experienced no such conflict: he concentrated all his efforts on learning how to draw and paint realistically.

But George did admit to believing that 'he produced his first important paintings in 1939, at a time when he was becoming deeply interested in the work of the modern French painters, particularly Monet, Degas and Cézanne.'[3]

He did, indeed, learn by inspiration derived from established masters, but he did not imitate them as such. If one unexpectedly comes across even one of his earliest paintings, one's immediate reaction is: 'That's a Melhuish.' However, there is a deal of truth in Hutton's statement that the budding artist used colour plates in magazines as a basis for portraits of personalities whom he could not hope to paint from life. One of his closest and most enduring friendships resulted from this.

Bristol in the early 1930s was a city much less affected than the industrial North by the results of the Depression. Life continued to be comparatively prosperous, a fact confirmed by the amount of house-building that took place as the comfortably-off drifted away from the immediate city centre to the newly-built suburbs. A vivacious young adolescent Barbara Lloyd (later Barbara Thorne) moved with her parents to a house at 15 Wimbledon Road in Westbury Park and discovered that her new neighbours at 1 Stadium Road were Stanley and Florence Seymour and their two daughters Kay and Tenny. Barbara liked the gentle and considerate Kay, but it was her younger sister Tenny who had a lively and outward-going personality that matched her own. They became the closest of friends. One day, some months after their first encounter, Tenny came to show Barbara a wonderful drawing of Greta Garbo which her cousin had done for her. It seemed so true to life as to be positively photographic – as, indeed, it was. Barbara was impressed and also surprised that any member of the Seymour family should share her own artistic inclinations. (The Seymours, apart from George's mother Elsie, were unashamed about their lack of interest in art at anything but the simplest, most representational level.) But George's talent was obvious even to the most indifferent.

About eight months after the revelation of the Garbo drawing, Tenny announced that her cousin George was painting her portrait. Tenny was evidently most concerned about how she looked in her best dress but, when the portrait neared completion, Barbara became impatient to see the work of art and meet the artist. Tenny took her down to 75 Spring-field Road to see the canvas. Although one feels that it was something of an apprentice piece (the face is unusually serious, almost lugubrious, and the bottle-green colour of the dress reflects rather biliously in the skin tones), Barbara Lloyd recognized at once that she and Tenny's cousin George were fellow travellers in the world of art. George was Barbara's senior by only eight months and instantly the two felt a tremendous rapport with each other. Overnight Tenny Seymour lost a boon-companion as Barbara and George enthused endlessly together about painting, about the Impressionists, the Post-Impressionists and the Fauves, even the Surrealists, to which their teenage minds were just beginning to be exposed. The Seymours thought the whole thing bizarre and Barbara's family, though more used to her exotic, extrovert behaviour, wondered about George's suitability as a friend. They worried about the intensity of the friendship. George and Barbara would engage in marathon discussions that would break off then continue in intermittent sessions on the telephone throughout the day, until they could resume in the flesh in the evening. But at no time was there ever any suggestion of a close emotional relationship. George was not seen as a potential boyfriend. As a result, their relationship plumbed depths of meaning that a romantic attachment might not have achieved. But part of the reason why this question did not arise was that George still looked very pale and sickly, scarcely built in the image of the romantic hero. Barbara's down-to-earth father always called him 'the Maggot' because he looked so white. (It was only the first of many curious nicknames that George accumulated during his lifetime.) But Barbara was unconcerned. Already she was devoted to her new-found soul-mate. She allowed George to make considerable demands on her patient friendship. Since he could seldom afford to pay for a model, she used to pose for him for hours as he concocted some Degas-esque composition. Over the next decade he frequently painted her in various stages of dress and undress, and she appeared on some remarkable and surprising canvases. When a selection of his paintings was published in book-form in 1946, the cover illustration was a hot-coloured portrait of a 'Negress'. Barbara had acted as the model for it. All this activity resulted in the build-up of a collection of many fine pictures. George may have claimed that he only began to produce important work in 1939, but he was confident enough to submit, and have accepted by the prestigious Royal West of England Academy, a study entitled *Gladioli* for the ninetieth annual exhibition in November 1935 in its imposing classical building at the bottom of Whiteladies Road. George's contribution was an artistic success, if not a commercial one (he asked only £5 for the picture). The Bristol *cognoscenti*, never quick to warm to anything avant-garde, realized that a remarkable newcomer had joined the artistic scene.

It would have been difficult to ignore George. He stood out in a crowd. His physical characteristics were striking: his pale Rupert Brooke-type features; his long fair hair, flopping over his face; his almost ethereally frail, even sexless image. (Indeed, did he even shave?) Added to that George cultivated the appearance of a Bohemian. He wore very brightly coloured suits with exaggeratedly baggy trousers. He had a collection of velvet coats, top hats and floppy bow ties with daring spots. He had a liking for jewellery, the more gaudy and colourful the better, although in the 1930s he confined himself to wearing some eye-catching links in his cuffs. He went nowhere without his rolled umbrella. In an age (and in the traditionally puritanical West Country) when one dared not wear a green shirt for fear of being suspected of deviant sexual leanings, his appearance was considered ostentatiously outrageous. He merely considered it part of his image as an artist and felt comfortable with it, despite the embarrassment of uncles, aunts and cousins. Friends who expressed their reservations did not last long as such.

However familiar, George remained an eye-catching figure in public. He was always busy about his quarter, from early morning when he used to do all the shopping for his increasingly crippled mother, until evening when he invariably went for a constitutional stroll in Redland Park. A young neighbour, Margaret Carl, thought him intriguing but she was made aware that not everybody found his eccentricities acceptable. As she later recalled,[4]

> to me he was 'grown-up', but I suppose in actual fact he was no more than twenty. My sister and I were absolutely fascinated by his unusual 'arty' appearance, and for reasons best known to children, we called him 'Sea-lion'!
>
> One hot sunny evening I was outside our home, Grove Villa, Southfield Road, Cotham, with my Mother when I saw Sea-lion coming up the road. As he drew near he addressed my Mother and then to my surprise patted me on the top of the head and quietly murmured, 'Beautiful colour, I should like to paint it' – meaning by this my hair, which was then amber and had the Victorian thickness of my Grandmother's. This remark seemed to alarm my Mother and I was rushed indoors!

But nothing deterred George. He had no intention of hiding himself away. Until the end of his days he was a great wanderer, preferring to amble round the living streets of Cotham and Clifton than to immerse himself fashionably in nature.

Recreation formed only a small part of his existence. Most of his day was taken up with painting or preparation for painting. The only luxury that he allowed himself (and one that was regarded as unusual) was constant music. If there was nothing on the wireless, he would play records on his gramophone. The sight of him painting away to a Bruckner symphony on records that had to be turned every few minutes without getting paint on them was mildly awe-inspiring. But then George was always a very meticulously clean painter. Paint seldom splashed off the Victorian marble-topped table that he used as his palette. The paint was applied cleanly to the canvas by means of big, broad-headed brushes or a favourite Edwardian table knife which he found ideal as a palette knife.

Everything was also spick and span as far as his personal hygiene was concerned. Not a subject that normally would call for comment, but the extraordinary thing was that from a very early age George never took baths. He refused to immerse himself in water because, he claimed, it was bad for the skin and made one susceptible to colds. He did, however, wash himself meticulously all over. He always looked clean and neatly turned out. He was ahead of his age and class in his liberal use of colognes, some of them unusually pungent and exotic. Yet there was nothing effete about him. Painting, despite the outsider's impression, is a physically demanding activity.

George was also fascinated by the logic of mechanical things. He took time to study radio (and later became something of an amateur astronomer). He planned a practical application for his knowledge, building what was for the time an extremely high-powered radio, which was so successful that it enabled him to listen to performances of operas from continental broadcasting stations. Perhaps less successful was his attempt to construct a recording machine by reversing the function of an old gramophone. He achieved results, but not of the quality for which he had hoped. This partial failure was easily compensated for by his evident skill as a photographer. Despite the antiquity of his equipment, striking results emerged from his dark-room.

He was inventive in another way. Money was always in short supply, but he was constantly devising methods of supplementing his income. Fairly legitimate was his habit of rooting round junk shops and buying cheaply any old pictures that he could find. He then cleaned away generations of grime and varnish and resold the paintings at a relatively handsome profit. Less legitimate was his habit of tapping his Grandmother Seymour for as much as he could get. By the 1930s she had become so old and incapacitated that her family went to the expense of keeping her in a comfortable nursing home. Every Sunday afternoon George's Seymour uncles visited and grandmother received her spending money for the week. However, George was waiting in the wings and, as soon as they had gone, he would arrive, and a substantial proportion of grandmother's pocket money would change hands again. This used to enrage the Seymours. Their only consolation was that he had to pay a penalty for his deviousness. Grandmother Seymour always insisted that he should have a glass of port with her before leaving. He was then not a great lover of alcohol and the heady drink made him feel sick.

But he persisted in cultivating his grandmother in the expectation of long-term gains in addition to periodic hand-outs. However, when his grandmother finally died in 1947, George's hopes were disappointed. The Church of England beat him to the post in the legacy-game. He found it difficult to forgive his grandmother (who clearly thought more about the future of her immortal soul than about her grandson's pocket). He never forgave the church. Ironically the church ill-repaid Caroline Seymour's generosity. She was buried alongside her husband William in St Andrew's churchyard and an elegant marble cross was erected over the grave, but two decades later, when the building was demolished in 1969, the cemetery was cleared. The remains were reburied in a common grave and the costly headstone disposed of, leaving the family very upset. However, George himself was fairly indifferent to the conventions that attached to death and its aftermath.

The truth was that at about the age of sixteen he had undergone a crisis over the question of religious faith. Until that point he had often attended the local church with his traditionally devout mother. His father was more of a sceptic and confined his attendance to the more conventionally ceremonial high-points of the church's calendar. For the budding adolescent rationalist mind there seemed to be no point in the blind acceptance of a faith that held out unguaranteeable hopes of a future life. Like many youths of his years, the growing awareness of natural sexual urges ill-accorded with the church's teaching on morality in the narrow sense, and then in its broader aspects. But he never ceased to think about religion and the possibility of some sort of spiritual existence. The subject intrigued him and, as his agnosticism tended radically towards atheism during the war years, he liked more and more to discuss the question with interested friends. Barbara Lloyd was convinced that, despite his protestations of doubt, he 'felt that knowledge which had been accumulated over a lifetime could not be lost in death but that this must somehow go on in a spiritual way'.[5] Once, during the apparently godless war years, he and Barbara were hotly disputing the existence of God. After hours of debate he announced: 'I've decided, Barbara, that there is no God.' At that precise moment the shilling ran out in the coin-operated electricity metre and the flat was plunged into total darkness. They both thought it highly amusing.[6]

But George was never a convinced atheist and the controversy over his undoubted agnosticism continued even after his death, despite the fact that in his first philosophical book *The Paradoxical Universe* (1959) he makes his views on organized religion quite clear. He used its final pages to question conventional concepts of God and the exclusive claims of the churches:[7]

Any concept of God or the world will itself be a conceptual image, and, as in the end no one conceptual image can claim metaphysical priority over any other, to attempt to disentangle God from the world or the world from God would be an operation that merely pays homage to the paradox . . .

Can the philosopher or logician take seriously the way in which one religion usually tries to refute another? An examination of the history of theology does not seem to disclose anything very convincing. For what is usually attempted amounts to no more than a call to accept something on trust, and, as each separate religion demands the same act of trust, one's choice would appear to rest upon the arbitrary matter of paying your penny and taking your dip. The arbitrariness of religious choice is usually masked by the fact that most people inherit their religion and as such tend to take its particular truth for granted.

Whether one agrees with them or not, there is little doubt about the agnostic tenor of his considered views.

At a more terrestrial level George's philosophical views were coloured by immediate political considerations. He was always apolitical in the formal sense, but the events of the 1930s horrified him, particularly the emergence of totalitarian regimes under Mussolini, Hitler, Franco and Stalin. At the time, if anything, George was inclined to be more left than right of centre, but in a rather passive way. There is no suggestion that he ever gave much thought to the plight of the suffering masses either in his own country or overseas. But on one issue he was absolutely clear. He hated all forms of violence and he was vehemently opposed to war. One suspects that his reasons were almost purely personal: he could not envisage himself engaging an enemy in hand-to-hand conflict, even though he might, given his political stance, be ideologically pledged to destroy aspects of the civilization that he, in fact, held dear. Not even the fascinating years that his father spent in the Royal Navy (albeit in a strictly non-combatant capacity) moderated his views on military matters.

After the fiasco of the Munich Agreement in 1938 George made a political commitment unique in his experience: he actually joined the Peace Pledge Union. A young student of chemistry, Peter Tiley, was struck by the sight of George at a local PPU meeting which they had both decided to attend. A week later they stumbled across each other in the public library in Cheltenham Road. Peter Tiley's interest in areas of life wider than science and pacifism attracted George and, although he did not share his particular passion for literature, he asked the youth along to Springfield Road to see the paintings in his studio.

A warm friendship developed just at the point when the cultural and intellectual life that they cherished seemed threatened. Something would have to be done about it.

PART TWO

1939–1945

CHAPTER FOUR

CARRYING THE TORCH

When war was declared on 3 September 1939, George and his friends of all persuasions had no intention of letting it destroy or erode all that they valued. Their response was so positive in approach that their previously disparate activities co-ordinated themselves into a coherent 'movement'. Indeed, the side-effects of war on Bristol brought some enormous cultural benefits.

George, Barbara Lloyd, Peter Tiley and a curious pacifist friend of George's called Norman, discussed the situation. What could they do to keep the torch of civilization burning during the dark war years? They decided to set up a group for like-minded individuals with as wide a scope of interests as possible, provided that they were more or less actively committed to the arts. It was apparently Norman who suggested adopting the name 'Torch'. What emerged was a well-run, but self-regulating and highly relaxed club, with as active a social side to it as a serious cultural one. The nucleus group cast out its net to catch any young people sympathetic to their aims. They were almost all in their twenties or even younger. (Norman, the shy civil-servant, who played an important role in initiating the idea, but who was very retiring and older than the rest of the friends, faded quickly from the scene.) In the meantime, Barbara had placed an advertisement in the *Bristol Evening Post*, announcing Torch's existence and encouraging enthusiasts to join in its activities. Torch's aims were wide but distinctive. It was intended as a forum for young people interested in music, art, literature and philosophy, but politics and religion were forbidden subjects.

Until its demise, Torch's activities followed a set pattern. It used to meet in the Melhuishes' drawing-room every Sunday afternoon at 3 p.m. for a session at which one of the members (or occasionally an outside speaker) would give a paper on a subject of interest to himself. Volunteers committed themselves two or three weeks in advance and most papers were carefully, if hurriedly, put together. After the paper there would be a discussion starting from the basis of the subject in question, but veering off in any direction as the spirit moved. Afterwards Mrs Melhuish used to serve tea and cakes or biscuits, for which everybody paid 4d. (a charge later inflated to 6d.). On Wednesday evenings at 6.30 p.m. the group would gather again but usually for a less formal session. There might be a 'brains trust' with Barbara in the chair or, more often, a musical evening with live performers or simply a 'recital' on George's gramophone. One of the leading members, the artist Deborah Jones, worked in the BBC record library for the early part of the war and used to borrow records overnight for the company's delight. Often George would play gems from his own collection, mainly of symphonic music and concertos. But he had an extremely mischievous sense of humour and he used to insist upon playing a piece 'blind' and making the audience guess what it was. Even the most expert musical mind could be thrown into confusion as the name of the most familiar of pieces refused to fall into place. George caused his friends many an embarrassed red face. Of course, he himself never engaged in the guessing-game because he already knew what the records were. (One cannot imagine why the group did not devise some method of getting its collective revenge on him.) After these sessions most of the members ventured out into the blackout for a drink at the local pub. George, however, was invariably conspicuous by his absence because he disliked drinking beer and, besides, he could ill afford to do so.

For a while the group met on 'neutral' territory in a little studio in Boyces Avenue that Barbara Lloyd rented for the group at 5s. a week. A snug attic room, it was the scene of many a jolly gathering and relaxed party until a German bomb obliterated it in the blitz one night after everybody had left. The group then decamped back to the Melhuishes' red drawing-room and George's mother was back in the business of supplying tea and buns.

There was nothing static about the group. Because of the exigencies of war there was a steady turn-over in membership. As some were called up or moved away from Bristol on official war work, influxes of newcomers hit the city. King's College was evacuated from London to Bristol, effectively turning it into a city that boasted two universities – and two student populations. Sections of the BBC, most intriguingly the BBC orchestra under Adrian Boult, also enriched cultural life until moved for greater safety to Bedford. The result of this was that there were a large number of young people in the city whose intellectual yearnings, particularly in the case of the undergraduates, were not entirely fulfilled by the necessarily utilitarian gallop through a truncated academic course.

Several artists gravitated to Torch, although, curiously, never a sculptor. Deborah Jones, Edna Orchard, Bernard Perrin, Dennis Reid, Hubert Dole and Peter Reyner Banham (later a distinguished architectural historian) were all accomplished painters. Eric Webb, John Sheppard and Robert Reid (a fine violinist) added their own peculiar talents. Among the undergraduate contingent were a number whose background was scientific or economic, and that seemed to make them avid for a cultural outlet. Nancy Barber was a brilliant mathematician who later went on to do high-powered government work. When the first German turbine was brought down over Bristol, she was taken to interrogate the pilot. One wonders who was the more daunted by the experience: Nancy always used to wear the most severely masculine of clothes and in the evening was never without a dinner jacket and black tie. She was, however, at times known to take her clothes off. Apart from anything else, George valued her as a willing model: she had crisp sculptural lines and entirely classical proportions. She must also have been hardy if she could bear the ordeal of posing in his chilly studio. Although reading for a degree in commerce, a local girl, Patricia Daly, evacuated back to Bristol as a King's College student, was already showing promise as the fine writer and poetess that she would subsequently become. Alexander Gordon-Burne (always known as 'Tuggy' Burne) was a cherished addition to the group. A scientist with a bright mind, he stimulated the philosophical side of Torch. Everybody liked him. Unfortunately Tuggy experienced within himself a philosophical conflict that was difficult to resolve. He came from a long line of high-ranking military men but, as his personal political views veered more and more towards the left, he seemed deliberately to reject everything in his family background (except his ingrained breeding, as it later transpired).

The whole purpose of Torch was to permit the free flow of ideas and nothing (and nobody) was allowed to inhibit that. The result may have seemed a little haphazard but, controlled by the set-pattern of the meetings, everything worked coherently. Since there was seldom a lack of volunteers to give papers, no formal rota had to be imposed on members. In early days young Peter Tiley found himself volunteering to talk on Oscar Wilde and he gave papers on T.S. Eliot and Gerard Manley Hopkins. Or was it a joint effort on Hopkins and Wilfred Owen? The *Faber Book of Modern Verse* had only recently appeared and was an endless source of inspiration. Even George, with his arid attitude towards literature, was seduced. He was particularly drawn towards Wilfred Owen, whose description of death in the First World War trenches he saw as an anti-war polemic. But there George's literary interest ended. Peter Tiley tried to involve him in some of his own literary 'passions', such as D.H. Lawrence and Aldous Huxley. 'Why not try it, George?' he would say. But the invariable reply was: 'I'm sorry but I just can't get into it. It doesn't capture my attention at all.'[1]

However, George's views were not allowed to prejudice the rest of the group. A surviving ticket announced that on 21 September 1941 an artist friend, Rollo Ahmed, would give a talk entitled 'Colour', very much a subject close to George's heart. Then the following Sunday, 28 September, John Sheppard was scheduled to introduce the subject of Somerset Maugham. That was met with general enthusiasm, despite George's air of studied indifference. George did, however, show a glimmer of personal interest when the session was given over to Barbara. She had been experimenting with writing short stories and tried them out by reading them to a potentially critical audience of friends. They were all impressed by their vitality and they all (even George) regretted that she did not develop much further her budding talent as a writer. But there was not always time to cultivate literary impulses and George was the most demanding of anybody of Barbara's time as a secretary and car driver.

Another budding writer was Peter Reyner Banham. Patricia Daly later recalled that he 'was a wonderful writer at the time, and he read aloud three of his short stories, which were tremendously good and very powerful. And we all thought that Peter was going to become a writer. I don't know: I think he went off the idea of imaginative, creative writing. But then again I think that he was probably inspired by the atmosphere of Torch, and we gave him a real appreciation.'[2] If his dwindling interest was a loss to the world of literature, the world of art history was the beneficiary. After he left Bristol in 1945, he achieved a remarkable reputation in the field of architectural history and ended up as Professor of Art History at the University of California, Santa Cruz. His achievement in the art world was paralleled by that of another Torch member: a painter, Jack Washbourne, distinguished himself, once popular television established itself in the 1950s, as a presenter of his own series on art. In retrospect his success was seen as a Torch success.

Indeed, Torch itself was regarded as an extraordinary Bristol phenomenon. Although each meeting might not attract many more than between twelve and twenty members, as wartime conditions often committed them elsewhere, Torch was seen as a remarkable achievement, still talked about as something vibrant and very special, even in the subsequent sophisticated decades of mass entertainment and communication. But Torch was not all seriousness. The formal discussions were never conducted in an atmosphere of moral earnestness. It also involved a fair number of official social activities and one or two more personal ones. From time to time the members would hold lively parties. A lot of drink was consumed. And what kind of drink was served from the Melhuish cocktail cabinet? Oh, none, they were strictly bring-your-own-bottle affairs. And members were not discouraged from bringing along outsiders as guests. Barbara Lloyd was the most adventurous. Until alluring American officers appeared on the scene, she added spice to the proceedings by bringing along a swarthy-looking bandleader. The bandleader (and, strangely, George) looked less than relaxed.

Inevitably the group engendered emotional entanglements. Some were not always happy: an attempted suicide by a rejected lover, nervous breakdowns for similar reasons, the odd unwanted pregnancy. George took an avid interest in these goings-on. And if what one did was particularly shameful, one made sure that he did not learn of it. A number of matches, not all to his liking, were made. The ravishing Edna Orchard became engaged to and subsequently married the artist Richard Macdonald. They moved away to London and then to Hollywood, where fame and fortune in the film industry awaited a talented designer. George was initially upset by this match because he worshipped Edna, but very much from afar since she was never aware of his infatuation (nor did she learn until after his death that he kept one of his portraits of her on the wall of his bedroom).

The background of war could be emotionally distracting. The fiancées of two of the men in the group thought their prospective husbands, 'too close for comfort'. They were probably mistaken and this did not prevent the women from marrying them. Even George astonished the company when he admitted that, when he saw the strikingly handsome Dennis Reid wearing a particularly smart suit, it was the only time that he could remember having physical feelings towards another man. But there was certainly nothing serious about the attraction. On the other hand, the rest of the group did not take any of his other involvements very seriously. He had a lady-friend who had been a neighbour of his for years. She lived conveniently close in the next street, Victoria Walk. Also convenient was the fact that her husband was away in the forces, and George was having what he called 'lovey-dovey' with her. But none of his friends ever quite understood what 'lovey-dovey' meant. The general concensus was that, whatever vagaries he got up to, he did not venture as far as having actual sexual intercourse with anybody at this period in his life. The Freudian symbol of the Torch remained for him an almost purely cultural and intellectual emblem.

CHAPTER FIVE

WAR ART

The experience of war affected George's friends in different ways. At first Peter Tiley had been an ardent pacifist. He was to be seen selling *Peace News* in the centre of Bristol on Saturdays. Among the Torch group he found a number of fellow pacifists, Tuggy Burne and Eric Webb, to mention only two whose stance was most politically motivated. However, despite disagreement on the subject, pacifism was never a point of dispute among the members. They respected each other's views, even when they underwent a change in complexion. Peter Tiley began to rethink his position once the bombs started falling on Bristol. He was still young, but he enlisted in the Royal Air Force and by early 1941 he was winging his way to Canada for training. Mercifully, he was kept on as an instructor and did not return to England until almost the end of the war – with a lovely Canadian wife and the promise of a promotion to the rank of squadron-leader.

But before Peter Tiley flew off to fight for king and country, George also received his call-up papers. He, however, had no intention of serving in the forces and made this quite clear to the authorities. In due course he was summoned to appear before one of the specially constituted tribunals designed to examine the cases of individual pacifists and conscientious objectors. They were not organized as regular courts of law. The 'accused' could not be legally represented by a barrister or solicitor, but he was allowed to bring with him a friend as a supporter and as witness to the proceedings. Peter Tiley bravely agreed to accompany him. George appeared before Home Office Judge Ernest Wethered, chairman of the South-West Tribunal under the National Service Acts, and was subjected to rigorous, if fairly kindly, questioning as to his motives and intentions. He explained simply that he did not approve of war as a means of settling man's material disputes. There was no religious foundation to his conviction, purely an ethical one. The judge did not seem unduly offended. Would George agree to serve in the forces as a non-combatant? No, he did not approve of even that. The tribunal noted his arguments and registered him as a conscientious objector. He was not even required to engage in war work of a kind useful to the nation, although he did evolve his own alternative means of contributing to the war effort.

There were two ironies about this situation. Even his most anti-pacifist friends respected him. They thought him brave and honest to go before the tribunal because he would never have passed the medical examination for the forces anyway. But in that way he could not have made his philosophical point. The other irony was that in later years he became quite friendly with Judge Wethered's artistically inclined son and took great delight in inviting the judge and his wife to one of his post-war exhibitions, where they were all photographed together as a record of happier days.

At first it seemed as though George intended to cope with the war by ignoring it. If it had not been for the idealism of Torch, his position would have seemed rather negative. But there was a comic side to it. During the war it was customary for people not serving in the forces to do duty as wardens under the Air Raid Precautions regulations. The ARP people met with no response from George and eventually came to visit him. They knocked on the door and explained that they wanted him to join their duty-rota. George quite simply but courteously replied that that was not convenient. The ARP people reeled back in speechless astonishment as he shut the door in their faces. But he did not escape for long. He did eventually take his turn as a warden and, in later years, he seemed proud enough to list his ARP activities on his *curriculum vitae*. As in the case of Peter Tiley, bombs were great persuaders.

The first year of the war was deceptive. The inactivity of the Phoney War left the British confused until, in the spring of 1940, friendly nations began to collapse before the might of Hitler's *Wehrmacht* – Denmark and Norway first, then the Netherlands, Belgium and France, all within a matter of weeks. The evacuation from Dunkirk and the battle for control of the skies seemed remote to Bristolians in their westerly position. After all, were not London-based companies and institutions being moved to the city for safety? But this was a false assumption. Bristol was an obvious target as a great commercial port with a significant transatlantic orientation. It was also a centre for heavy industry vital to the war effort. In suburban Filton the Bristol Aeroplane Company was working at top speed to manufacture tens of thousands of fighter planes for the air force. The distribution of spare parts alone was a major operation, managed apparently almost single-handedly by Barbara Lloyd in her lowly secretarial capacity in the Ministry of War. From September 1940 German bombs started dropping in earnest on Bristol and raids reached a climax in the great blitz of November.

George was holding a Torch meeting at Springfield Road on the evening when the air-raid siren sounded. Since it was impossible to leave, the little company had to lie with their heads under the table as the raid continued throughout the night. An uncomfortable and alarming experience, but at least Deborah Jones was glad to have been there. Her own house off Pembroke Road in Clifton was completely burned out that night. She was left with only the clothes in which she stood up and the little teddy-bear that she always carried around in her pocket for luck. It certainly worked that night.

George's own house was also damaged in the air raids of November 1940. A bomb landed nearby, damaging the front and blowing part of the roof off, but the Melhuishes emerged unscathed. Nine of their neighbours were not so fortunate: they all died that night. George's parents must have wondered what fate had in store for them. It had been quite kind to them so far. After all, they had just celebrated twenty-five years of happy marriage on 29 September. How much longer did they have? Almost 1,300 citizens were killed by bombs; 3,000 homes went up in smoke. The Melhuish house only came into the category of 'bomb damaged' – and there were 90,000 of those. At first light, on the news of the disaster, George's friends rushed round. He seemed philosophical, but stressed the cost of the losses sustained. Reassured, the friends went their own way, their pockets lighter by a few pounds.

The roof was soon repaired, but the blitz had long-term consequences for his life and career. He later confessed to finding it 'tragic but exhilarating' to witness the bombing and insisted that it began the whole process that moved towards his emergence as a notable abstract painter in the early 1950s. The journalist Max Barnes later recorded George's experiences:[1]

> Looking out from his Gold Room window across the rooftops of Montpellier . . . his whole personality had been moulded. For it was here watching Jamaica Street go up in flames during the blitzes that his artistic vision was fused in a fiery cauldron.
>
> Until then he had been painting portraits and drawing his inspiration from Nature. During the war his art underwent a dramatic change. The lines of his paintings became less clearly defined and often cloaked in smoke and flames. The latent violence of his abstract period, until now locked away, had been released by the spectacle of a city consumed by fire.

The immediate effect was upon his developing interest in painting urban landscapes, a genre at which he excelled and which many still regard as the most spectacularly successful of his career as an artist. The editor of *The Artist*, Raymond Sawkins, alluded to this involuntary process:[2]

In the winter of 1940 Bristol . . . was under German bombardment, and Melhuish would sometimes wander out after the raids to see how high explosives had changed the face of his old town. He found many of the buildings, semi-destroyed, had assumed fantastic shapes that gripped his imagination. He set to work painting them and produced some fine paintings. By using strong colour and handling his brush boldly Melhuish expressed his subjects with a feeling of power: his buildings often possess a massive strength and in some of these paintings there is the feeling that the buildings belong to some other world – as indeed they did – the world of the blitz. When he paints a building, he makes you feel that this is a particular one, with an individual character which distinguishes it from others.

Whether they are studies of individual buildings, such as *The Bombed Ballroom*, *The Belisha Beacon Blitz* and *Bristol Theatre after the Raid*, or more general views of bombed townscapes, such as his distant view from across the Avon of a traumatized Bristol, the buildings themselves take on the characteristic attitudes of human anguish. The people who once occupied or frequented them have now gone; their former haunts remain as the victims of inhumanity, terribly still, posed as a reminder of deliberate destructiveness.

About the same time George, surprisingly, tackled one or two paintings with a religious subject-matter. A lurid-coloured *Crucifixion* puzzles the viewer: despite its jarring tones, it has all the formal structure of a Russian icon but none of its transcendental spirituality. Much more moving was an enormously complex study, the *Entombment of Christ*. It consisted of five full-size figures, including Mary Magdalene, Joseph of Arimathaea and the Virgin. The neighbour's wife, with whom George claimed to be having 'lovey-dovey', was inappropriately cast as the Virgin; Barbara Lloyd less flatteringly as the Magdalene. George's friends posed willingly as he painted with his customary energy. Unfortunately it was not always possible to predict what emergency commitments his models might be expected to fulfil and, just before one full session, his Christ was called away. Barbara offered to save the day. By this time the United States had experienced the shock of Pearl Harbor and had joined the Allies. American soldiers suddenly appeared on the

English landscape and some of the officers found themselves billeted in private homes. Barbara discovered that a staid but highly intelligent doctor, a colonel in his mid-thirties, had been lodged in the house where she had a flat. Carl Cope knew George well, liked his paintings and attended some of the Torch meetings, but he tended to spend most of his time alone, working on plans to administer the German health service after the war. Cope was sure to oblige George as a stand-in Christ. Barbara rushed round the corner and up the stairs. She called out: 'Oh, come on, colonel, you've got to be Jesus Christ!' Cope was fond of George, so he obliged. In the studio he was stripped to his jockey shorts as George fussed around arranging the drapery on the other figures. That was no problem, but something seemed wrong with the colonel lying prone in the mourning women's arms. George announced: 'Of course, El Greco's Christ didn't have a loin-cloth.' The colonel sat up abruptly: 'Well, Melhuish's is having one!'[3]

Despite its comic aspects, George's hesitant experiment with his *Entombment* is revealing. It is his bombed buildings, not the mute and static life-group, that constitute a series of real *pietà* studies. The depersonalized images of the torn and broken townscapes are somehow more tragic and telling than human figures, posed to represent distress. George realized that he had a vocation as a war artist. He saw his recording of the horrors of war as his war work. Interestingly, this went beyond the eloquence of gutted and damaged buildings. He also executed a number of canvases on industrial subjects. From the 1942–4 period his *Blast Furnaces* and *Turbine Furnaces* are immensely powerful statements of a positive response to negative forces. A solidly-built Reyner Banham was immortalized as the model for the stoker in *Turbine Furnaces*. That particular canvas, acquired by the Imperial War Museum, is a breathtaking work whose violent magenta tones are unimaginable in the black-and-white reproductions usually available.

George saw his war paintings not simply as a vehicle for making a personal statement, but also as a means of augmenting his meagre income. He never sought or enjoyed the status of official war artist. But when he thought that any of his work might appeal to the War Artists Acquisitions Committee, he submitted it for consideration as the work of an independent artist. What Deborah Jones described as George's 'wartime Vlaminck' style[4] appealed to the panel, who agreed to purchase some of his submissions for the small sums that they could afford. One sometimes wonders how George's motives as a war artist could ever have been pecuniary. The effort of lobbying sympathetic committee members, such as Sir Kenneth Clark, and the cost of packing and transporting the canvases that might well be rejected was prohibitive, as his correspondence with the committee officials reveals. But he did gain a certain satisfaction when his work was accepted, accompanied by a certain pride when it was assigned to his own city of Bristol as part of the locality's official war art collection. His work was also shown with that of the official war artists in an exhibition at the National Gallery in 1944.

Throughout the war George found that regular income could be made from painting portraits. He realized that potential sitters were often subconsciously impelled to have themselves immortalized in that age of uncertainties. From George's point of view, they were not pot-boilers. Even though he needed the money, he would not allow his subject's vanity to compromise his artistic integrity. He did, however, evolve a remarkably successful sales patter. Many of his friends from Torch found themselves being talked into having their portraits painted. Dennis Mickleburgh had initially become involved in Torch because he was attracted by its musical activities (his family was prominent in the piano trade in Bristol) and, in 1943, when George realized that the young man's twenty-first birthday was imminent, he suggested painting him as a unique celebration of the event. Dennis was beguiled by the idea. Another passing member of Torch took a little more time to make up her mind. Jean Glenn's first job was in the reference section of the Central Library on College Green, where George was a regular reader and they came to know each other. He invited her to Torch and finally suggested that she might like her portrait painted. She later recalled:[5]

I agreed to this after some consideration! – and went to his studio in his mother's house in Springfield Road, Cotham, for several sittings. (I went on my bicycle since it was wartime!) . . . When the portrait was completed, he sold it to me for four guineas . . .

When he suggested painting me, he remarked at some stage that he was interested in 'ruins' (he had painted some vivid blitz scenes) and 'types'. He never said which he considered me to be!

His portraits could have an emotionally catalytic effect. In 1939, when his friend and fellow music-lover, Ronald Reed, was mildly courting a young beauty called Ruby Harding, George suggested that he might capture the lady's heart by having her portrait painted. While George executed the work (on aluminium), Ronald and Ruby got to know each other better and then married. The result was years of happiness and a total of six children.

Less successful was George's attempt to paint the portrait of Dorothy Irving-Bell, the vivacious wife of the Senior Assistant Medical Officer of Health for Bristol. He had been introduced to the Irving-Bells by the poet and flamboyant eccentric Trevor Blakemore, who had gone into voluntary exile in Bristol in order to be with his companion, Anne Driver, the children's broadcaster. Blakemore admired George as an artist and suggested that he might do a very good study of Dorothy Irving-Bell. She consented and three or four times went for sittings to George's house. He made her sit on a kitchen table. She did not mind particularly, but became rather restive as long session followed long session. Then she made a fatal mistake: she looked at the painting before it was finished and she could not hide her reaction from George's sensitive eye. She was clearly unhappy about his distinctive style. He gave her no more sittings and left the portrait unfinished. Nothing was heard of it again, wartime shortages probably compelling him to re-use the canvas. However, the incident did not sour the relationship at the personal level and he remained friendly with the Irving-Bells for decades to come. Her reaction to his work is perhaps a little surprising because she had plenty of examples hanging before her eyes on the walls of his house: a double-portrait of his parents (plus the cat, Fluff); an individual portrait of his cigarette-smoking father; a deceptively severe one of his mother; and a perfectly ravishing self-portrait, with a red bow tie and a remarkable blue shirt (remarkable because George used blue in his paintings as little as possible). But these portraits were from earlier days and by the mid-war years his style and use of colour had become much more aggressive.

Another person who was taken aback by his portrait of her was Kathleen Beer. Kathleen moved more in Bristol's musical circles than the art world, having a beautiful singing voice. She starred in the London première of Falla's *Master Peter's Puppet Show*; sang in Rutland Boughton's long-running *Immortal Hour*; and coped with Dame Ethel Smyth's constructive criticism of her performance in *The Wreckers* (shouted from one end to the other of a crowded London bus). But devotion to ailing parents and commitment to the family's ladder business, founded by her grandfather, a great friend of Isambard Kingdom Brunel, brought her back permanently to Bristol, where for nineteen years she worked as a highly successful director for the Bristol Opera School. A young Rita McKerrow, already a professional singer of note, was performing in St George's, Brandon Hill, in a nativity play by Irene Gass with music by Eric Thiman. After one performance, Kathleen invited her round to the studio of Methven Brownlee, herself a successful photographer, and, for some reason, George was present, although he had not attended the play. Rita McKerrow was not overly impressed by his appearance. The spotted bow tie was passable, but his hair looked rather lank and, worse, his front two teeth were missing, having gone the way of all flesh. By way of compensating for nature's deficiencies, he had a plate with false teeth, but he had developed the habit of taking it out when he thought that he was in relaxed company. What Methven Brownlee thought of his informality is another matter; she was not the type of woman to put up with male vagaries. But that scarcely mattered, since the Brownlee set and his own, younger one tended not to mix (with the notable exception of Deborah Jones, who looked on 'Brownie' as a substitute mother). However off-putting his appearance, Kathleen Beer found herself being induced to sit for her portrait. Her father was in poor health and she thought that her picture would make a charming present for him. She did not reckon with the wilfulness of George's artistic impulses. A gentle, modest individual, she found herself transformed by him into an imperious figure whose fair complexion had become almost swarthy and whose cherished sage-green dress had turned red. But Kathleen was enough of an artist herself to try to understand his interpretation and, as a work of art, the portrait is successful.

Even more important was George's portrait of Adrian Boult. Boult was a good friend and former colleague of Kathleen Beer's and, when the BBC orchestra was evacuated to Bristol and he took a house on the Downs called Cook's Folly, their friendship revived. George was genuinely fond of music and admired Boult. He regarded it as an achievement to get him to pose for the portrait. The result was impressive. With other famous London evacuees, George had less success. He approached some and met with a discouraging response. Paul Beard suggested that, if he wanted, he might come and make sketches in the green room, but George preferred to work in a less public place and nothing much came of the project.

Torch members continued to provide a supply of models for portraits. Reyner Banham took off his stoker's dungarees and posed for him. John Sheppard also sat for him, although George seems to have been more interested in listening to Sheppard's gossip about their friends than in the painting.

His portrait-studies of his two close women friends, Barbara Lloyd and Deborah Jones, are among his finest achievements in the genre: Barbara in a straight portrait and in another at her dressing table; and Deborah, again at her *toilette*, fixing her hair, the arms above the head framing her exquisite classical Greek features. A double-portrait of George with Deborah Jones at a café table is a superb piece of craftsmanship.

George confessed to being less confident of himself with men's portraits. Barbara asked him to paint her new beau, Barrie Thorne. He obliged but found the job unusually difficult. The result, however, was an extraordinarily lifelike canvas.

He seems to have had slightly fewer problems with other male portraits. He painted Peter Tiley's picture in the winter of 1939–40, just after the outbreak of war. He is a scholarly-looking youth, with a withdrawn, distant look. (This was a fairly characteristic feature of George's earlier portraits.) A second portrait of Peter was painted after the war in 1945. Still in his uniform and sporting a truly awesome moustache, the subject has clearly been precipitated towards maturity by the experiences of war. But in stylistic terms a comparison of the two Tiley portraits instantly reveals the extent to which George himself had matured as a painter, with a sureness of touch and control of colour that makes the 1945 portrait stand out as a work of infinitely greater mastery than the earlier one.

George's fee-scale had also developed during the war. He tended to sell his work to impecunious friends at much lower than the commercial rate, but even here fame and inflation were catching up. The 1940 portrait of Peter Tiley cost 30 shillings; the 1945 one commanded a fee of £20. But George would soon earn considerably more than that for his work.

CHAPTER SIX

A QUALITY OF DYNAMIC ENERGY

During the war Bristol experienced a high point of cultural vibrancy. The mass of Bristolians were conservative in their tastes and suspicious of anything new and extravagant. But pressurized by the need to maintain a community spirit and given an intellectual shot in the arm with the influx of academic and artistic evacuees, the city came to life despite German bombs. There was a healthy disrespect for the *Luftwaffe*. As Barbara Lloyd recalled, 'going home from Torch one night after a blitz, I remember kicking great pieces of shrapnel – just kicking them as we went on – with the whole city in flames. Awful! We all quite enjoyed it . . . The quality of courage and fortitude that it brought out in people was marvellous.'[1] Patricia Daly found it heartening when her father (who, in his free time from his job as chief engineer at the BBC, ran the Home Guard) told her that his 'men' could not enjoy a rank based on their professional standing in the outside world. Apparently Adrian Boult's appointment to a rank above Leon Goossens, a mere lance-corporal, had caused some friction. But petty rivalries had no lasting significance. The main thing was to work together towards a common aim. As Patricia remarked, 'it was a curious set-up altogether during the war because people were thrown together so much. . . . The blitz had broken down a lot of barriers.'[2] None the less, barriers did remain. There tended to be a divide between the cultural orientation of the two universities and that of the Art School, which was a hive of general artistic activity. Patricia Daly recalled: [3]

The interesting thing about Bristol in those days was that, if you wanted to know about avant-garde literature, you did not go to the

University, but you would hear all about it from the Art Group people . . . This was typical in those days: the Art School [abounded with] really advanced ideas in literature and in music. I mean, *Façade* was very popular at the Art School, whereas at Bristol University they were still mainly centred on madrigals . . . A shutter came down with Vaughan Williams and the Elizabethans. But the Art School people (and George, of course) were interested in modern music, Constant Lambert's *Rio Grande* and *Façade* and Delius and really interesting modern music as well. And in literature you'd find much more advanced ideas in the Art School.

George had many contacts with the Art School set. A number of regular Torch members came from that background. They were, of course, very much of the same age group as himself. Contact with the older, more traditional clubs, such as the Bristol Savages, was more of a problem. Originally a late-Victorian foundation for poets, painters and singers, the Savages (with all the cult paraphernalia of categories of membership differentiated by different colours of feathers) occupied their own building in the centre of the town. It was called 'The Wigwam'. But for George they were a world away from the early twentieth-century *apaches* of the Parisian avant-garde whom he admired from a distance of time and geography.

Perhaps more exciting (and more sympathetic in terms of age) was the Clifton Arts Club. Deborah Jones had warm memories of it. She was intent on becoming a successful artist, yet kept her well-bred but impoverished body and soul together by modelling for artists. Strikingly beautiful, she later recalled what happened:[4]

I left boarding-school just before I was fifteen . . . in 1936; and immediately I got entangled with the artist lot in Bristol. I used to sit for the Clifton Arts Club, and in those days it was really something: it wasn't just a gang of old faggots dabbing away for dear life . . . We had some very good painters. We had Donald Hughes . . . and artists like Mary Fedden, Maisie Meicklejohn, Biddy Cook . . . and Bernard Perrin . . . All sorts of people, but they were good. And they had a super place, a whole building, complete with a ghost in the attic . . . The ground floor was a shop, on Park Street, the corner of Charlotte Street, a lovely big Georgian house . . . And the whole of the top was burnt out in the blitz, so we often wondered about the ghost.

George was a welcome visitor to the club but, in time, his egocentricity and his personal mannerisms caused the members to lose patience with him. They particularly disliked his apparently chronic shortage of cash that seemed to give him the licence to call on their material support whenever he needed it. What irritated even more was the knowledge that he was developing (and clearly could afford to develop) a parallel life outside Bristol.

George had always been attracted by what he called 'the glamorous life'. His greatest ambition was to make a base for himself in Paris, the acme of perfection as far as he was concerned, but that was impossible until hostilities ceased. In the meantime, he enjoyed the sophisticated company that had abandoned the metropolis for Bristol. Among them, Dorothy and Ronald Irving-Bell's friends Anne Driver and Trevor Blakemore were a source of constant social stimulation. Blakemore, who soon became a familiar figure round Clifton Village with his flowing cloak and broad-brimmed 'poet's hat' that scarcely concealed an ill-fitting toupee, had come down to Bristol to be with Anne Driver after children's broadcasting had been evacuated from London. What did he do? Nothing much except float around doing his best to pretend that food shortages did not exist. When Blakemore decided to move in formally to Anne Driver's place in Rodney Cottages, Ronald Irving-Bell found himself inveigled into transporting his extensive wine-cellar. As a senior medical officer, he not only had a car but also the petrol for it. The wine had arrived; the gourmet Blakemore devoted himself to nosing out the most unavailable of foodstuffs. Then the invitations to dinner were issued: 'To hell with this *pro patria* stuff! We're going to have a jolly good dinner.'[5]

George found himself the recipient of some of this 'illegal' hospitality. He also found Blakemore's dinner-table repartee entertaining, if start-ling. Anne Driver used to sit at table, let his 'frightful language' wash over her, and then only mildly remonstrate with him for using all sorts of outrageous words. At times the guests would pretend not to know what they meant (although they knew perfectly well) and say, 'What's this odd word you're using, Trevor?'[6]

Blakemore had a good friend, John Peil, a sedate Greek scholar, more at home in the groves of academe, but he did join the party each Christmas. The cottage was not large, so Peil was accommodated next door in the Rodney Hotel. Predictably, Blakemore would announce that Peil was staying at the 'Sodney Hotel'. Just as shocking for a sensitive soul were the extraordinary 'fatal gifts' that he prepared for his guests and left wrapped in coloured tissue paper by everybody's side plate. The gifts consisted of plasticine models of various different appendages of the human body, such that even a qualified medical man, like Ronald Irving-Bell, found eye-opening. The poor, staid scholar received a model of a clergyman wearing a dog-collar, with a caption that read, 'Father Up, the Catholic Priest.'[7] All this was light-years away from Anne Driver's world of 'Listen with Mother'.

For the day, that level of humour was considered outrageous and, normally, quite unacceptable, but George seems to have taken it in his stride, even though he was not a particularly witty person himself. There is never a hint of levity either in his paintings or in his philosophical works and, in the social context, his humour tended to remain at the teasing or mischievous level. The problem about George was that it was a full-time job to induce others to take him seriously. And they did, as far as his work and achievements were concerned. Behind his back, people tended mildly to poke fun at him. The Blakemore set gave him yet another nickname, 'the Gull'. They thought that the way in which he responded to ideas with a double exclamation 'Yes! yes!' sounded like a seagull's cry. Truth be told, George never lost his rather flat Bristolian accent, even after years of socializing far from the West Country influence. In a curious fashion the way in which he seemed to grind out his words, slowly rolling his 'r's, suited his almost pontifical manner of making a point, serious or otherwise.

Another set of arrivals on the Bristol scene who fascinated George were the American soldiers. From 1942 a number of them, billeted in private houses, caused quite a stir. He was particularly intrigued by the black soldiers and made a number of studies of them: the warmth of their skin-tones struck a sympathetic chord at a time when he was employing a rugged, expressionist style and a bright, colourful palette. He wandered into the realm of the imagination and Barbara Lloyd found herself transformed on canvas into an alluring Negress. But the American soldiers' influence went further than George's studio. Carl Cope, lodged with Barbara's landlady, Mrs Clare Jenkins, in her big house at 75 Cotham Brow, made a big hit with everybody despite his reticence. Patricia Daly and Barbara were introduced by him to an extraordinary book, *The Circus of Dr Mayo*, 'which had a cult following in America in those days and since has become quite fashionable here'.[8] George, needless to say, did not join the hierophants. Even the fascinating Colonel Cope could not induce him to delve into it.

George did, however, delve into another area of cultural life. Looking to the future and knowing that his reputation as more than just a local artist depended on self-advertisement beyond the confines of Bristol, he set his sights on London, since Paris was still inaccessible. His motives were not simply self-seeking. He also felt the need for exposure to the new stylistic influences and stimulation that the capital could give in a way that Bristol could not. In 1943 he took a studio in Chelsea, at

45 King's Road, and plunged into a world of artists, gallery owners and cultured socialites, such as he had previously only dreamt about. He enjoyed himself while he pursued the serious business of painting and having his work exhibited and, he hoped, sold.

Though less chic than in subsequent decades, the King's Road was then well placed from the social point of view. Tite Street and Cheyne Walk were comfortingly nearby. The road itself contained convenient shops and pubs. The wartime social set were to be seen making a bee-line for the latest pub that had acquired its gin ration. George saw pubs mainly as social rather than drinking centres. He appreciated a little more 'the wonderful, old-fashioned dining-rooms nearby'.[9] These were highly necessary because, although George did cook for himself in the studio, his kitchen facilities were primitive in the extreme. Barbara frequently visited him there over a number of years and recorded her memories of the place. The studio was above an optician's premises and was set 'in a row of early Victorian houses with shops underneath . . . It was just one big room on the first floor with windows looking out onto the King's Road. And you went down a sort of half-stair and there was a lavatory and basin, but that was all.'[10] The rent was ludicrously low, so nobody was surprised that there was no light on the stair. The water was never hot and, worse, George had to share the conveniences with 'another person living in the building, a lady who was very dictatorial, a fellow tenant'.[11] She was always complaining to or about George. This was scarcely surprising, since he had to clean up after painting in the communal sink.

But George had to cope with other hazards. Barbara often used to come up to London to visit him. There were frequent air raids and, when the sirens went, she would laugh as he pulled on his long-johns: 'Come on, Barbara!' And they 'used to rush down and go into the Circle Line and ride round and round while the blitz was on'.[12]

London inspired another departure for George in terms of his art. The surroundings of beautifully constructed Georgian streets and squares made his mind move more and more away from buildings blitzed beyond recognition to the image of buildings in the absolute stillness of undisturbed history. One seriously doubts if he imagined that, as the war drew nearer to its end, he was projecting forward to the hoped-for tranquillity of the future. More likely, he was intent on preserving a record of past human achievement, should the ultimate holocaust occur. The result was that he executed a series of stunning architectural landscapes, often at night with dark, menacing skies and always containing a dramatic vibrancy of their own, simply by virtue of the fact that they were impressive products of a worthwhile civilization. His pictures

Belgrave Square (1943) and *The Port of London Authority* (1944) are particularly striking examples of the drama of structures. Like the blitz paintings, they contain – and deliberately so – no 'narrative element'. George scrupulously avoided inserting human figures and even transitory human artefacts, such as motor cars, into his scenes. Only occasionally does one gain the impression that some form of human activity is going on 'behind the scenes'. Back in Bristol, in the early winter months of 1944, he availed himself of Anne Driver's cottage as a base from which to paint a snow scene of Rodney Place. The street is, predictably, deserted but from the windows yellow light glows out, indicating some human dimension, warm in contrast with the cold scene outside. This painting also illustrates something characteristic of George's use of colour: although a snow scene, he manages to confine his use of white to a minimum amount of superficial streaking brush strokes; there is also practically no use of blue.

George's studio in the King's Road did not mean that he became London-based. More often than not he was in Bristol, since he felt that his mother should not be left unattended for too long. She was increasingly crippled with arthritis and, although his father was still alive, he too was incapable of heavy domestic work. Besides, he loved them both and did not like to be parted from them for any length of time. However, he did use his London flat as a base from which to make painting expeditions out into the countryside. Basically he disliked country life and had little respect for nature as such. He would end up painting buildings such as Doddington Church, Winchester Cathedral and Reculver Church. Even canvases with titles such as *Landscape* invariably have a building, such as a ruined castle, as their focal point. A painting entitled *Flint Castle* is of a more dubious inspiration. George certainly did not visit Flint in person. (Indeed, he never travelled further north than Birmingham. And even that was a mistake: he fell asleep on a train and had the shock of his life when he awoke to find himself in New Street station.)

This period illustrates how the relevance of nature-in-the-raw gradually receded for George. The last 'nature paintings' that he attempted all date from before 1946. But even by then natural objects only retained any significance for him if their forms had some anthropomorphic quality. In his introduction to George's published collection of paintings, *George Melhuish*, his devoted friend, the editor of the *Bristol Packet*, Richard Hutton, goes on at inordinate length when discussing a 'nature painting' entitled *Tree and Fungus*:[13]

The eye of the person beholding this picture is alternately recognising and agreeing with the familiar and rejecting, for a time, the unfamiliar . . . All objects have private meanings as well as common meanings to those who see them. An object such as a tree has a common meaning . . . a meaning which makes the majority agree that it is a tree and nothing else. The tree has a private meaning too and this meaning, based on memory and the subconscious mind, varies in each person . . . But for the artist there are no private meanings and he is only concerned with the meaning of the tree that strikes his artist's eye. He has to contend with all the private meanings of all the people who will see his painting of the tree and he has to subdue these obtruding private meanings and substitute his own.

In the case of *Tree and Fungus* no such effort was necessary. A study of a 'nature object' it may have been, but even the most unfreudian of eyes would recognize it as a female form in a none too dignified pose. One thing is certain: George's paintings were all 'unnatural' in as much as he invariably produced the finished product in his studio and very seldom out of doors. But he had one great advantage. As Raymond Sawkins pointed out, he was 'in the habit of . . . making quick sketches in oils outdoors on unprimed paper before returning to the studio to paint the final version'.[14] By the end of the war and even more noticeably in the post-war period a development in technique took place:[15]

His method was to make pencil sketches which attracted him out-doors, with scribbled instructions as to colours, and then return to a studio . . . to paint direct in oils . . . His interest has enabled him to cultivate an excellent memory for colour: while walking about he will make a mental note of some colour scheme – perhaps seen in a woman's costume or flowers in a park – and he is able to file away these colour 'references' in his mind until he needs them.

London was just as important to George as a base from which to publicize himself. The exhibition of his work was a pressing priority. He had already exhibited in Bristol and nearby towns, but he knew that the eyes of the art world tended to focus myopically on the capital. In 1942, even before setting himself up in Chelsea, he had some of his war paintings exhibited at the Leicester Galleries. The owners were impressed enough to show more of his paintings the following year, as did the Léger Gallery. Also in 1943 he had his first one-man exhibition in London, by courtesy of Jack Bilbo at the Modern Gallery. Foyle's, the adventurous bookshop in Charing Cross Road, mounted a one-man show of his work in its prestigious little gallery in 1944. The introduction to the catalogue proclaimed:[16]

His aim is high – namely, a return to the heroic dignity of the Masters of the past, and his present art has been achieved by constant struggle and meditation towards this end. Both his landscapes and portraits are painted in a style of great vivacity, and one feels instantly that here is something which has been wrought by a powerful and confident brush, a competent draughtsman, dominated by an unusually aesthetic mind . . . I cannot help feeling that George Melhuish is on the threshold of great achievement . . . in his best paintings he has carried his finished work onto a plane unique in the history of painting today.

The enthusiastic writer was a certain Barbara Addison, whose views might reasonably be expected to be biased, since she was, in fact, Barbara Lloyd. On a recent impulse, she had married one of her group in Bristol, Alfred Addison – or 'Alfie Ad', as she always called him. He disappeared off to his army unit next day and only re-appeared several years later when an annulment had to be worked out. Meanwhile, Barbara wrote under the name of Addison, more often than not in connection with George's work. Predisposed to it she certainly was, but her comments were fair and balanced, reflecting the growing public respect for the artist.

Outside London, George had held exhibitions of oil paintings in the Cheltenham Art Gallery and in the Co-operative Education Building in Bristol. But possibly more important were the hangings of individual canvases in 'establishment' galleries in the capital. During the war he regularly had paintings accepted for the Royal Academy Exhibition. The first was his *Houses under Snow* in 1943, and in 1944 he exhibited another canvas entitled *Snow Scene* along with his study of Deborah Jones's *Toilette*. Sedately translated into English as *Girl dressing her Hair*, it caused quite a stir. In June 1943 he had one of his paintings exhibited in an Artists' Aid for China show, organized by Lady Cripps in Hertford House. The editor of *Connoisseur* reviewed the exhibition and reproduced an illustration of George's painting, 'a lurid representation of *Bath Abbey* enduring its blitz, a convincing first-hand impression.'[17] George was in good company; his picture hung cheek-by-jowl with artists such as George Harcourt, Augustus John, Feliks Topolski and Jacob Epstein. On display in the Chinese Section was a 'very attractive rose quartz carving of a flute player given by Her Majesty Queen Mary'.[18] Lady Louis Mountbatten contributed a white jade bowl. The Royal Society of British Artists also twice exhibited his work. And in 1944, when the National Gallery's Official War Artists' Exhibition showed their purchases, the *Turbine Furnaces* made a particular impact.

News of George's success reached Bristol. His friends, on trips to London, would slip into the National Gallery and find themselves confronted by his paintings hanging alongside the illustrious. They experienced a vicarious frisson of pleasure for him. Some of his friendly rivals back in Bristol ill-concealed their jealousy at what he had achieved before them, for all their years of academic training. As Patricia Daly commented, 'he was on very good terms with people like Sir Kenneth Clark. He just took his pictures to show people and evidently his work was recognised as being outstanding . . . even though untutored. Whereas the academics of the Royal College, or the students, I should say, and Bristol were perhaps more hidebound, although some of them could be very good. But at that time . . . there wasn't the encouragement towards experimentation.'[19] George was nothing if not uninhibited and entirely unabashed about what he had achieved. When his book *George Melhuish* appeared in 1946, he listed on the back cover quotations from reviews of his work over the preceding years: 'One of the younger of our eminent artists, whose work is virile and exquisite in colour' (*The Artist*); 'Melhuish brings into British Art a quality of dynamic energy, even violence, that is far from a national characteristic' (*The Studio*). The *Daily Telegraph* commented particularly on his 'snowscapes of power and breadth'. *Queen*, faintly grudgingly, commented: 'I admit you've learned your use of red, Mr Melhuish . . . Certainly, too, I'll congratulate you on your negro nudes.' In Paris the journal *La Revue* took up his work: 'Although he may be a believer in modernism, he reveals his knowledge of the Great Masters of the past, and works ceaselessly to perfect his craft.'[20]

George was particularly proud that his work was being discussed and illustrated in French journals. With the liberation of Paris this seemed like a promise, a prophecy of things to come.

CHAPTER SEVEN

WRITING ON ART

The war period witnessed George Melhuish's emergence as a writer and philosopher. He was always extremely hard-working as an artist, painting with a speed and energy that surprised anybody deceived by his fragile appearance. However, he seemed to need no excuse to divert his attention away from the serious business of painting. In 1943 he decided that his career might benefit from a diversion into the world of art journalism. His motives were partly pecuniary, partly self-advertisement. But, more important, he had begun to feel the need not only to be a painter but also to rationalize his philosophy as a painter and, as it soon transpired, to formalize a whole philosophy of life.

The editor of *The Artist*, Raymond Sawkins, commissioned him to do a series of articles on the technique of painting. Those who considered George as an 'untrained' artist thought this rather presumptuous, but that did not prevent him from producing six well-turned pieces, aptly illustrated with his own work. The first appeared in March 1944 and the rest in five subsequent issues. They focused almost entirely on the architectural painting that preoccupied him at the time and at which he excelled. In his prefatory article he discussed 'the necessity for developing outlook'; he revealed his historical antecedents, beginning with the Italian primitives and the Renaissance painters, but 'it was not until the rise to eminence of landscape painting at the beginning of the seventeenth century that we have paintings in which buildings often predominate in the composition'.[1] He went on to point out how Claude, that master of landscapes, made 'fine and outstanding use of temples and ancient ruins in many of his big works, often with much dignity and grandeur, while many Dutch painters of the late seventeenth and early eighteenth centuries painted with great precision, but with little emotion or imagination, the neat and clean streets of Holland'.[2] George harked back to the time of El Greco in whom, 'with his beautiful and mysterious views of Toledo, we see for the first time the city panorama produced as a painting of fine emotion'.[3] He then projected forward to his own position on the subject, though taking care to pay due homage to his particular hero, Turner, perhaps the greatest master of architectural subjects. He lectured his readers. The artist's response to a scene was what mattered:[4]

> This should always be one of spontaneous interest and enthusiasm. The subjects that have for some time appealed to me have been the fine and dignified Georgian streets of cities such as Bath and Bristol. These streets often have a mood all of their own, perhaps of a delicate nostalgia or deep richness . . . Georgian architecture . . . offers strong yet simple lines in composition, often with subtle new colour harmonies, as, for instance, when late afternoon sun plays upon an old terrace with, perhaps, some houses an ochre colour, some grey and one, say, a delicate pink or green . . . Late afternoon sunshine is often productive of some of nature's most interesting lighting effects on buildings, often combining richness with an interesting shadow pattern caused by the relative lowness of the sun.

Finally, the perspective created by a skilful painting of the sky was all important: 'the weakness and indecisiveness of many landscapes of all kinds is often due to the sky not having been properly treated. The sky must always be considered as an intrinsical part of the composition.'[5] Perhaps an obvious point but an important one that George, as a painter, could not be accused of overlooking.

The subsequent parts of the series explained in more detail the approach essential for success with urban landscapes. Some knowledge of architecture as a discrete branch of the Fine Arts was 'a good thing', but balance in arranging one's composition was almost more important. Indeed, knowledge of architectural principles 'should be used with discretion, never allowing any such knowledge to override the mood, dramatic set or conception of an individual painting'.[6] He promised a discussion on the use of colour: 'Do not be afraid of using strong colour; your pictures will be more powerful . . . Remember that, in architectural subjects, we have to handle fairly big masses, and for this reason their colour values must be carefully watched and suitably arranged, otherwise any one mass might throw the whole picture out of harmony.'[7]

The whole of the article in the May issue did, in fact, centre on the question of the use of colour. Again, while he had a great deal of practical wisdom to impart, he did allow his distinctively post-Impressionist concept of the drama of colour to carry him away in a fashion that might have surprised readers who still regarded Monet as an avant-garde discovery. From a man with an eye for brilliant reds, hot yellows and bright greens, it is not surprising that he was prejudiced against the ultra-violet end of the spectrum:[8]

> While not necessarily agreeing with Sir Joshua Reynolds that a painting can never have dignity where blue is the predominating colour, I think, since the 'finds' of the Impressionists, that purple and blue have been thrown all over the canvas, often with very little meaning and much vulgarity to the colour scheme. Blue and purple are, of course, fine colours when used with good taste, but many landscapes have been rendered rather worse than they may otherwise have been by gaudy blue sky or monotonous purple shadows.

The article in the July edition of *The Artist* is interesting because, although it deals with what George calls the 'extras' of architectural landscape, like human figures, trees and skies, he has some apposite warnings to make as well as some positive advice to give. As he remarks, these extras, 'if poorly or shoddily treated . . . will ruin the quality of any work'.[9] The human figure in any kind of landscape was anathema to George, but he does try, to begin with, to be objective about the matter:[10]

> A very common mistake made by students when introducing figures into landscapes, when the scene is already more or less finished, is to forget to draw the necessary shadows relative to the rest of the work, or else forget the shadows altogether; the figures then seem as if they are stuck on the canvas.
>
> My own reason for not using human figures in my landscapes is not that I fear being able to co-ordinate them with the rest of the landscape but, in the kind of mood I try to present in my compositions, they would usually be ambiguous.

George, who spent most of the rest of his life meditating on concepts of ambiguity, was being a purist for once – but with remarkable effect as far as his own urban landscapes were concerned.

His comments on the painting of trees in landscape meant that he was treading on dangerous ground, for the simple reason that, unless a tree was the focal point of the composition (in which case the treatment would veer towards the abstract), he was himself not always comfortable when painting them, so he was well aware of the problems involved:[11]

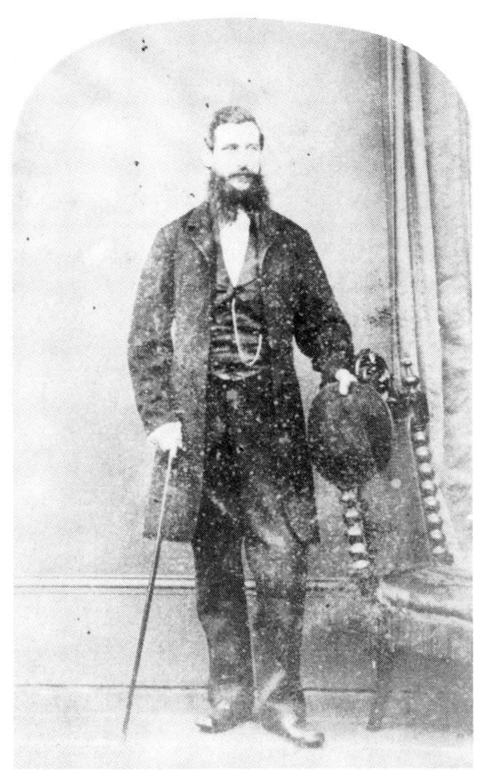

1. George Melhuish (grandfather),
    c. 1872

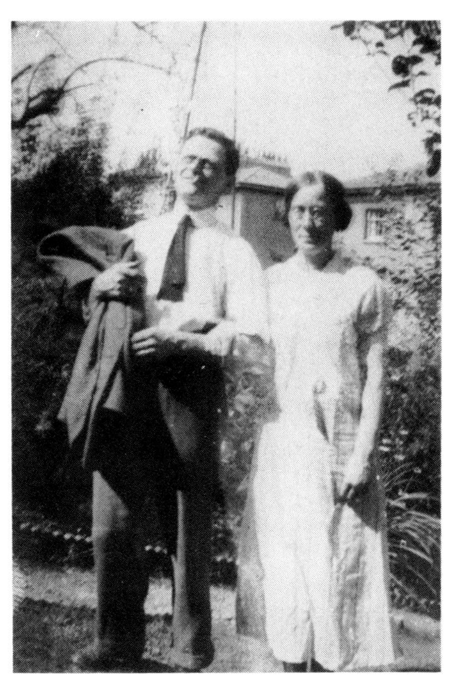

2. George and Elsie
    Melhuish, *c.* 1930

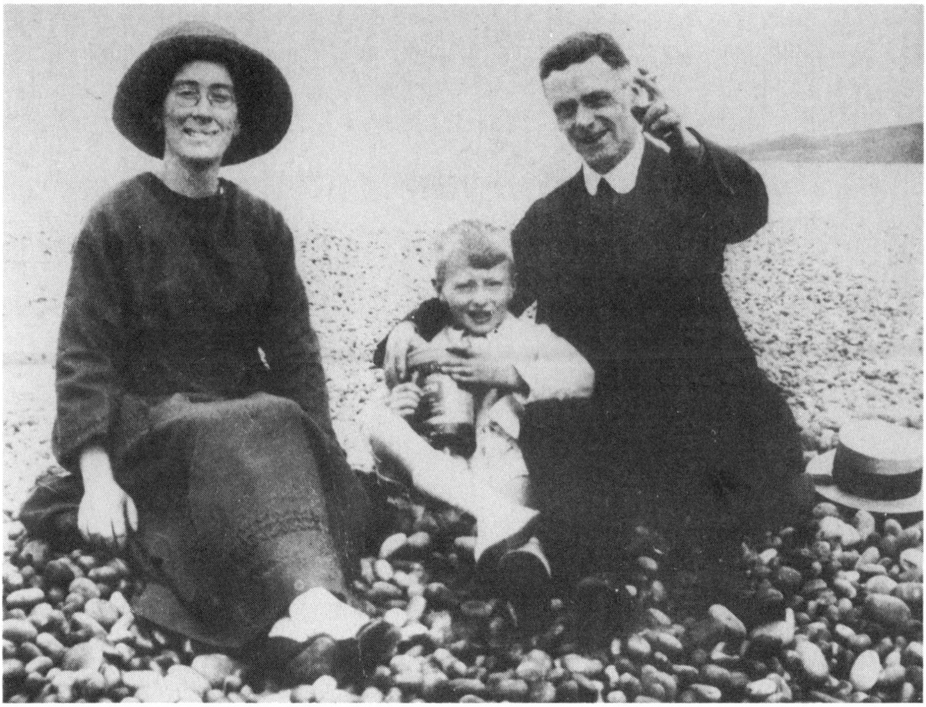

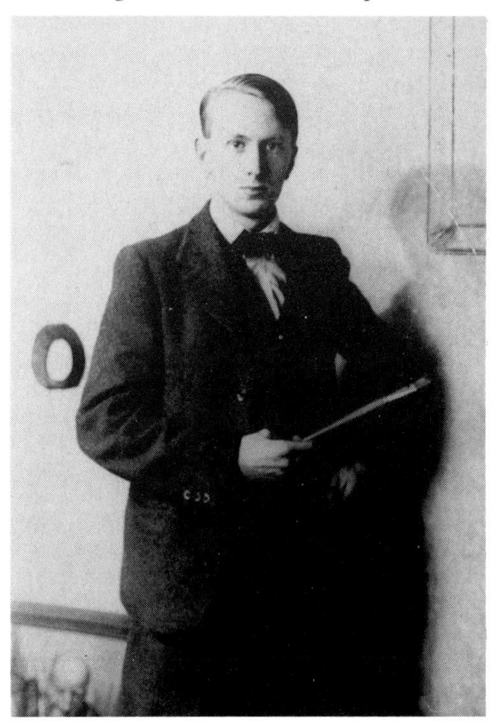

3. George Melhuish with his parents, *c.* 1922

4. George Melhuish, *c.* 1935

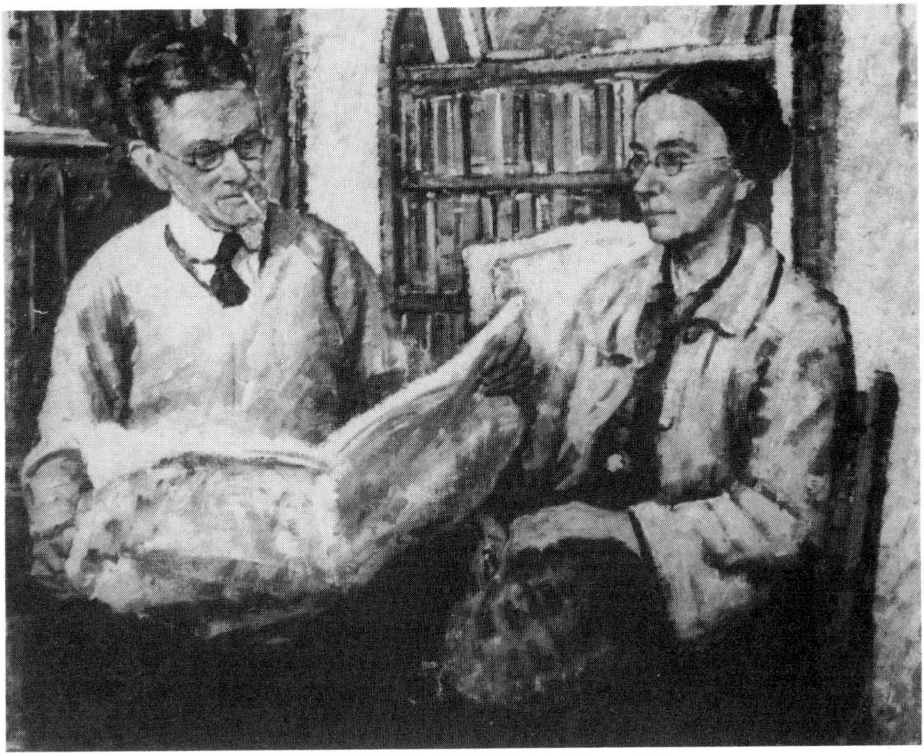

5.   Double portrait of George and Elsie Melhuish, *c.* 1938

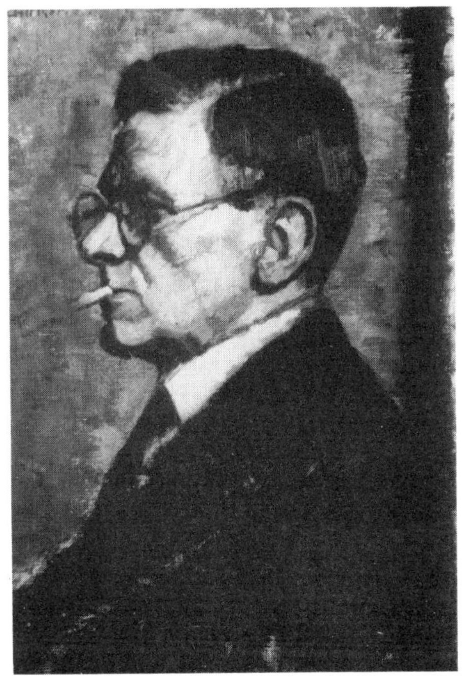

6.   Portrait of George
      Barnett Melhuish, *c.* 1938

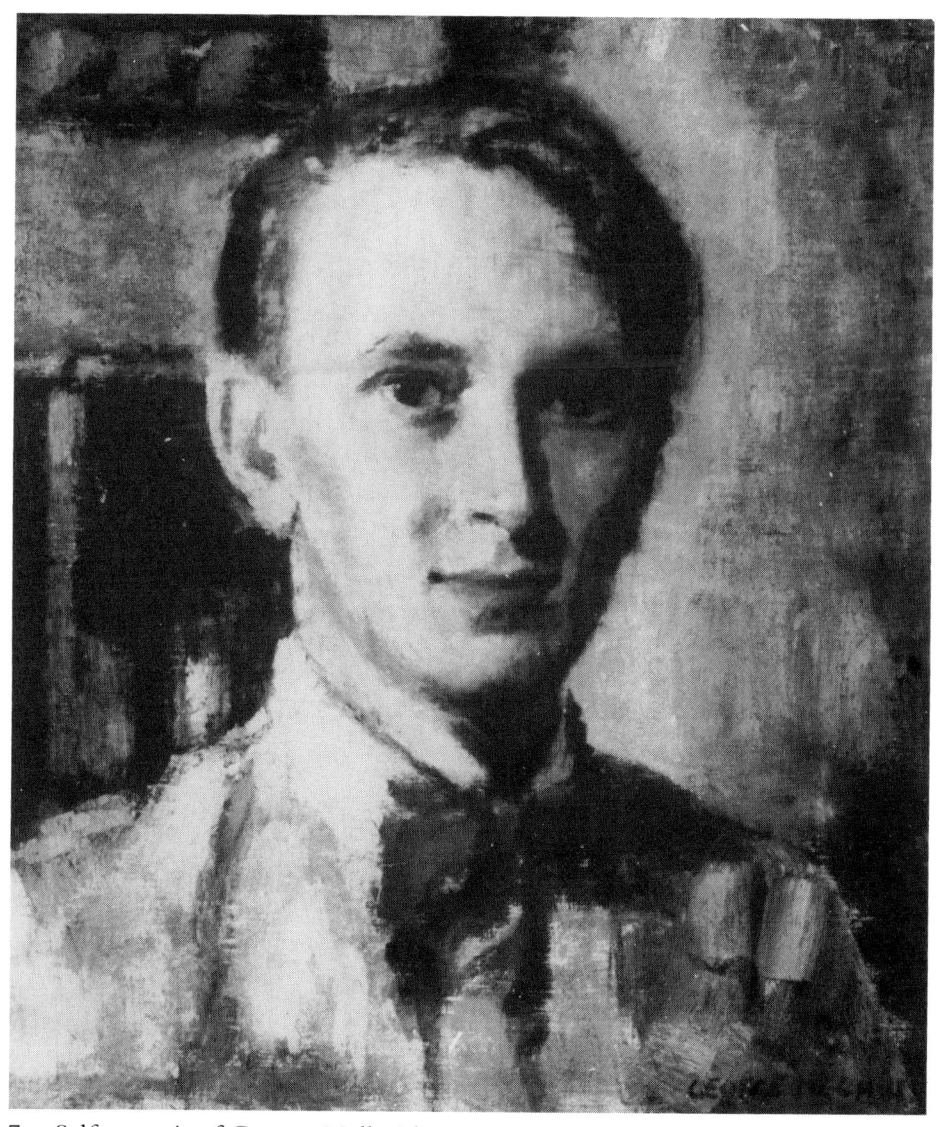

7.   Self-portrait of George Melhuish, *c.* 1938

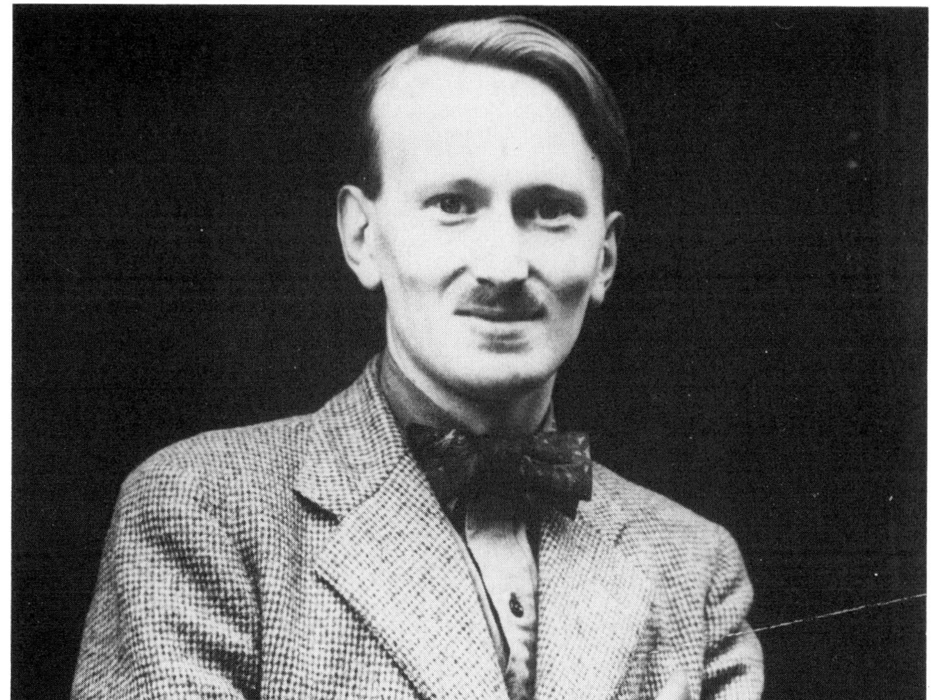

8. George Melhuish, *c.* 1942

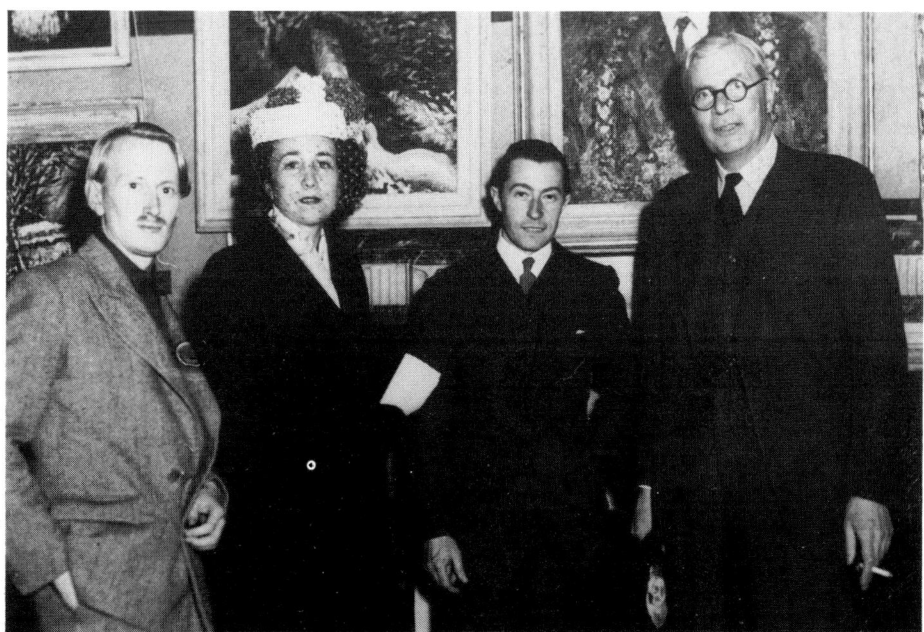

9. George Melhuish with Lady Rose, Sir Francis Rose and the Hon.
Oliver Stanley, MP

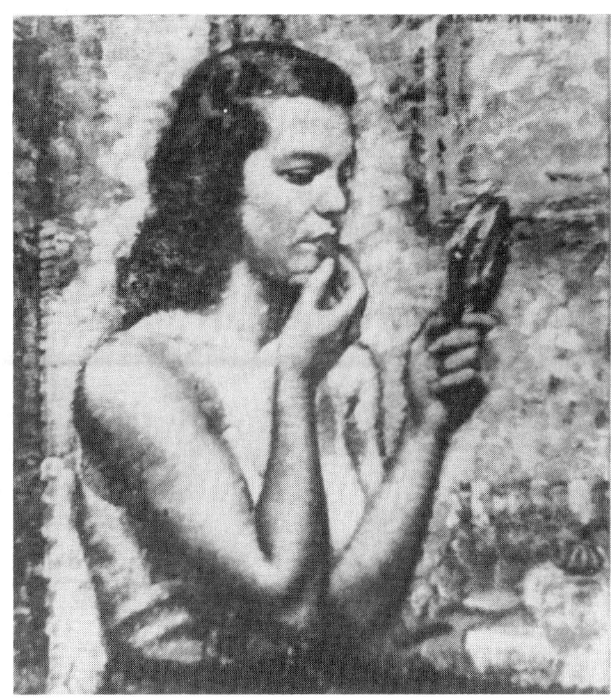

11. Portrait of
    Barbara Lloyd
    (later Thorne),
    c. 1941

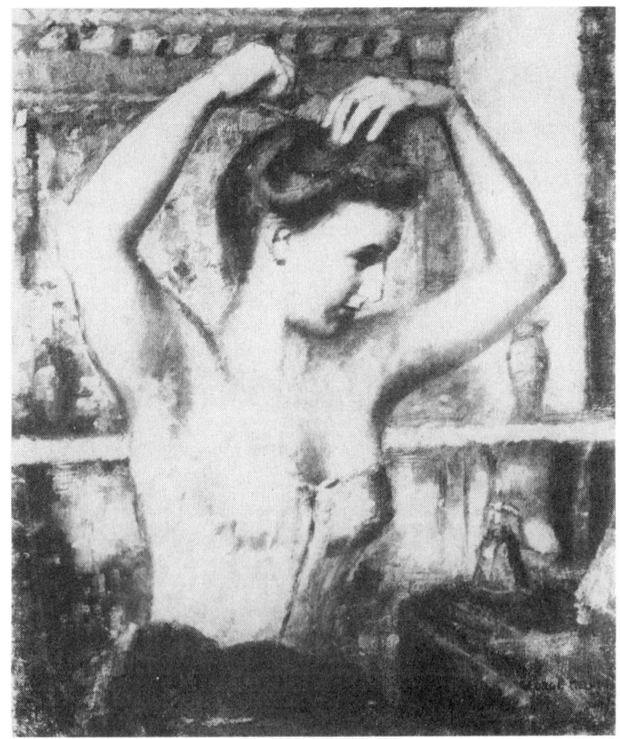

12. Portrait of
    Deborah Jones
    (*Toilette*), 1941

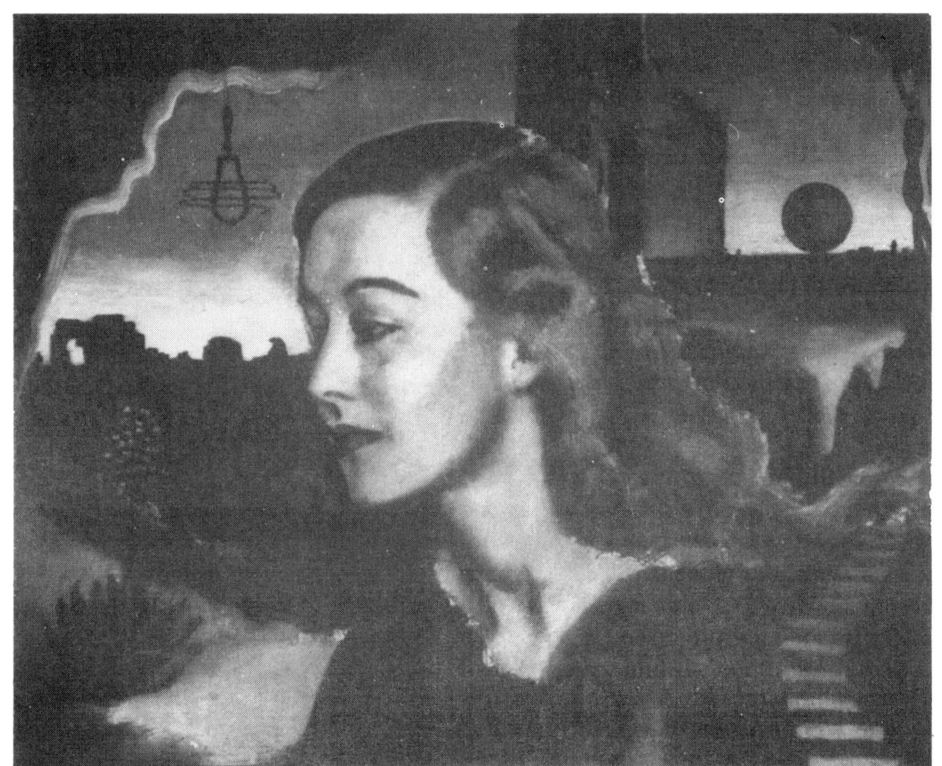

10.   Portrait of Edna Orchard (later Macdonald), 1939

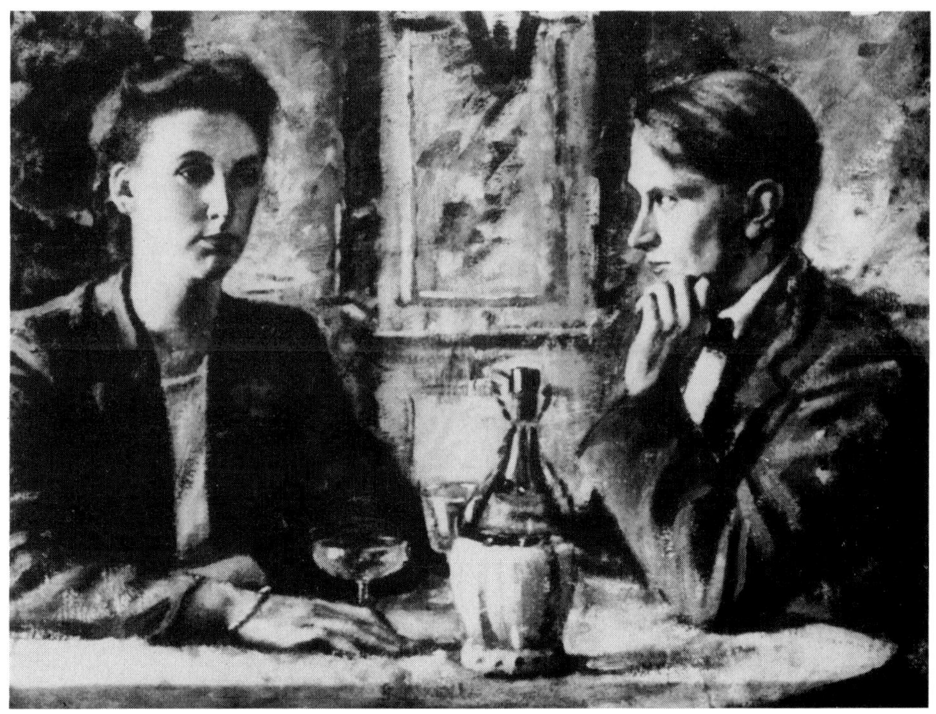

13.   Double portrait of Deborah Jones and George Melhuish, 1942

> Try not to get too many colours mixed on one tree, as this often makes
> for indecision and sentimentality. The English painter, Wilson Steer,
> could do this successfully, but some of his trees are formless; Cézanne
> was a great master of tree painting. Give special attention to the edges
> and shadows of the foliage, as they are important in suggesting the
> anatomy of the tree.

His mention of Cézanne is revealing: one cannot imagine George as a
tree-painter without his influence. Also revealing is his preoccupation
with the real problems of painting foliage. He, in fact, was most
successful when depicting leafless trees in winter landscapes, then
nothing detracted from their anatomical structure and form.

The concluding article in the August issue summed up the series with a
number of entirely practical hints on mundane subjects, such as choosing
one's site for *al fresco* painting with care, and how and when to clean
one's brushes. But more important was the warning on the dangers of
slavishly imitating the style of favourite masters. George made no bones
about his profound admiration for the work of Paris Bordone, Claude,
Poussin, El Greco, Rubens, Turner and Sickert. He also spoke warmly
of the achievements of 'more modern artists', such as Vlaminck, Utrillo,
Kokoschka and Soutine, throwing in an admiring reference to John Piper
and Graham Sutherland. However, one must beware:[12]

> The influence of various artists on your work is to some extent
> inevitable and indeed . . . some influence is desirable; but your attitude
> to the masters of all periods should be one of learning and not of
> copying. Do not copy the mannerisms of a painter but try to expand
> some idea his work may have suggested to you. The French Impres-
> sionists learnt from Constable and Turner without copying them.

The irony is that, as a painter, George took his own advice to heart and
never imitated the style or mannerisms of other artists, even though
some of his closest friends were heard to say that he 'went through the
phases of Manet and Monet . . . And then we were on to Matthew Smith
and Kokoschka and, as [other] people came up, George used to copy
them.'[13] One does feel that this is unjust, since he scrupulously practised
what he preached on the subject of imitation in this final article.

The off-shoots of this diversion into journalism were varied and
interesting. For one thing he came to know a fellow contributor to *The
Artist*, Adrian Hill, father of one of his greatest friends of the future,
Anthony Hill, an artist like himself. A second point was that the exercise
forced George to learn the craft of expressing his ideas on paper. One

suspects that his smoothness of style (with only an occasional infelicity of phrase) owed a great deal to Barbara Addison's 'editing'. She certainly typed and retyped endlessly his early drafts. He had already evolved the habit of roughing out his ideas in note form and then dictating the 'final version' straight on to the typewriter, if he could find a willing and capable typist. The problem was that it did not help him learn the art of honing his own prose, nor did it help him to evolve a very literary style. Barbara did the double job of typist and editor – and all in the name of friendship. Payment did not enter into the matter, although occasionally, after some arduous piece of work, he would reward her with the gift of one of his pictures. He was quite unabashed about this 'exploitation'. He was constantly on the telephone to her and, whenever he knew that she had a slack period in her work at the Ministry of War supply depot in Victoria Street by Temple Meads station, he would come trotting down with some more work for her. The burly lorry drivers, whom Barbara supervised as she sent them off to the four corners of the realm with vital supplies for the RAF, used to find the sight of George, eccentrically dressed as always, highly amusing. They nicknamed him 'Charlie 'Arry', because of the way in which he walked, and constantly pulled his leg, but they were fond of him. And they saw a lot of him because, once he had the writer's bit between his teeth, there was no stopping him.

But it was Barbara who did all the hard work. Indeed, before George burst into print again, she had published an article of her own in *The Studio* in July 1944. An expanded version of her introduction for the Foyle's catalogue, it was designed to project George further into the limelight of the art world. She stressed, with no hint of contrived flattery, his rapid intellectual and stylistic progress:[14]

> To the onlooker, his advancement . . . has been almost sensational and perhaps the War years have seen his greatest achievements. Melhuish is his own severest critic and this, coupled with his passionate interest in all modern movements, may account for his outstanding advancement . . . Melhuish has developed a fine, broad and easy verve; his colour is unusually outstanding. He is a master of technique, excelling perhaps in the oil medium . . . A dramatic and simple emotional directness pervades his handling, whose recent ancestors are to be seen in the work of such painters as Van Gogh, Vlaminck, Kokoschka, Rouault. It is this humanism of application that may serve him well in the future and save him from becoming, as perhaps it is only too easy to become, in these days of artistic idealism, only a clever vehicle for aesthetic intellectualism.

There was certainly little danger of that, even though George's mind was veering more and more towards intellectual pursuits. Barbara revealed that he was 'at present engaged upon writing a treatise on the technique of modern painting'.[15] This may have been some substantial elaboration of his articles for *The Artist*. However, nothing came of the project. There is no surviving draft of any such work. What most likely happened was that his philosophical inclinations gained the upper hand and relegated it to oblivion.

CHAPTER EIGHT

PHILOSOPHIC BEGINNINGS

On the appearance of his first book on philosophy, George told Jasia Reichardt of *Art News and Review* that he had come into being as a philosopher at the age of thirty-one, that is, around 1947–8. The deduction of a firm age (and therefore date) at which the transformation took place is misleading. It would be just as incorrect to give the impression that the philosopher superseded the artist in the second half of his active life: he continued to paint and to develop his artistic style until the middle of the last decade of his existence, although, granted, by then the philosophy enjoyed a clear priority. On the other hand, the philosophical beginnings occurred much earlier than the 1947–8 period. A more likely date would be 1932, when he was only sixteen, the point at which he rejected the conventional moral and religious assumptions with which he had been brought up. That was not an easy process because, he insisted, he had to unlearn all that he had previously taken for granted before being able to construct a positive alternative in its place. Given his later preoccupation with the validity of dream experiences, it comes as no surprise that, as he confided to his friend Vicky Malins, 'he had an important dream. It changed his life. He woke up wondering "what the truth of reality was".'[1] Perhaps not uncommon as an experience for a thinking being but, according to another friend, Muriel Ward-Jackson, he was insistent that his philosophy originated in a dream. A mutual friend, Elizabeth Clough, confirmed this and revealed that George had put a more or less firm date on the episode: it had, indeed, happened when he was sixteen, at the very point at which a 'new' philosophy was desperately needed if life were not to become a black intellectual void. Until the day he died, he went on developing and refining his ideas, but there can be no doubt that they began to gestate at this early juncture.

He always maintained, as a kind of boast designed to shock, that he was 'fundamentally arrogant'. In the end of the day this arrogance, this conviction that he had something significant to say, first in his painting and then in his philosophy, was the motor-force behind his achievement in both fields. However, in the case of the philosophy, at first there were drawbacks. As he sought to develop the ideas derived from his initial inspiration, he tended to look only to philosophical sources that confirmed it and helped him to build up his own metaphysical structures. As a result he could by-pass philosophies that apparently added nothing to the tenor of his thought, or he referred to them selectively as a contradiction in the dialectical working-out of his thought patterns. One again wonders if he might have benefited from a more rigorous and formal intellectual training. But that might well have stunted his originality as a philosopher. What did happen was that, from his mid-teens until the middle war years, he evolved what he thought was a relatively original philosophy, independent of parallel modes of thought outside in the wider world. Only after this period did the ideas of Niels Bohr, Alfred Korzybski, Luitzen Brouwer, Stéphane Lupasco and even Alfred Einstein come to him as a revelation that encouraged him now that his own thought was sufficiently advanced to benefit from their influences.

By 1944 George felt confident enough to contemplate putting his ideas on paper. After one or two attempts at articulation, at the expense of Barbara Addison and her long-suffering typewriter, early in 1945 he finalized a statement of his ideas, a form of manifesto of what he, as a nascent philosopher, intended to elaborate. His friends, including most of the Torch devotees, who were fairly philosophically inclined, failed to appreciate the way in which his mind was working. They had the greatest difficulty in grasping the elaborate terminology that he had already begun to evolve. Those who tried but failed to understand it even went so far as to suggest that he was trying to perpetrate a hoax on them. But Barbara struggled gallantly to help him spell out his ideas – literally and metaphorically. Another friend who responded sympathetically was Tuggy Burne. A scientist by training and now a committed Marxist, he had a sharp mind that remained open to new ideas. He really believed that George had hit upon something of great originality and lent him his support. George was less inclined to reciprocate. Given the nature of his philosophy and his acknowledged debt to Kant and Hegel, one wonders if, simply from the methodological point of view, George did not find the Marxian concept of dialectic intriguing. If he did, he none the less rejected it and he never alluded to it in any of his writings; it was too materialistic in orientation and, worse, it appeared to base itself too much on stereotypes – the very things that he had set out to question. Nothing of his early philosophical writings has survived. Either he decided to destroy them or, after his death, somebody presumed to make the decision for him, but this is probably less of a loss than it may seem (except from a historian's point of view). All his early ideas were preserved and presented in, one imagines, a much more refined form in his first published monograph *The Paradoxical Universe* in 1959. He explained that his aim was [2]

> to demonstrate the balance of the world of occurrences . . . It is necessary for those who have attempted to describe the universe as finite to see the balance of reality as a bias, that is, a balance through selection, as in a finite universe only certain peculiar things can occur.
>
> But for the concept of reality which accepts an energetic antithesis as its precedent, ultimate truth can never be merely a dogmatic entity. For in this universe particular bias always has to be equated, as paradox is the scale and ambiguity its principal logical tool.

Basically what George was trying to suggest was that historic philosophical traditions had shied away from concepts of paradox in an all-too-human impulse to discover absolute concepts of truth. He may have seen himself as a Pontius Pilate asking the question, 'What is truth?' but he was concerned that [3]

> the fear of paradox has been elaborated by virtue of the fact that the epithets 'true' and 'false' have usually been labelled as independent entities, that is functions with some absolutely basic mission to fulfil. Whereas the authentic place of 'true' and 'false' with regard to particular value is always relatively ambiguous. The traditional view of things has led to an effort to define a universe sustained by particular forms of law and with strict non-paradox as its truth-condition.

In essence he was seeking to modify the tradition of logic that derived from Aristotle's 'laws of thought', and particularly the three most fundamental: [4]

1.   The law of identity (That everything is what it is).
2.   The law of contradiction (That a thing cannot both be and not be so and so).
3.   The law of the excluded middle (A thing either is or is not so and so).

George did not reject this simple, mathematical logic as such, but he was intent on suggesting that there was an infinitely more subtle operation of received black-and-white logical patterns than philosophers looking for the 'truth' cared to admit. He was concerned to demonstrate that, since everything in the physical world is in a state of flux, paradoxes and negation, which might appear to contradict or be in conflict with the operation of 'pure' logic, are, in fact, an integral part of the dynamics of change. He was certainly not the first metaphysician to attempt to describe the world through a logic of 'contradiction'. In Ancient Greece Zeno, with his paradoxes, and Heraclitus may have set that particular ball rolling (or arrow flying) and even with the predominance of Judaio-Christian thought there remained an impulse to explain apparently paradoxical physical (and spiritual) states. George may not have agreed with Cardinal Nicholas of Cusa's effort, in his *De Docta Ignorantia* of 1444, 'at uniting reality through a balance of opposites', but he did find it 'interesting, if illegitimate'.[5] By the twentieth century the forces critical of Aristotelian laws of logic were infinitely more vigorous and less deferential, even if in a minority position and criticized in turn. At this point in George's life he still had to discover what place he himself occupied in the 'school', but he was nothing if not confident about the direction of his philosophical thought. He stated bluntly:[6]

> The logic of the paradoxically energetic state had been developed by myself as an alternative to the assertion that the basic significance of reality is itself *biased truth*. An effort is made to show that the force of this logic is not barren, but may lead to a new potential of possibilities such that whenever 'nothing' or mere negation would appear to be the case, this negative will then be seen to be implicated by an operational antithesis into becoming 'something', so erecting an energetic bipolarity between the most primitive antithetical states that it is possible to pose.

At this stage George was concerned to explain the dynamics of the physical world, but, in as much as he saw an explanation in a definition of 'nothingness', he was already well on the way to being a metaphysician in the classic sense. Indeed, his projected work had the provisional title *The Double-Meaning of Nothingness* (a title which he abandoned and then re-adopted for his final major enterprise). He was intrigued by the idea that the universe came into being out of nothingness (even Genesis suggested that). The problem was how to define a concept of nothingness that admitted of a subtlety that was more than just simple negation. He explained:[7]

> To state that the universe of existences was developed or was preceded by a pure 'nothing' or nothingness, that it is sensibly legitimate to speak

of the beginning and the end of the universe, is really to say no more than that nothing(ness) has an alternate relationship or circularity with something(ness). For if a 'situation' such as the whole universe is posed as evolving from a true 'nothing' to a universe of 'something', then this relationship cannot be a referential one. It follows that, as conceptual images, beginnings and endings are not *ultimately* legitimate in themselves, for the only class of statement that can arise will be obliged to take the following form, 'the time between the universe of "nothing" and the universe of "something" was *no time at all*', 'the space between the universe of "nothing" and the universe of "something" was *no space at all*', etc. In a regression from 'something' to 'nothing' or a progression from 'nothing' to 'something' if the status of 'something' is the case or it is asserted that what is the case is 'something', then to say that the ancestor or inheritor of a specific 'something' was or will be the state of 'nothing' is to endow the negative reference with negative energy – that is energy through paradox.

Many of George's acquaintances seemed deliberately intent on misunderstanding the basis of his theory; others were intellectually incapable of grasping it, even though it was, in many ways, commonsense in its approach. One of his friends used to flutter around uttering key-words such as 'paradox', 'ironical' and 'ambiguous'; for her the decision-making process became intuitive and anti-rational, full of glaring contradictions, simply because she imagined that he had kicked over the traces of all rationality. That sort of situation did not worry him unduly, although it caused considerable awkwardness for the other parties involved. He had a remarkable facility for brushing aside anything that appeared like a lack of understanding or any criticism that added nothing constructive to his own ideas. He was adept at picking holes in others' theories, but took less kindly to having the tables turned on him. As Barbara remarked, 'Old George was like the kid with the wickets and bat saying: "I'm not out and, if I *am* out, I'll take my wickets and bat away"!'[8]

By drawing up his statement George showed clearly that he intended to take his wickets and bat off to play a more significant game than any possible on the intellectual playing fields of Bristol. He persuaded Barbara's fiancé, Barrie Thorne, to make fifty copies of his statement on 'non-duality' and he spent a weekend at the end of January 1945 sending them 'to various persons and publications, including Jeans, Joad, Bernard Shaw, Sir Henry Livingstone, the Royal Society, the Faculty of Philosophy at Oxford, Cambridge, Edinburgh, Yale and Harvard, *The*

Times, the *Telegraph, Discovery, Nature*, etc.' He had a number of replies; however, as Barbara added, 'for the most part the statement is not fully understood but nobody has spotted any flaws'.[9]

Tuggy Burne was upset by the lukewarm nature of the response. He felt that the academic establishment had ganged up against George as an 'outsider'. His ideas 'did not conform to accepted dogma at that time and he was not a professional philosopher – any more than Einstein!'[10] Truth be told, it is always difficult to assess the potential of any non-professional, especially when his work (as was the case with George's) is still in an unrefined state. He himself was much less upset. He went straight ahead to plan the next stage of his project. As Barbara revealed to Patricia Daly, 'George now wants to write a short book on the subject, which we are starting tonight. We intend doing one hour per day and he thinks, by doing this, we can finish it in a fortnight.'[11] This scenario was not over-optimistic. A few weeks later Barbara was able to report to Patricia: 'After a fortnight's hard work (almost two hours every evening), George and I have finished his book on the theory of non-duality. It has been rather boring for me as I haven't understood much of it and the words he uses!'[12]

With a sigh of relief Barbara turned to slightly less taxing intellectual pursuits. She continued her work with the Bristol Astronomical Society, of which she and George were founder members. The society had begun on a small scale with a group of enthusiasts arranging lectures and visiting the observatory on Royal Fort Hill. George enjoyed gazing at the stars in bomber-free wartime skies, but Barbara's approach was more practical. As soon as she finished work on his book she felt free to spend more time on astronomy. On 27 February she wrote to Patricia Daly:[13]

Tonight I am going up to Cotham School for the second of the series of lectures on popular astronomy run by the BAS. So many people turned up to the last one that we didn't know where to put them all. I hope to have things arranged better this week; have got Dr Bush to take the chair and a larger screen. The Education Authority is interested in these and, with a bit of luck, may help us financially.

But after what George's work had demanded of her, this was a mild and pleasurable preoccupation.

There were certainly lighter moments to life as the war perceptibly drew to its close. One Saturday afternoon Barbara and George induced Tuggy Burne to come on a trip to Bath. Walking the streets made them hungry, but where to eat, in an age of food shortages, was something of a problem. Barbara hit on a bright idea. She spent her days working with lorry drivers, so she knew what to do. She later recalled:[14]

I said to George: 'The best place to get something to eat in Bath is a transport café. There is one round here that our drivers go to, which is jolly good.' So George and I trundled round there with Tuggy and went to this place. And it was a proper transport café with American cloth on the table. And Tuggy said: 'I'm not eating in here. I'm not going in this place!' George and I turned round on him and said: '*You*, the communist, will not eat in this working-class café!' – whereas we were quite happy to go in. 'Oh!' he said, 'I'm not going to eat there!'

George and Barbara were annoyed but secretly amused. Tuggy seemed to them typical of a type of intellectual, upper-middle-class communist who apparently had little idea about working-class living conditions, whereas Barbara, who spent her days happily organizing work for droves of lorry drivers, had a fair insight into their way of life; and George always evinced an almost voyeuristic interest in working-class culture. But they both knew that Tuggy was going through an agonizing psychological experience in which all the apparent contradictions in his make-up struggled to find a solution. Alexander Gordon-Burne came from a long line of high-ranking army officers. His father and brothers were all actively fighting for king and country, while he was an avowed pacifist and a card-carrying communist. But the inner conflicts had a curious side-effect. He started to have fainting fits for which there seemed no physiological reason, so he consulted a psychiatrist. The analyst, on hearing of his family's military background, suggested that his pacifism was eating at him as a kind of guilt-complex and causing the fainting fits. Such was Tuggy's faith in the man that he immediately joined up and the fainting spells stopped. Perhaps the 'cure' had something to do with the fact that he had just become engaged to Joan Brett-Smith, but even the prospect of married bliss must have seemed uncertain, because he was duly issued with tropical kit without knowing his destination or how long his tour of duty might last. However, he had less to worry about than most of his military contemporaries: he joined up just as European hostilities ended and when the conflict in the Far East could not last much longer.

George did not follow his example. Instead, he hailed the new era of hope by buying a very grand second-hand Railton motor car. In time he would become much more discerning about the used-car business; the Railton turned out to be suffering from every conceivable mechanical disease and was certainly not roadworthy enough in time to celebrate Germany's capitulation on 7 May 1945 in the grand manner that he had planned.

PART THREE

1945–1950

OLD FRIENDS AND NEW HORIZONS

Even before the formal end of the war a general air of anticipation and excitement began to affect George's friends. The bonds that had bound together Torch as a group, though always fairly loose because of inevitable comings and goings, slackened still further. Matches and marriages were in the air and they tended to distract attention away from the group's activities. Peter Tiley returned but devoted himself to his new wife rather than to Torch activities. Tuggy Burne was desperately anxious that his friends would also be his fiancée's friends, but had not succeeded in this aim before setting out for tropical climes. Some members became rather too politically motivated as a socialist future began to seem a distinct possibility. Eric Webb, whom nobody had ever regarded as a sparkling personality, re-appeared after spending the last two years in Cairo (not by any means the safe posting that it might seem, as Lord Moyne learned to his cost). The group welcomed him back. 'We took him the rounds one evening and he seemed to enjoy himself, although he is a rather stolid sort, a Rationalist and a Communist – his conversation would suit Tuggy – and he stayed with some Party members at Knowle by the name of Gumball – they would be Party members with a name like that!'[1]

Politics was still against the rules, but it was not always easy to calculate the side-effects of personal political inclinations. Nancy Barber and two severely tailored female friends, fellow mathematicians, invited themselves to stay with Barbara Addison; they were returning to Bristol to attend a meeting of the Association of Scientific (and Clerical) Workers as it lurched towards the far left. Barbara's friend, Barrie Thorne, was worried for another reason. When the three changed their minds and stayed with another woman, he exclaimed: 'Jesus, I'm glad they decided not to stay with you.'[2] Barbara thought the implication rather unworthy: men tended to make judgments based on faces and figures. But she did not conceal her own relief at having avoided the hazards of an attentive hostess's duties.

Some of the friends were distracted by more material problems. Bernard Perrin had married a fellow-artist, Audrey White, and they found themselves forced to apply their professional skills to making ends meet. Barbara learned that 'George called on them . . . and was amazed to see, all over everywhere, hundreds and hundreds of curiously shaped wooden things, all gaily coloured and drying. Bernard had apparently bought up a lot of loom bobbins which he was constructing into skipping ropes!'[3]

Deborah Jones had plans to supplement their income. They had a spare room and she hoped to rent it. She felt that after years of work on a lathe she had made her contribution to the war effort and was determined to avoid humdrum employment at the expense of her art. But this meant that she too lived in relative poverty. Barbara gleaned some information about her from George:[4]

> Deborah must have been thrown out of Pembroke Road because she is now living in a barn place at the end of Princess Victoria Street. She invited George round one morning (he met her in Queen's Road) so he just went with her out of curiosity. He says there is a number of ramshackle buildings about there, quite cut off from the houses, and she has one of these. Drain-pipes weave in and out in all directions; there is no water or heat; furniture is a few odd boxes, a barrel and an old bed propped up with wood. The roof is falling in; the walls are damp and peeling; the floor rotten, but it is evident that she prefers living in this squalor to working.

Barbara clearly did not approve of this, but she herself was not above criticism – though unjustly. She had, at last, found a real soul-mate in the form of Barrie Thorne, but they could not marry immediately because she was still technically married to Alfred Addison. She was horrified at the thought that her husband's return from the army might mean that he would want to create a proper union out of their hasty and ill-considered marriage.

George realized with regret that the old intimate atmosphere of Torch could not be recaptured. He continued to organize meetings but, since he was less and less in Bristol, it was not easy to hold them on a regular basis. When Barbara married Barrie Thorne in 1947 and became permanently based in London, the group finally ceased to exist – except in the affectionate memories of all who had participated in its activities. George recognized that time had moved on and, while Torch still existed, he tried to parallel, or rather complement, its activities by holding *conversazioni* in the red drawing-room. Patricia Daly knew nothing of this when she invited Barbara for a few days in London. Barbara had to refuse:[5]

> Very many thanks for your invitation but you obviously have not been told about the great social event scheduled for next weekend! George is emulating our old friend Mrs Proudie and having a *conversazione* on Sunday evening to which he has invited all the elite of Bristol. Donald and Ellard Hughes, Kit Gunton, Dr and Mrs Bodman, Dr Bates, Anne Driver, [Richard] Hutton, Mrs Linton and etc., about twenty-one persons in all and most of them have accepted. I dare not stay away, although I am not too keen on attending, as I have promised George to serve the coffee for him – nobody but me being allowed into the bowels of [the] Melhuish household.

The event duly happened on Sunday, 23 July, but Barbara was not impressed. It certainly could not be compared with a Torch meeting:[6]

> Personally, I did not consider it as successful as it might have been, although George seems to think that everybody enjoyed themselves. In the first place . . . there were far too many people present to handle or seat comfortably; secondly, you were quite correct about some being allergic to others – they were – and consequently formed into little cliques, leaving odd people out here and there. The Cliftonian element, which consisted of various doctors and their wives, while not being snobbish, did not mix with the Elaine, Joan Lansdown-Harvey element, which was younger and more flighty. There were several people on the sort of middle plane who had nothing to say at all and a couple of men who didn't seem to know anyone but George. Thirdly, there was not enough coffee to go round. Had I been giving a coffee party, I should have commenced serving it early on and gone on serving it most of the time; George didn't serve it until nine o'clock and then only one cup each and there wasn't enough for Pat Coe or me (not that we minded but there should have been). There was no really interesting conversation, mostly small talk, gossip about people other people didn't know and Jack Bilbo. There will be another one in three weeks' time and I suppose I shall have to go, although I should prefer to stay away. I feel so uncomfortable for the people who feel uncomfortable, if you know what I mean.

But Barbara and Patricia had other things to think about besides George's playing at being Mrs Proudie. Barbara was apprehensive about the possible consequences of her errant husband's re-appearance in London. Patricia was elated at bursting into print for the first time with her edition of *Penguin Parade*. Meanwhile, George held his second *conversazione* on Sunday, 13 August. Barbara sent her apologies: 'I did not attend and neither did all the more dignified persons who came the last time; [George] said it was more like a Torch meeting, Elaine and a friend Margaret Bees, Litzie, Pat Coe and Peter Tiley, but it was quite enjoyable.'[7] However, this was effectively an obituary on Torch. There could be no going back. Barbara was particularly nostalgic about the group: 'The more I think about it, the more I think what strong friendships were forged during those years. We really all grew to know each other.' And it was her fiancé, Barrie Thorne, though a latecomer to the circle, who put his finger on the point: 'It is so pleasant to be sometimes with real friends as against the passing acquaintances one makes in bars and places.'[8]

Perhaps George had accepted the inevitable: his attempt to cultivate Bristol society outside the young artistic and intellectual set had to be abandoned for the time being until it was revived some years later as a means of advertising – and selling – his paintings. In the immediate post-war period his mind was on several other projects. He was still not satisfied with his little book on the theory of non-duality and, in the process, he was driving Barbara to distraction. She confided in Patricia:[9]

> As you know, I am extremely fond of George but sometimes I get too much of him and this is one of my overdose periods. You see, we have been working upon this wretched theory of his for months now (any normal person who hasn't a typewriter writes his work out and then has it typed, but George dictates it straight to the machine, corrects it and then I have to type it all over again, and when you consider that this is the third time I have done it, you will forgive the adjective 'wretched') for about one-and-a-half to two hours every night and what with that and the trials of the Railton, I feel a vacation from George for a couple of days would be a good thing.
>
> It was awfully amusing on Tuesday. I told him that I was ill and couldn't do anything (having a large amount of housework to do . . .), went home, girding myself with an apron and attacked my stairs, clouds of dust whirling around and George arrives to see how I am!

One wonders if he saw the amusing side of the incident. He was rather too earnestly intent upon having himself taken as a serious figure of substance, a social mover and one with style. The reference to the Railton explains a great deal. He had a passion for luxury motor cars that amounted to a form of manic pretentiousness. He judged them by their external appearance, as he hoped that he, as owner, would be. When he cared to put his mind to it, he could understand the mechanical workings of car engines, but he disdained that. Moreover, his attempts to learn to drive were not notably successful. (They finally ceased when he found that he – and his car – had demolished a telephone kiosk.) The surprising thing is that the Railton ever got on the road. The garage men informed him that it had everything wrong with it; it was only fit for scrap. They offered him a derisory sum to take it off his hands. He demurred and persisted. Finally in August 1945 it was semi-roadworthy, but the basic hazards remained. Barbara gave up in despair:[10]

> After my trip in her I washed my hands of driving it or teaching him as he acted in an infuriating and childish manner about the thing; also things kept going wrong with it and I don't think anyone but a very expert driver and mechanic should have charge of it. George seems to want everybody to do jobs on it for nothing and at the moment has a man called Gard driving him around at night whilst George and woman recline in the back seat! This man Gard is a flashy individual whom George has told to wear his best suit when he is with him (I imagine he sucks his teeth and wears rings) and is a twister also, but that's none of my business.

A few years later George's motor car obsession took on even greater proportions – and considerably more profitable ones. Meanwhile, one of the reasons for his wanting a stylish car had to be abandoned. He and Barbara had planned a trip to Corsham to see the painter, a fellow war artist, Lord Methuen. Methuen was not only a fine and highly productive painter, but he was also active in the promotion of the arts in the Bristol area. He became the president of the Royal West of England Academy and one of his first achievements was to persuade the new Prime Minister, Clement Attlee, to return the academy's fine headquarters on Queen's Road. (During the war it had been requisitioned by the Inland Revenue.) In 1946, after a hiatus of six years, the annual exhibition was able to begin again with a renewed vibrancy that contributed enormously to general artistic life in the city. But George's motives were entirely personal. He was planning to publish a volume illustrated by the best of his paintings from the war period and he wanted Lord Methuen to write a foreword to it. Both George and Barbara had high hopes that he might agree because George knew him well (from the war artists' exhibitions in London) and Methuen had been a patient of one of his *conversazione* guests, Dr Bodin, whose wife Muriel's portrait was due to figure among the illustrations. Methuen was apparently too busy to comply with his request, but this did not prevent the project from going ahead. And a fairly ambitious project it turned out to be, though in keeping with his overpoweringly egocentric consciousness-raising drive. Barbara explained the plan to Patricia Daly:[11]

> The book, which will consist of about thirty-six plates in black and white and eight in colour, will have just a short biography (like the Penguins) in front and this is being done by Hutton, editor of the *Bristol Packet*, who is getting out the book. Incidentally, the book is being got out by subscription, we have to get 200, which I think will be fairly easy with the number of people that George knows, before the printers will do it; I think the price will be 12/6. Hutton (who is a tremendous 'doer') will get out a pamphlet all about it and you will get one in due course. Hutton, in case you don't know him, is a Bristol Aircraft Company man, primarily interested in Bristol and literature and his . . . *Bristol Packet* is a small magazine, I gather, got up by Bristol writers, poets and so on. This is his first venture into the visual arts and he is very keen. By the way, if George starts to tell you anything about this, I haven't told you as you know how secretive he is.

George could not be secretive for long. The Bristol Writers' and Artists' Association, under the chairmanship of one of his oldest friends and patrons, Leslie Urquhart-White, with Richard Hutton as honorary secretary, took over the organization of the project. Hutton was quick to produce a leaflet inviting subscriptions and introducing George to anybody who did not yet know him: 'George Melhuish has achieved much in the World of Art, and now stands on the threshold of a period which leads to maturity. At such a time a young Artist needs recognition in the practical form of a permanent record' – hence the proposed book. He outlined George's achievements to date and informed potential clients that 'a quality of the work of George Melhuish is a virility created from use of his great knowledge of colour and this gives his canvases a uniqueness among contemporary paintings'. Hutton then added a curious comment: 'This individual quality springs from the fact that, as a painter, Melhuish is outside the general trend of the day and finds inspiration in Bristol rather than in the Metropolis.'[12] Was Hutton trying to rouse local interest? Certainly George drew a great deal of inspiration from his native city, one has only to look at his architectural landscapes to see that, but he had already proved that his sights were set well beyond Bristol – and soon beyond the national boundaries. The citizens of Bristol, however, did not fully appreciate his potential and, although subscriptions did come in, it fell to a few of his friends to put up £50 each to float the project. There was, of course, the promise of a share in the royalties, but, predictably, there were none.

Perhaps the venture was overambitious, especially in the post-war years of austerity. Hutton promised that the book would 'consist of sixty-four pages, of which there would be fifteen colour plates and numerous half-tones, together with a critical appreciation of the Artist and his work.'[13] When the book appeared in mid-1946, it was roughly half the promised size with seven colour plates and twenty-six half-tones, together with eight pages of introduction from Hutton. However, it was an impressive production, containing a well-balanced selection from George's various specialist genres: portraits, nude studies, blitz paintings, architectural landscapes and a few 'nature' studies. Barbara achieved pride of place by having the canvas of her as a negress reproduced on the cover. And Richard Hutton himself appeared anonymously under the title of *Portrait of a Young Man* (1945). A striking, full-face portrait, its basic colours of lime green, golden yellow and blazing red are so arresting that one wonders if it were designed to say more about the artist than about the sitter. The point is that, although the book is nowadays a collector's item, for all his hard work, Hutton's introduction rather lets the side down. It is so ponderous that, to begin with, friends wondered if George had ghost-written it. He undoubtedly had a hand in it because it is redolent of the self-advertising bombast characteristic of his general approach to his public. In a way, this approach was successful, even if couched in a form of language that now seems overpowering. The *George Melhuish* book appeared just at the right time to complement the new series of shows in which he planned to exhibit the work of several highly productive years at his easel.

CHAPTER TEN

PARIS EXPOSURES

In 1946, the year in which George's book of paintings was published, he celebrated his thirtieth birthday. It was a period of fevered activity for him, but friends were glad to see that he was not neglecting his personal life in his pursuit of public recognition. After all, he needed a woman-friend to sit beside him in the back of the Railton. Then something serious apparently happened. He began a 'hectic friendship' with a girl called Edwina and speculation was rife. Would they marry? But his schoolboy vow was not forgotten and, after five weeks of this 'hectic friendship', they fell out. Barbara knew him well enough to surmise that he had been largely to blame for the rupture: 'At heart, I believe Edwina is a kind person, and would not deliberately injure anyone.'[1]

George was too preoccupied with other matters to be upset for long. The Bristol Writers' and Artists' Association, organized by the indefatigable Richard Hutton, mounted under their auspices an exhibition of most of the works illustrated in the book. The show was opened by the MP for Bristol East, the President of the Board of Trade, Sir Stafford Cripps. One might have thought that the affairs of state during that period of intense political activity would have prevented Cripps from accepting the invitation, but George already knew him well through Lady Cripps' China Relief activities and Sir Stafford was sensitive to the need to cultivate his constituency base: socialists had to appear to be civilized – and, after all, George's was the first major art exhibition in Bristol since the war, though he was no socialist himself. How artistically inclined Sir Stafford was was another matter, but Barbara Addison, who had written an introduction for the catalogue, found herself being gently berated by him for being too uncritical of George's works. Perhaps her prose was a little over the top:[2]

George Melhuish is a modern painter in the broadest sense of the word. His bold brush-work and virile colour leave behind the uncertainty and esoterism of some of his contemporaries. His canvases reflect his opinion that painting should have a 'paintingly' [sic] quality about it. He reflects, in our opinion, the young spirit of a new civilization now being achieved from the ruins of the old by people who are alive to these days of promise and opportunity.

Cripps could scarcely have objected to the sentiments contained in that last sentence – nor could George: he was on an all-out publicity drive. He had managed to get himself elected to the exclusive Sesame Club and had been immediately pressed to give an address on 'Modern Portraiture'. His friends thought that this was something of an honour for 'Our George', especially since, in April, the next lecture in the series was to be given by Anne Driver's old friend Edith Sitwell, 'speaking on English poetry' – in other words *her* poetry.[3] Afterwards she invited a galaxy of literary and artistic 'stars' to dinner at the club: John Lehmann, Henry Moore, George Barker, Louis MacNeice. T.S. Eliot was a guest of honour and Dylan Thomas was also invited, mainly in the hope of healing the eight-year-old rift between himself and La Sitwell. But Thomas' boorish behaviour towards the retiring Eliot meant that the hostess had a nightmare of a time. George enjoyed circling round on the fringes of this set and, in fact, got to know the inebriated Dylan Thomas quite well. He even invited him down to Bristol to stay at Springfield Road, but it is doubtful whether the poet even got as far as Paddington station.

The Sesame Club contact was of great help when George's paintings were shown in a one-man exhibition in London at the Alpine Club Gallery at 74 South Audley Street. The show was opened on Tuesday, 4 June, by yet another local MP, Oliver Stanley (a true-blue Conservative, the new member for Bristol West and heir to the earldom of Derby – George was nothing if not apolitical!). The opening turned out to be a glittering occasion. He had worked hard to attract 'important' guests. He asked Richard Hutton to invite L.R. Bradley, the Director-General of the Imperial War Museum, in the hope that he might purchase more of his war paintings. Mr Blaikley, the museum's man in charge of pictures, did attend but did not respond well to George's work. One suspects that he found them too exotic and disturbing in the 'brave new world' atmosphere of post-war Britain. However, he was not in the majority. Barbara, though obviously sympathetic, reported to Patricia Daly that 'George's show . . . was a great success both from a publicity point of view and from a financial one.'[4] And her very next sentence unconsciously revealed things to come:[5]

We are all now Paris-mad and brushing up our French. I am deeply shocked to find that I have even forgotten how to conjugate the most basic verbs such as *avoir* and *être*, whilst George's pronunciation would make you die – *depuis* being 'de-poo-is' to him! . . . I cannot, no matter how I try, get over that truly British trait of feeling an utter fool when speaking anything other than my Mother tongue. Now I shouldn't think you would suffer from this feeling of embarrassment because, when you used to give us readings at Torch, you always read with the correct accent – or dialect when it came into the conversation.

The point was that George, who had long seen French painters as his closest artistic ancestors, was fixated with everything French. He was determined not only to go and work in Paris, but also to make his mark there in artistic as well as social circles.

The one person who did most to precipitate him into his Paris phase was a fellow painter, Sir Francis Rose. Rose was seven years George's senior. He had inherited his baronetcy in 1915 and with it a considerable fortune. Much of his life from his wayward childhood onwards had been spent in France and had consisted of one long pursuit of the most colourful of pleasures. As a teenager, he was one of Isadora Duncan's bosom-friends, and in 1926 Jean Cocteau organized a special seventeenth-birthday party for him at the Welcome Hotel in Ville-franche. Francis danced the night away in the arms of an American sailor. However, his lifestyle detracted in no way from his career as a prolific painter of great skill and vibrant imagination that bordered on real genius. His work was almost always figurative and was shot through with an element of fantasy that emerged in everything he produced, in a style that could be alternately hard and virile or seductively feminine, alarmingly grotesque or delightfully decorative. For a while Francis Rose was tutored by Francis Picabia, and then in the early 1930s he was taken up by Gertrude Stein as her second major 'discovery' after Picasso. Francis, as a painter, was very different from Picasso and, frankly, the Stein patronage and propaganda did him more harm than good. For the moment he was not much concerned about that. He spent most of the 1930s observing at first hand Hitler's consolidation of power and then travelling for a year and a half in the Far East. He returned to Europe to find that his fortune had almost entirely disappeared as a result of his wild extravagance and the malversation of an American financier. Francis took all this philosophically in his stride. He managed to survive and to enjoy himself (invariably at other people's expense), even though he never recovered his financial position. Most of the first half of the war he spent as an NCO in the RAF until he was invalided out, at which point he married a woman who was as intelligent as she was beautiful, the writer and historian Dorothy Carrington. (From the time of her marriage she was known as Frederica, after her illustrious father Major-General Sir Frederick Carrington, since she felt that to be called Dorothy Violet Rose was overdoing the floral theme.)

George first met Francis and Frederica early in 1945 when they attended a meeting at the India Society in Victoria Street. The British Empire was still intact (though only just) and a source of pride for some. George had never forgotten the tales about the Far East that had fascinated him on his father's knee as a child. Now he could reciprocate when he returned home to his ageing parents in Bristol. Francis Rose, of course, had visited both India and China and was about as sinophile as one could be. The India Society, however, was dominated by rather conventional ex-colonial types. One typically Edwardian gentleman said to George: 'Ah, this evening we've got artist-persons . . . I must introduce you to Sir Francis Rose.'[6] Francis recognized George as a fellow artist of equal talent and soon drew him into a social circle that was more exciting than anything that Bristol could provide. Even in the deprived post-war years the Roses managed to give the most entertaining parties in their flat in Rossetti House in Flood Street, not so very far from George's humble King's Road studio. It was here that he first met the Dylan Thomases, Cyril and Patricia Conolly, the Henry Moores and (the stars of Francis' firmament) His Excellency the Chinese Ambassador, V.K. Wellington-Koo and his ravishingly beautiful wife, Huilan.

George was mesmerized and it is no exaggeration to say that he fell in love with Francis Rose. In fact, contact with Francis and Frederica brought to the surface a basic ambiguity in his nature. He worshipped the coolly classical Frederica from afar. (She was never aware that he had any feelings for her.) But he was totally fixated by Francis and even his less 'aware' friends soon realized that he lived only for the next time that he would see him. George's feelings were undoubtedly homosexual. However, there can be equally no doubt that there was never any tangible expression of these feelings on his part. There were several cogent reasons for this. On the one hand, though Francis cherished George as a friend, he was distinctly not his 'type': George was refined and delicate, whereas Francis had a nose for working-class boyfriends – the rougher the better. On the other hand, George was too frightened ever to contemplate engaging in any physical act of homosexuality. For somebody who considered himself to be a free-thinker, he was remarkably hide-bound by the moral prejudices of the day. He shied away from the cloak-and-dagger atmosphere in which an unsympathetic legal system forced most homosexuals to conduct their private lives. Francis Rose suffered from no such inhibitions and seldom noticed how his behaviour shocked other people. George recounted a revealing story about him:[7]

> He brought this boy round to my studio in the King's Road one day and stayed so long; then the boy went. And he turned to me and said: 'You think he's beautiful, don't you?' Now, to me he seemed like – we don't hear the phrase so often nowadays because it doesn't apply — he seemed like the sort of man who would have brought in the coal, if you were having some delivered. And I was naive enough to say that. I said: 'He's only like a man who would deliver the coal.'

However, he quickly realized that it was a case of opposites attracting and never again raised an eyebrow at anything in which Francis became involved – at least, in the sexual sphere. But the incident says almost as much about George's nature as it does about Francis's. One suspects that, even in his heterosexual moments, George was too inhibited to consummate any relationship – and, latterly, he was physically incapable of doing so. There may have been osculatory and masturbatory aspects to his 'sex life', but he was generally detached about personal involvements. This did not prevent him from having an insatiable curiosity about the sexual antics of people close to him and the beloved Francis unwittingly provided him with a great deal of vicarious pleasure.

Francis also provided him with something more tangible. He had a rather elegant *piano nobile* flat on the Quai d'Anjou in the very centre of Paris on the Île Saint-Louis. Almost as important, he had the *entrée* to a society of talent and glamour such as George had previously only dreamed of. From time to time he used Francis's flat when it was available but, once familiar with Paris, he was almost more content to stay at the Royal Condé, a beautiful old-style hotel which he discovered at 10 rue de Condé in the Latin Quarter, just next to the Odéon. Because of his parents' increasing age and infirmity, however, he did not like to stay away from Bristol for lengthy periods. He would visit Paris in spells of two or three months; four months was an absolute maximum. He could not contemplate setting up a permanent studio of his own in France. In fact, he saw Paris primarily as a social base. But he did do a great deal of painting in the city as well as deriving enormous inspiration from its forms and colours, and this was reflected in the canvases that emanated from his English studios up to the early 1950s. In May 1948 Raymond Sawkins, the editor of *The Artist*, described the effect of the city on his art:[8]

> The Latin Quarter, with its quaint architecture and colourful atmosphere appealed strongly to him. His method was to make pencil

sketches of scenes which attracted him outdoors, with scribbled instructions as to colour and then return to a studio which he had rented to paint direct in oils. While in Paris he painted a number of churches, including the famous Notre Dame.

One might get the impression that George was churning out sugary lollipops for tourist consumption. Not at all. There was nothing of the pretty 'artists painting in the Place des Ternes' type of original or reproduction. Admittedly, in 1949, he did have some of his French scenes published and sold in special folders under the title of *Images*, but they were disturbing works of enormous vigour. Eventually his Paris landscapes would dissolve into fascinating patterns of light and lines. As one critic put it,[9]

> his paintings are multi-coloured diffusions or dazzles of light, held together by constructural lines – sometimes like the filament wires in a lamp, sometimes like the bars of a brazier. These lines and surrounding tones of colour are intended to establish the depth of the scene and mark the form of the bridge, the hill or the street sky-line.

The *Scotsman* critic also commented that 'the city emerges from shadows, but is illuminated by lights apparently reflected from the sky and the streets, though really lit up by the mind of the painter, who finds drawing so easy that he rubs out some of the structure of his paintings to emphasize the evanescence and sense of dissolution'.[10] One is, of course, looking ahead over half a decade of artistic development, but it is clear that even in the earliest Paris landscapes George's fixation with abstract forms and striking juxtapositions of colours was already pointing him in the direction of his great period as an abstract painter.

He found Paris equally inspiring from the social point of view. Naturally he wanted to induce the city's artistic and social set to take an interest in his art. His motives were partly pecuniary. If they attended his shows, even without buying, others might be induced to purchase. But basically he loved the glamorous life and, perhaps surprisingly, achieved quite a success in the salons. His French – or lack of it – may have been a problem, but most of top society spoke at least a word or two of English and, besides, he had a certain allure as an artist. He also had the advantage of Francis Rose's patronage. Francis certainly introduced him to Picabia, Braque and Picasso. And Cocteau was susceptible to cultivation. He and George seem to have responded well to each other. George was slightly guarded about their acquaintance: he knew of Cocteau's reputation; he also knew that it was Cocteau who had 'brought Francis Rose out' at the age of seventeen. George commented: 'Cocteau . . . I found quite interesting, as one would.'[11] For many years afterwards he preserved a small bundle of Cocteau's notes written in purple. (They apparently contained nothing of great intellectual substance, but one cannot be absolutely certain because they have now mysteriously disappeared.)

In addition to this artistic set, George also hovered on the more adventurous fringes of high society: the Princess Alexander of Yugoslavia; the Comtesse Tolstoy; a fellow painter, the Iraqui Princess Fahrunissa Zeid el Houssein; and the Princesse de Rohan (big in high fashion and in patience: she later had to cope with a damaging scandal caused by Francis Rose's fantasizing about international frauds involving Suez Canal shares). The eternal Princesse Nina Mdivani (at the time simply Mrs Conan-Doyle) became a good friend. But the high point for riches and glamour was Marie-Laure, the Vicomtesse Charles de Noailles. If for nothing else, she and her husband were 'notorious' for having helped Cocteau produce his film *Le Sang d'un poète* in 1930, for which the viscount was duly expelled from the exclusive Jockey Club. George found Marie-Laure fascinating for her sharpness of mind and high style, if not for her looks. Francis Rose took him to parties at her mansion in the Place des Etats-Unis. George had never before visited a private house where vast canvases by Rubens, Delacroix and Goya adorned the walls, apparently indifferent to the illustrious company that their owner kept. After all those grand noblewomen, the nobleman with whom his friend Jane George tended to stay in the rue Boissonnade seemed to make for a refreshing gender change. But no: Jane George always insisted on calling him '*la baronne maudite*', which left George in no doubt about his sexual proclivities.

Meeting the witty journalist from *The New Yorker*, Janet Flanner (alias Genêt) and her formidable girlfriend Solita Solano, and the intriguing Christian Dior, almost matched the excitement of rubbing shoulders at parties and private views with the famous film stars who drifted through Paris; Dora Maer was on George's visiting list as well as Lauren Bacall and Martine Caroll, but it was Humphrey Bogart whose acquaintance George always cherished – and immortalized in an impressive portrait (done from memory and photographs).

More important was his contact with some of the great creative geniuses of the day, people who had been distant sources of inspiration; now he met them and saw their works 'in the flesh'. Picasso and Braque (whom he particularly idolized) he came to know almost at once. Then he was introduced to Constantin Brancusi, Marc Chagall and Ossip Zadkine. Two significant friendships for George, as artist and budding philosopher, developed with Michel Tapié and, through him, with

Georges Hugnet, the surrealist poet. He was enthusiastic about George's work and soon the walls of his apartment in the Boulevard du Montparnasse were hung with his paintings.

There were, however, three gaps on George's visiting list. He planned his first visit to Paris for the summer of 1946, but the amount of work involved in his Alpine Club exhibition meant that he, more sensibly, delayed his departure until late September – the beginning of the 'Season'. Francis Rose had equipped him with letters of introduction, the most important being to his adored mother-substitute Gertrude Stein. Unfortunately, by the time George reached Paris, Gertrude had died, on the operating table, on 27 July 1946. Francis Rose was devastated. But with an admirable degree of pragmatism, he urged George not to be deterred but to present his letters instead to the grieving 'widow', Alice Toklas. George did and subsequently came to know her fairly well. When in Paris she would invite him to call at the flat in the rue Christine. One wonders just how highly George estimated Alice. She had not yet achieved the standing of the formidable high-priestess of the Stein cult, but he could tell that she was 'rather a fiery customer', even though he realized that it was a bad time to visit her because 'she was very knocked back by Gertrude's death'.[12] However, Alice did derive pleasure from showing the young Englishman Gertrude's famous collection of paintings. On the walls there were early examples of Francis Rose's works alongside the Picassos and Braques. 'They had hung Picasso's portrait of Stein over the mantelpiece. It was still there. It hadn't gone to the Metropolitan yet . . . It was quite a memory.'[13]

The second social 'near miss' for George was Francis Poulenc, original member of '*Les Six*' and, arguably, the best of the bunch. Poulenc lived opposite the Palais de Luxembourg, just round the corner at the top of the rue de Condé where George spent so much of his time. They had a number of friends in common, most notably Cocteau and Francis Rose, but by this time the 'reformed' Poulenc was fairly distant from the unregenerate poet. As for Francis, he was fond of music, but it was not his artistic first-love. He apparently thought that it was not worthwhile introducing the two men, despite the fact that George was a committed, if none too avant-garde, music-lover. Surprisingly, during his years as a visitor to Paris, he did very little on the music scene. He was most attracted to opera, but he scarcely ever went to the Opéra or the Opéra-Comique. Perhaps the tickets were too dear: he would never contemplate buying cheap seats; he would rather do without.

A further great disappointment for George was not meeting Christian Bérard. Overweight, unwashed but with all the style of the true eccentric, Bérard scarcely bothered to clean the paint off his hands before going out into society. He had been an enormous influence upon Francis Rose as a boy in the Cocteau set and they had remained friends. Francis insisted that George should telephone and introduce himself. During the next three years of regular visits and frequent telephone calls, however, George did not once succeed in getting through to the idolized artist. Francis himself had no such difficulties in consorting with his old friend and he was with him in January 1949 at a lighting rehearsal for Molière's *Fourberies de Scapin* when he bent over to tie a shoe-lace and collapsed dead. Francis was distracted with grief and commemorated his friend by making an enormous drawing of him on his death-bed as a little man was working on his death-mask. It was a bizarre but touching tribute to the alluring painter. 'Bébé' Bérard had a wide range of admirers. Crowds gathered in the street to watch his funeral cortège pass. An ex-jailbird, Jojo le Javanais, straight out of Jean Genet, had been one of Bérard's closest friends in the distant past. As Francis Rose later recalled:[14]

> Jojo was extremely ugly, but magnificently built, and showered presents on Bébé and all his friends . . . I will never forget him when he was a middle-aged man and quite bald, battling through a police cordon and stepping into the middle of the road modestly to throw a bunch of lilies of the valley in front of the flower-laden hearse carrying Bébé's coffin in procession along the densely crowded streets. He threw another bunch from the top of a lamp-post as the coffin was being carried to the family tomb in Père Lachaise cemetery. Cocteau, Dior and I persuaded him to descend and invited him to come with the family and friends to the grave, but he refused saying that he had not seen Bébé for twenty years.

George missed that emotional experience, but he was afforded the opportunity of meeting Bérard's live-in companion, formerly Diaghilev's devoted secretary, Boris Kochno. Alas, the circumstances for a close friendship were not auspicious. Francis Rose, who effected the introduction, was angry with Kochno for not choosing what he considerd Bérard's best paintings for the memorial exhibition held in Paris soon after his death.

However, by this time George had begun to consider himself something of a Parisian personality. After only a few months' acquaintance with the city he was given a one-man exhibition by René Breteau in his exclusive gallery at the far end of a charming little courtyard at 30 rue Bonaparte. When the show opened on 8 January 1947, it attracted a deal of attention. Paris-based critics rushed to publish their appraisal of this unknown's work. They were all struck by the power of his canvases. The critic of *Cette Semaine* wrote:[15]

George Melhuish affirms . . . the breadth of his conception in the generous impasto. He exaggerates the head of a Spanish woman in a black mantilla or a woman with dishevelled hair; he emphasizes the heavy shapes of a nude's back-view; he strains towards a vermilion when painting the skies behind 'Notre-Dame' and 'Sacré-Coeur'. There is ardour in the spontaneity of his pictorial temperament.

The *Nouvelles Littéraires* echoed these phrases: 'the English painter George Melhuish manifests the sympathetic temperament of an ardent colourist who is not afraid to admit to a robust sensuality. However, let him guard against the intellectualism of some of his recent pictures.'[16] Guy Dornand of *Le Spectateur* pronounced: 'G. Melhuish, liberal with colour, can be classified as a semi-expressionist. It is from colour that he brings out the design in the voluminous forms of his nudes and in the evocative force of his landscapes. The vigour of his temperament is designed more for mural painting than for the easel.'[17] The arts man from the *New York Herald Tribune*, not normally the kindest of critics, commented:[18]

Foreign painters, more than ever, seem to be drawn to Paris, attracted by its 'ambience', and their reaction to it is always of interest, no matter what form it takes, when it is reflected in the works of an artist worthy of the name. George Melhuish . . . offers an interesting case in point. The direct methods he chooses seem arbitrarily exaggerated to express a certain spirit of revolt which one senses in his work . . . All this means that he is still a young and gifted painter, and that his strong artist's temperament simply needs a self-analysis that time and an artist's experience invariably bring to bear. His portraits are strong and vigorous. They show great promise and reveal his real worth.

George was flattered by so much critical attention. Whether or not he really was seeking 'to express a certain spirit of revolt . . . in his work' is another matter. He certainly liked to think of himself as a painter pushing back the frontiers of artistic style, but he would scarcely have seen himself as a social rebel. But during that January in Paris, rebels and reactionaries alike were primarily concerned about one thing: how to keep warm. The winter was bitterly cold and post-war fuel supplies were scanty. But George lingered on shivering in his hotel room until the exhibition closed on 31 January. He wanted to savour every moment of what was his first Paris triumph.

CHAPTER ELEVEN

LIFE ON A SHOESTRING

Despite finding his spiritual home in Paris, George had no intention of neglecting the artistic scene in England. He was one of the first to exhibit his paintings in the Royal West of England Academy when it launched itself again with its annual exhibition on 16 November 1946. He never made any effort to have himself elected as a member and, therefore, had no automatic right to hang his pictures. But each year up to 1954 he had at least one (and often two) of his paintings chosen 'blind' by the selection committee, even though over this period his style began to change radically and possibly became less appealing to provincial art officionados. He treated the matter with a degree of panache. Soon he was asking and getting the highest prices of any artist in the exhibition. From his point of view this was in keeping with his growing international reputation. It also reflected the fact that his canvases tended to be bigger than the others displayed. Because of the alphabetical proximity of their names, he and Lord Methuen found themselves catalogued and sometimes hung side by side. Perhaps George benefited from this coincidental association with his illustrious friend but, fine though Methuen was as an artist, George had no difficulty in putting his and most of the other exhibitors' work in the shade.

His Paris experience was now showing a two-way artistic effect. His Galerie Breteau exhibition introduced Parisians to some striking English scenes among the urban landscape canvases. A few of his Paris scenes were also included but not as a significant element. When he returned to England, he had built up a sizeable collection of paintings inspired by his French experiences and he continued to work on further ones once he settled down in his studios in London and Bristol. The result of all this activity was that he was able to mount a one-man exhibition in London at the Gallery Jabé in Jasons Court, Wigmore Street. Billed as 'George Melhuish in Paris', it opened on 1 October 1947 and ran for a whole month, attracting a great deal of attention from a London public that found in the colour and romantic allure of Paris a means of vicarious escape from the grey austerity of post-war Britain.

The general tragedy had passed. In 1947 George had to cope with two personal bereavements. His grandmother, Caroline Seymour, finally died in April in her nursing home at 10 Salisbury Road. She was eighty-seven years old and had been infirm for a long time, but George's life so far had been singularly untouched by the death of loved-ones: he had no recollection of his Seymour grandfather's demise in August 1917, since he was scarcely twelve months old at the time. His Melhuish grandmother, Emma, died when he was an impressionable adolescent in 1933, but he was not quite as close to her as to Caroline. Yet his feelings about her were decidedly mixed when he was told the contents of her will. There were no such equivocal feelings when death struck again (immediately after the close of his Gallery Jabé show on 28 October and before the opening of the Royal West of England Academy's exhibition, with his *Cathédrale de Saint-Jean, Lyon,* on 19 November). His father's health had been poor for years and finally he died at home with George by his bedside on 15 November 1947. The cause of death was not the lung disease that one might have expected of a heavy smoker, but uraemia caused by interstitial nephritis, not a pleasant death for somebody who had spent his seventy-one years in complete harmony with his fellow-men. George adored his parents and was devastated by his father's death. However, in practical terms, it seemed likely to cause problems. Although his mother, Elsie, was still only fifty-seven when widowed, she was severely crippled with arthritis and virtually incapable of looking after herself. She was a willing and uncomplaining soul. Barbara Thorne recalls her efforts to serve her a cup of tea by holding the cup between her two sets of clenched knuckles. Treatment in a homeopathic hospital only produced false hope and, when the agony in her knee-joints became quite unbearable, her doctors suggested that she should have an operation to fix them permanently in one position, straight or sitting. She chose the latter: at least it meant that, when George held his parties, she could be wheeled in and seated sedately as the centre of attention for young and old alike. Everybody admired her for her selfless and gentle nature. Her ailment only heightened her appreciation of life's pleasanter aspects and she could express this in the most tellingly simple words. Writing to Patricia Daly at a time when she was in particular distress with a septic ulcer on her arthritic knee joint, she told her with girlish pleasure: 'I went for a nice motor ride one evening last week with some friends. We went to Aust. It was a glorious sunset. The sky was full of beautiful colours.'[1]

At first George had thought that his father's death might mean an end to his Paris expeditions, so soon after they had become possible. But Elsie Melhuish refused to allow filial duty to spoil the career of the son whose achievements she saw as possibly fulfilling her early messianic concept of him. If he wanted to go away for periods of work, she would induce some kind friend or neighbour to attend to her basic needs or, as latterly, she would go to stay with friends like Ronald and Ruby Reed and their six children, or to a nursing home. However, from time to time George used to overcome the dilemma by taking his mother with him on his trips. He frequently transported her to London by motor car, to stay with him in the cramped conditions of the King's Road studio and, to everybody's astonishment, he took her to Paris with him on at least two occasions. He was not a happy traveller at the best of times and how he coped with his mother in a wheelchair is hard to imagine. There was no question of taking an aeroplane, so mother and son had to negotiate their way by boats and primitive trains. Once in Paris a hotel with no lift seemed a minor inconvenience. Travel on the Métro, of course, was out of the question, but most of George's contacts and all the Left Bank galleries were within easy wheelchairing distance of the rue de Condé. His mother thoroughly enjoyed the fuss and attention that she attracted.

The problem of his mother's welfare had at first seemed intractable. One can see that from the fact that he sub-let his London studio on a temporary basis or lent it to friends. When he had to visit London, he was faced with the dilemma of finding some place to stay. Deborah Jones came to the rescue. After the war she had lingered on in her distinctive flat in Princess Victoria Street, Bristol, still apparently happy to concentrate upon her (as yet) unlucrative painting. She had lost none of her sparkle. Unfortunately it often extended to her gossiping about her friends' peccadillos, real or imagined. It always seemed to be George who learned the latest gossip. One of the reasons for this was that, as a portrait painter, he used to chat constantly to his sitters – and, in turn, they chatted to him. In January 1946 he was painting a girl called Muriel Wilson. Although she had never met Barbara Addison, she innocently let slip a titbit of speculative gossip about her. Deborah had been her source of information. George was furious for Barbara's sake, but again failed to realize that he would have been better to hold his tongue. The resultant falling-out was only temporary. Deborah decided that the charm of life on a shoestring was wearing thin, so she packed her bags and went off to London where she obtained a job at the Royal Opera House, just as it was being reconverted from its wartime ballroom status. She applied her remarkable artistic talents to making the lavish headdresses and stage jewellery that were an essential part of the glitter required of post-war opera and ballet productions. She came to know everybody who mattered in all aspects of the theatre world: Oliver Messel, Bernard Miles, Walter Hodges, Christopher Fry, Kurt Jooss; the list was long and varied. She even encountered professionally the delightfully eccentric composer Lord Berners and the just as delightfully eccentric Francis Rose in one of his stage-designing periods. She was always being asked to do lucrative free-lance work, so she decided to set up her own independent business supplying theatrical ornaments and jewellery. It was enormously successful.

However, Deborah took a long time to establish a settled domestic base. As she later recalled, 'I was living with a ballet company then . . . the International Ballet Company . . . It sounds a bit excessive, doesn't it? I'd met some of the boys when they came down to Bristol . . . And when I went up to London, I slept on the floor of the big room with five or six others. That was at 11 Ladbroke Gardens.'[2] And that was where George came in. When the ballet company went off on tour, he could come and stay at the house during a period of relative calm. But there were horrors lurking unseen. Deborah remembered (and George did not quickly forget) one particularly 'dreadful discovery':[3]

> In the kitchen . . . there was a rather nasty little cupboard under the sink and something . . . pale was coming out at the top . . . George said: 'I don't know what it is, but it's getting bigger.' And when we opened the cupboard, it was absolutely full of a red cabbage that had grown inside the cupboard. It was absolutely beautiful. It had grown out of itself, like a bolting lettuce that grows on and on. Those things grow out of themselves because they have their own heart to grow out of. And this leaf was growing bigger and bigger and coming out of the top of this cupboard door.

George was horrified, but secretly amused. He made sure that, from then on, the King's Road studio was always available when he wanted it. He could put up with primitive conditions, but he was becoming increasingly fastidious about domestic cleanliness. Part of the reason was that he was worried about his health. Already the signs of the terrible diabetes, which later tyrannized all aspects of his life, were beginning to show. (It was finally diagnosed in November 1950.) This meant that he became careful about what he ate and drank. It also meant that he was less relaxed about moving in a society in which dinner-parties again became the order of the day – or, rather, of the night.

Perhaps this was no bad thing as far as the Bristol scene was concerned. The grander the society, the less he met with a sympathetic response to his art. Even *cognoscenti* like the Professor of Pathology, Tom

Hewer, and his wife Anne found themselves out of their depth with George. They lived at Vine House in Henbury in such grand style that the professor was called 'the Baron' behind his back. Their great passion was the garden, which they made into a work of art, but they also had something of a reputation as connoisseurs of painting. George set out to cultivate them. The Hewers always considered themselves to have a discerning eye for 'modern art', but what they meant by that and what George meant by it was not necessarily the same thing. When he asked if he might paint Tom Hewer's portrait, they found themselves agreeing. The result, 'rather more than life-size, in orange and green', did not please the Hewers, although they agreed to buy it.[4] The basic problem was that two different forms of individualism had come uncomfortably up against each other and neither bent to the other. As Anne Hewer recalled, 'he was very eccentric as a young man, as well as when he got older, which in itself is always an interesting thing, but we did not find ourselves on the same wavelength at the time of the portrait painting (which can in fact be a time when one gets to know an artist well) and the opportunity never came later either.'[5]

One of the reasons for this failure to 'gel' was George's indefatigable approach to the commercial side of art. He tried to mix socializing with salesmanship. The Hewers clearly could not cope with this. Others of their social set were more sympathetic, but only up to a point. George was never happy about using agents to sell his pictures. He thought that they took too large a cut for their efforts and so, when his work was not being hung in exhibitions, he tended either to pursue private commissions or to hold large *soirées* at 75 Springfield Road, when a glass of wine mellowed guests as they examined his latest paintings, hung, already priced, round the walls. Often his most appreciative 'patrons' came across his work by chance. One day in 1948 Dr Kenneth Smith, an eminent psychiatrist, was doing an outpatients session at Bristol Royal Infirmary and the hospital secretary, knowing of his interest in art, said: 'If you don't have anything to do after clinic's finished, George Melhuish is holding an exhibition of his paintings at his house. Why don't you come along?'[6] Kenneth Smith and his wife, Vera Apter Smith, duly descended on Springfield Road. He recalled the occasion[7]:

There was George in a room full of paintings, all over the place, and a lot of people – people whom I knew – so we bought a picture on the first occasion, a relatively minor piece . . . . I had vaguely heard of him then. We rather took to his paintings. And it was a bit of fun, the *soirées* and that sort of thing . . . For three or four years we bought some of his pictures and advised some other people to do so.

One of those who took his advice was his brother, Canon John Smith, rector of St Albans, Westbury Park. They took him to one of George's selling parties and he was impressed by the paintings – if not by the wine. He remarked to George that he would not be surprised if his work were to be chosen for the Royal Academy's summer exhibition. George said nothing, but thought it 'very droll' (to use one of his favourite expressions). He had, of course, already exhibited a number of times at the Royal Academy. Indeed, the Smiths later acquired the stunning study of Deborah Jones, *Toilette*, that was such a success at the 1944 exhibition. He was fond of the painting and was unusually reluctant to part with it. But he was going through a lean financial patch and gave in.

Over the years the Smiths (who were highly discerning collectors of all kinds of art) acquired a sizeable number of his paintings. Canon Smith bought two: a flower piece and a view of the Île de la Cité. Kenneth and Vera Smith acquired work over the whole range of his styles, including some of his architectural landscapes. (One of them was an interesting study of the port of Marseilles – interesting because George never visited the South of France.) The Smiths also commissioned a number of works, some of them of an unusual nature, as Kenneth Smith recalled:[8]

Once or twice I had a couple of frames and I said to George: 'Would you paint me something for these frames?'

And he said: 'Well, it's not my way of doing things. But arbitrary painting is a good discipline, so I suppose so.'

So he did me a couple of pictures to fit the frames.

The Smiths had two lively sons, Paul and Michael, clever children who thought George enormous fun. He, unusually, responded to their enthusiasm and painted Paul's portrait at the same time as he executed a magnificent study of the boys' mother. (He later exhibited this in the Festival Exhibition of Contemporary Painting in Bristol in May 1951. When Sir Kenneth Clark opened the show, he made it clear that he thought the painting one of the best exhibits.) The Smiths got the impression that George was very short of cash. He gave the appearance of being run down, so they asked him to give their son Paul a course of eight lessons in painting. George accepted the commission. He was a born didact, yet he had no interest in face-to-face teaching: that was not the road to fame. However, in the late 1940s cash did seem to be in short supply.

With George it was difficult to judge from appearances, but the Smiths were genuinely concerned about him, while friends with less social panache might have been put off by his manner. Ever considerate, Vera

Smith would call at Springfield Road just to see how he was faring (and also to see his mother, of whom she was genuinely fond). She described what would invariably happen:[9]

> We did sometimes go round of an evening just to see what he was up to . . . And he would come to the door and he'd look at you as though he'd never seen you in his life before. And he would say: 'Oh well, now that you are here, you'd better come in.' He'd very unwillingly just open the door so that you would have to squeeze yourself in.

George was so self-orientated that he could not see how strange his manner appeared to the general public. He certainly did not expect it to meet with a reciprocal response. As the years went on he became more and more demanding. Diet, for him, became an increasing problem, but even understanding friends like the Smiths found some of his requests bizarre: 'He would demand the most impossible things, as if it were a restaurant.' He himself had no compunction about calling unexpectedly at their house in Howard Road. Vera Smith was surprised but amused by one particular incident:[10]

> One night he came in and we had finished supper. He came in and said: 'I'm hungry. I'd like some supper.'
> So I said: 'Would you like a sandwich?' – because I'd already cooked and washed up.
> 'No,' he said, 'I'll have a tin of best salmon.'
> And I'd never heard the expression 'best salmon' before. I suppose he meant red salmon, as opposed to pink salmon. I don't know. So I had to fish a tin of salmon out of the cupboard and he just ate that, not in any bread at all. He was really hungry. And we used to feel sorry for him. We thought: 'Poor chap, . . . he's very hard up.' Possibly he wasn't, but he seemed so.

Truth be told, it was more likely his health that caused his down-at-heel appearance as he went through a period of adjustment to his medical condition. And it was certainly not over a question of tins of salmon (best or otherwise) that his friendship with the Smiths tailed off. They failed to appreciate his development of an abstract style of art. It was so foreign to them that it seemed like the old story of the artist flinging a pot of paint in the public's face. They were honest enough to say so openly to him. He did not appreciate their candour because he knew that they, like many others, had simply not made the intellectual adjustment necessary for a proper appraisal of abstract works. But this period of cooling-off was still in the future. For the time being, the Smiths, parents and children, were among his most loyal friends.

Another little enclave of loyal friends came into George's life soon after the Smiths did. At the opening of the Royal West of England Academy Exhibition on 22 October 1949 he attracted a great deal of attention. His striking portrait of Sir Adrian Boult was on display; magisterial, yet kindly, the face was also familiar enough to a discerning public to be eye-catching. George found himself being photographed beside the painting with Home Office Judge Wethered, who had generously let him off the hook at the tribunal to which he had been summoned as a conscientious objector. Among the other exhibitors was an attractive young married woman, called Dorian Mogg. She had taken up painting only six months previously as an outlet for a creative urge that motherhood and an ordinary job could not entirely satisfy. George was impressed by her and by the painting, *Evening Flight*, that had crossed the academy's august portals after such a short apprenticeship. Before long she and her husband found themselves as guests at a number of his evening entertainments.

Dorian Mogg's abiding impression was that friendship with George was fun. She would invite him and his mother to spend the afternoon with her family, Elsie Melhuish having to be carried into the house. The two Mogg boys, David and Anthony, used to sit fascinated at her feet as she talked to them in the reassuring voice of a former schoolmistress. She would delight them by reading to them. Dorian would do her best to please George by providing something that he particularly liked at tea-time. And again it was salmon (fresh or tinned: he liked both) that invariably filled the sandwiches. As she later commented, 'It was pleasant. And my husband and I talked to George on all different subjects. It was very nice and informal – something you wouldn't expect of George, as other people saw him.'[11] These were telling words because his brusque public image did not endear him to everybody and, by this time, had begun to turn the Bristol art set against him. As time went on and he developed more radical modes of artistic expression, the staid Bristolians were less and less amused. George himself reacted by cultivating a style of friendship to which he was already inclined. Increasingly, friends ceased to be part of a wider group but were cultivated very much on a one-to-one basis. This was a natural outcome of his philosophical inclinations. The Socratic approach to dialogue seemed most intellectually stimulating. The great disadvantage was that a number of his closest friends not only never met each other but did not know of each other's existence. This made for problems, because a less than discerning person might imagine that he (or she) enjoyed a unique place in his life, whereas the truth was very different.

Dorian Mogg had no such illusions, even though she appreciated his individualistic tendencies. She came to know him at more than a purely social level by taking lessons in painting from him. She was clever enough to realize that, although she had had work accepted by the local academy, she would benefit from some expert advice on technique; she recruited another friend, a Mrs Howeman, and together they took lessons from George. Dorian's first and enduring impression was of the broad brushes that he insisted on their using. She found them awkward, but the lesson was well learnt. Although these sessions took place over a relatively short period – he was clearly not as impecunious as had been supposed – she spent enough time with him to do a number of formal exercises, such as a flower study of some daffodils and, more intriguing, a portrait of Elsie Melhuish. George was happier when the course of lessons ended and he continued the friendship with Dorian by painting a beautiful portrait of her. She was struck by how quickly he painted the highly finished canvas. The last thing that he wanted was to cut short their association: that was simply the way in which he worked most successfully.

However, by this time, he had realized that one could go on only so long keeping the wolf from the door. If his career as an artist were to continue to flourish and, increasingly importantly, his career as a philosopher, some sounder financial basis to his life would have to be found.

CHAPTER TWELVE

MOTORS AND MOTOR FORCE

In 1948 George hit on a plan to put his finances on a firmer footing. He started to buy second-hand cars with the idea of reselling them at a profit. Though no driver himself, he had always found motors fascinating, especially the grander, luxury models. His buying the Railton in 1945 had sown the seeds of the idea and when, in the post-war years, cars were still in short supply, a decent living could be made from dealing in used vehicles – at least until small, economical family cars became more available in the 1950s. There was always a demand for the more luxurious models, even when they might be ten years old and had suffered considerable wear and tear during the war years. These cars could be bought relatively cheaply but, when spruced up and resold, they tended to hold their value better than ordinary vehicles, which were much more vulnerable to changing fashions, not to mention overwork.

Somebody who observed George's technique of salesmanship at first hand was Percy Edgell. He described how cars brought them together:[1]

I was interested in the buying and selling of motor cars as a means of trying to make a living and I had the idea of setting up some sort of hire service, a Rolls Royce hire service. So through the paper I saw this advert for a Rolls Royce and I went along to look at it and the owner was George, of course . . . He'd bought it in London and had brought it down with the idea of making an honest profit on it. I looked at this pan-technicon and decided that it was not suitable . . . for what I had in mind.

George and Percy Edgell did, however, have a friendly chat and subsequently got to know each other well. When Percy learned that he was a 'struggling artist', he felt a degree of sympathy and gradually allowed himself to be used by George, who sensed that here was somebody with invaluable technical skills. After the Rolls Royce episode Percy began to see him at the weekly car auctions that took place at a garage and saleroom called Old Baker's. He used to observe, agog, his technique of buying and selling. At auctions he always wore a smart bow tie and he would always bid for items using a rolled umbrella. Good psychology, he claimed: it tended to intimidate rival buyers.

Having bought two or three cars, he would have to have them driven round to garages which he rented on Nugent Hill, just round the corner from his house. As a youth, Brian Jenkins, the younger son of Barbara Addison's landlady, Mrs Clare Jenkins, knew George fairly well as a visitor to the house on Cotham Brow. When he learned that he was interested in cars, his curiosity was aroused: he had always been fascinated by the mechanics of cars and motor cycles. One Sunday morning George invited him to come and see the silver-grey Railton that he still kept for his own use. He was duly impressed but, when a number of other cars came and went in fairly rapid succession, he was less happy. Years later he could still recall his reaction:[2]

> I was always appalled because he would never worry about the mechanics of the thing: it was purely the appearance. And that may have been the case with many of George's things: it is the appearance that matters. And because he wasn't mechanical – at least, I assumed that he wasn't mechanical – when I lifted up the bonnet and looked in at all the bits and pieces of botched repair jobs that had been done, I was appalled. I was left wondering what to say – to say: 'Oh, my goodness!' or whether to be pleased and keep him happy by saying what a marvellous car it was. Generally it didn't make a lot of difference. He was obviously pleased with its shape and the colour.

George was, in fact, quite interested in mechanics, but with the vintage motor cars salesmanship and external appearances were all that counted: that was why his customers were buying cars of that quality. Most would not have spotted defects even if they had taken the trouble to look at the engine. He made sure to discourage such inquisitiveness and, if something were glaringly defective, he would conceal it. Percy Edgell once spotted that there was a piston missing in a Rolls Royce which he had just bought. George simply got a mechanic (or, more likely, a compliant friend) to cover up the missing part with a metal plate. George was more concerned about the vehicle's visual effect. As Percy noted, 'He didn't have much equipment as a car-salesman. All he did was to bring them back; put on a coat of polish and some boot-black on the leather upholstery – or boot-polish, which shone it. And he used his artistic talents to touch them up.'[3] Percy thought this was a waste of his potential, but it did not stop him from helping him to make a go of the business. He was always having to lug around hugely heavy batteries that seemed constantly in need of recharging. If George bought a car out of town, it was always Percy who had to go and fetch it as his driver. George contributed to the hazards of such an operation by putting only one gallon of petrol at a time into his luxury limousines. The proverbial exclamation, 'Oh, we seem to have run out of petrol!' took on a new meaning.

Once back in the garage and duly smartened up, the car would be thrust on the market with a number of sales gimmicks. He would put an advertisement in the local paper that might read: 'Lady owner. Going abroad. Must sell.' It never failed to achieve the desired result. Occasionally there would be side-effects to these idle untruths. A few years later, at the end of his selling days, his great friend Charmian Deckers would help him with his sales pitch (and his driving). She laughed at the thought of it:[4]

I always remembered . . . if we sold an old jalopy very well. I used to give trial runs as if it were mine. 'Lady going abroad,' he used to say. And occasionally irate people would 'phone up and say: 'You're not a lady going abroad with a so-and-so to sell. We saw you off Lansdown Road last week.' Terribly funny! What could you say?

One of the advantages of Cotham as a centre of sales operations was that it was on a fairly steep hill. Having concluded a sale, George would set the car and the new owner rolling smoothly down the hill in the full knowledge that, when it reached the level or attempted to drive up the next slope, it might not function quite so smartly – if at all. He was prepared for this. He would promptly close up the garage and disappear round the corner. He did not want what he called 'squealers' coming back and complaining. Charmian Deckers reflected half-guiltily on the matter: 'But it was great fun. It was almost like Chicago in the old days. If we'd sold a car that was a bit of a dud, we used to go to and have tea at the Grand Hotel.'[5]

But, to be fair, not everything about George's car 'business' was suspect. He was a genuinely clever salesman and hit on certain selling gimmicks a great deal earlier than most. For example, he developed the habit of buying cars purely and simply for their number plates, if he thought that they might have a particular appeal to customers. He was certainly shrewder than the devoted Percy Edgell about the sales potential of certain used vehicles. Charmian Deckers recalls the sensation that he caused by buying a steam-roller at auction and driving it through Bristol. The great advantage of Percy's house was that it had useful parking space in the back garden, of which George availed himself (once the steam-roller was gone and as long as he considered it suitable). Percy's daughter, Rosemary, recorded that her 'mother's first memory of George Melhuish was of opening the front door to a thin, pale individual with a rolled-up umbrella . . . He wanted to know when it would be convenient for a car to be moved out of the back garden as apples were falling on the roof.'[6]

A lot of George's success depended on a form of unconscious affrontery. He was apparently unaware that his taking advantage of kindly friends was seen as such. When he had a big vehicle that he thought more suitable for the London market, he would ask Percy Edgell to drive him up from Bristol. Invariably Percy had to buy the petrol. He was almost used to that but, on one occasion, the last straw was laid on the camel's back when, half-way to London, George decided that he would like a drink. They stopped at a pub and George ordered the drinks, then immediately scuttled off to the 'gents'. He did not re-appear until after the waiter had brought the order and coaxed the money out of Percy.

Percy did, however, try to gain some recompense in kind. He suggested that George should paint the portraits of himself and his five-year-old daughter Rosemary. Several sittings for Percy failed to produce a completed study, but Rosemary's portrait turned out to be a highly finished, striking picture of an adult-looking little girl with a solemn, critical look on her face. Her later recollection of the experience was remarkable for the sharpness of its sense-perception:[7]

> I vividly remember being dressed up in a pale blue frock, with an artificial rose pinned on the front to have my portrait painted by George. I went with my father to a large Victorian house in Cotham for several sittings. The house was very dark and cold . . . It was so cold you could see your breath, especially in the studio, full of the accoutrements of the job, paint oozing from the half-squeezed tubes, palette knives of all sizes, assorted brushes, and a pervading smell of oil paint and turps. The working palette consisted of a marble washstand.

George was nothing if not realistic about the hard economic facts of life. While he would do anything to avoid paying cash for services rendered, he was remarkably unsentimental about his passions in life.

The Railton, the Jensen, the Delage and the prized Silver Ghost, though objects of love, came and went and, while the market held up, they provided him with enough money to survive and do what he wanted with his painting and philosophy. He continued to produce canvases as actively as ever. Perhaps for a short while he was less vigorous in seeking buyers at the international level, but this was a very active period for informal sales in the Bristol area. Yet that had only a limited appeal for him and the thought of one-man exhibitions or hangings was seldom far from his mind. In the spring of 1949 he organized an adventurous show in the City Art Gallery in Bristol, an 'Exhibition of Works by Contemporary Painters'. He persuaded the great and good either to lend exhibits from their private collections (such as Sir Kenneth Clark) or put their work up for sale. The result was that pieces by Matthew Smith, Julian Trevelyan, John Piper, Graham Sutherland, L.S. Lowry, Henry Moore, Princess Fahrunissa Zeid el Houssein, Cecil Collins, Barbara Hepworth, Ivon Hitchens and many more jostled for attention. Among the 'many more' was George's friend Sir Francis Rose, exhibiting three canvases. George limited himself to exhibiting only two of his own paintings. One of them, *Woman with a Lamp*, was chosen by the *Bristol Evening Post* to illustrate its notice of the exhibition and to reassure the public: 'All the painters represented in the exhibition have achieved some degree of national recognition. A John Piper, a Henry Moore, and Barbara Hepworth's *The Hands*, are three pictures of special interest, while Mr Melhuish exhibits some of his own work including a new picture of striking quality.'[8] As George explained in his introduction to the catalogue, he saw the exhibition as educative. He also reassured the West Country audience, to whom some of the painters represented were 'new', that they were all nationally acknowledged masters of their craft:[9]

> An exhibition of truly contemporary art should to some extent create in the observer an element of surprise and controversy. For in it we see the artists of the day working out in a new manner the age-old forms of a living aesthetic. Modern art does not represent one pathway but many. The present exhibition shows an interesting cross-section of what is being done in Britain today.

George expanded these comments when he spoke at the private opening of the show on the evening of 25 February. The West Country had, indeed, not seen the like for many years and the whole enterprise was regarded as something of a triumph for him. However, if he were intent on bringing the outside art world to Bristol, he saw his own road to fame and fortune as leading in the other direction. Harold Rubin gave him and his fellow artist, James Hull, a two-man exhibition at the chic Twenty Brook Street Gallery in Mayfair. The show was opened on 12 April 1949 by 'one of Britain's foremost aesthetic theorists and art critics Herbert Read'. George's canvases were well received. And the art critic of the *Bristol Evening Post*, up in town for the opening, used his column to castigate the worthy citizens of Bristol for their lack of appreciation of his work. While this prophet had not been received of his own, his paintings had been acclaimed in London and Paris:[10]

His work has appeared frequently – and has often been disparaged – in Bristol, but other national galleries and private collectors from France and America have found his canvases worth retaining . . . It would be unkind but certainly not unwise, to predict that, if the nation were to acclaim Melhuish as a painter, Bristol – forgetting past neglect – would hasten to acclaim him as a true son of the city, and bask happily in any limelight his stature might cast in her direction.

One imagines that Bristolians were too surprised at the startling mixed metaphor to notice the reprimand, but they could not help taking notice as the critic forged ahead with his panegyric on George's paintings:[11]

These . . . works are highly individual and promise a considerable advance from former expressionistic styles evolved by the French. In the main, they reflect highly emotional and violent expressions of atmosphere within semi-architectural scenes embracing churches, houses, streets and quarters in Paris, Bristol, Bath and the West Country. The large, turbulent canvases, painted in extremes of the colour scale, are heady, disturbing 'tours de force'.

The mood expressed in these tempestuous paintings will be more readily understood if the spectator is capable of imagining his sudden exit from a cool, dark sanctuary into a moving world drenched in hot light. Melhuish interprets a moment before the eyes fully adjust themselves to the apparent reality of the scene before them, leaving a vivid, forceful impression of a vortex of colour, light, movement – and the vaguest impression of architectural structure upon which the mood is built.

Such a feeling has been captured in *Maisons anciennes, Montmartre, Boulevards*, and other similar studies. Although this work is strong for the British spectator, it is more valid than the small 'respectable' national interpretations of extreme modern art which will become more popular as the tones are subdued, the canvases reduced in size and the frames painted quietly and tastefully to accord with the English drawing-room.

After that his co-exhibitor, James Hull, with fifty-seven works on show (to George's mere twenty-two) merited only a passing reference. However, when the Twenty Brook Street Gallery opened again in July 1949 for an 'Exhibition of Paintings by S. John Woods, David Strachan, John Barker and Artists of Today', the director Harold Rubin included in it canvases by both George and James Hull. Clearly he did regard them as part of the up-and-coming generation of young artists.

Bristol made a gesture to counteract the accusations of neglect. When an exhibition, entitled 'Bristol à Bordeaux' was held at the Musée de Peintre in Bordeaux in the winter of 1949–50, the city hastily retrieved one of the blitz pictures, which it owned (and which had been lent to the Museum and Art Gallery at Weston-super-Mare) and sent it as one of the exhibits. George's *Bristol Theatre after the Raid* had been painted after the bombing of the Princes Theatre in November 1940, but the collective memory of the war, which had a different significance for the great 'twin' centres of the wine trade, was still fresh. There was something prophetic about George's work being exhibited on French soil once again.

He put together an exhibition from his accumulated stock of paintings at the Art Gallery in Cheltenham. It opened on Saturday, 4 March 1950 and he was present to 'say a few words' to the assembled company. He was beginning to enjoy speaking in public on the subject of art, but on this occasion his mind was on other, more glittering things than the staid hoards of Cheltenham's art-lovers. As soon as the show closed on 27 March, he packed up his canvases and headed in the direction of France. By pulling strings with his illustrious Paris contacts he managed to secure an invitation to mount an exhibition of paintings at the most prestigious of galleries, J. and H. Bernheim-Jeune, at the heart of fashionable Paris, on the corner of the Avenue Matignon and the Rue du Faubourg Saint-Honoré.

The exhibition opened for the *vernissage* on Saturday, 15 April 1950 and ran for a successful two weeks. The French press twitched an inquisitive nose. A. de Falgairolle wrote that George displayed 'an ardour, a temperament and an enthusiasm which, while taking as a subject the sombre Palais Royal, turned it into something with feeling, almost romanticism. Melhuish brings life to skies of a lowering intensity.'[12] Another critic described the exhibition as 'pretty disturbing because certain canvases, delirious explosions of acid colours, are highly displeasing'. But that was only the first impression and the writer concluded that such painting simply needed 'a solid point of departure brought to bear on its disturbing air of mystery'.[13]

An American critic, Barnett Conlan, was less equivocal in his response to George's 'selection of Paris impressions'. He explained to his readers:[14]

He is an expressionist of a rather frenetic type, and in some instances the colours seem to explode on the canvas. In *Old Streets* the houses which blaze in incandescent yellows have an almost portentous air. In a canvas such as *Orage* this seems more appropriate. He can be stable and legible when he wants, as is seen in his pictures with arcades. Melhuish, who was one of the official painters of the last war, seems to have carried over something of his impressions of that period . . . His houses appear to rock and blaze and the effect of some of these paintings almost suggests Hiroshima.

George must have relished that as a compliment.

Geoffrey Fraser, the English-language art critic based in Paris, wrote an article on the Bernheim-Jeune show which was published in the *Bristol Evening Post*. He confessed that it 'proved a distinct surprise' and he noted a similar reaction among 'many French art lovers, including the Princesse de Rohan, who came to the varnishing day, and the many connoisseurs and art dealers who make the point of visiting regularly all shows staged in the Bernheim-Jeune gallery'.[15] They all apparently made the mistake of coming along with a prejudiced notion of what English painting was all about. Fraser explained:[16]

It certainly surprised me when I went to see it in the expectation of finding the usual humdrum collection of more or less talented paintings that, at rare intervals, a few English artists venture to submit to the verdict of Paris.

Mr Melhuish's work is very far indeed from being humdrum, for he strikes a particularly distinctive note of his own. He lays little weight on forms; forms are indicated rather than expressed. The medium of their expression is an often startling, but always attractive, combination of colours.

Perhaps the most characteristic painting shown is one entitled *The Saint Germain Quarter*. Mr Melhuish seems to me to have expressed the ardent, vigorous intellectual and artistic fermentation that is the mark of that quarter of youth and Existentialism as a kind of great flaming flower with just a glimpse of luminous houses between the sweeping flames. An original conception and a singularly attractive one.

Geoffrey Fraser was delighted to meet the artist in person at the opening of the show. He was impressed when George told him that he had already sold several of the paintings. Fraser himself noticed a dealer who specialized in buying paintings for South America 'manifesting a keen and promising interest'. Fraser then went on to explain the reason why his work had caused such a stir:[17]

Hundreds of artists stage one-man shows in Paris, but the percentage of sales is usually an exceedingly small one. This makes Mr Melhuish's success all the more remarkable.

It is amusing to note that the general impression of French visitors to the gallery has been astonishment at the fact that the artist is an Englishman. It is the firmly anchored belief of most Frenchmen that Englishmen utterly lack imagination, which explains the surprise felt at the work of this singularly imaginative English Impressionist.

The irony was that George was being lauded as an 'English Impressionist' at the very point at which his artistic style had travelled well beyond the point of Expressionism (let alone Impressionism) and was feeling its way towards the abstract. But his old friend the editor of *The Studio* chose to mark his Paris triumph by reproducing an unequivocally expressionistic study of the basilica of Sacré-Coeur.

The Bernheim-Jeune exhibition closed on 29 April 1950 and George was on the move again. On 15 May a one-man show of his paintings (again almost entirely of French landscapes) opened at the Galerie Parenthou at 14 Grand'Place in Roubaix, just outside Lille. He was billed as 'this celebrated young English artist'. And the catalogue that introduced him to the citizens of Roubaix continued in the same adulatory tone:[18]

George Melhuish astonishes with his vision of the world. According to him the entire material world breathes and regenerates itself. This is true not only of a visible life subordinated to the elements, to light – an undoubtedly pleasing image but also rather superficial – but above all of a powerful interior life, appropriate to each object and each mass. For this painter nothing is inanimate.

George the philosopher had clearly briefed the writer well beforehand. 'All these paintings throb with an intense and sometimes tumultuous life that fills the canvas or paper with its peremptory vigour . . . Even his buildings are living beings.'[19] The writer thought this all the more remarkable for an artist born in a land of mists and greyness and commended him for his exquisite use of colour, his respect for the principles of perspective and his rejection of stale intellectualism:[20]

The world created by G. Melhuish is a new and magnificently powerful world, colourful, musical and sensual, at times brutal, but it is always a source of strong emotion and pure joy. One cannot remain indifferent to it. It releases from this combination a comforting warmth for some that is too torrid for others. One is either for or against; there is no middle ground.

When the show closed on 31 May it was judged to have been a success. Unfortunately, as the unsold paintings were being transported back to England, a strange incident occurred. At Lille some of them were put on the train for Brussels. George pursued them hot-foot on the next train heading towards the Belgian border. However, by the time he arrived the paintings had completely disappeared. Nobody knew anything about them. He was totally at a loss to know what to do. His French was not good enough to pursue the search in person, so he took a rueful look at the Belgian frontier (which he refused to cross) and left the matter in the hands of the police. Only by a hair's breadth had he avoided adding another foreign country to his achievements as a traveller. That would have been a significant addition because, apart from Wales, France was the only foreign land that he ever visited.

PART FOUR

1950–1957

CHAPTER THIRTEEN

ABSTRACT EXPRESSIONS

In the early 1950s George continued to divide his time between Bristol, London and Paris. For a while his Paris trips had to be relatively brief as his mother's health deteriorated and he was reluctant to impose on friends, like the Reeds, for long periods. Otherwise she would have to go into a nursing home and that was a costly exercise. By this time he was earning a respectable income from his paintings, but he was dependent upon his motor-car business to supplement his budget. This, however, required him to be in Bristol or, at least, London. He had no inherited money. Even his father's estate, though meagre, had automatically gone entirely to his mother. His Lennox aunt died in 1953, but this brought him a legacy of only £36 – and even that was entirely unexpected.

After his French successes of 1950 he decided to build on the prestige that this, at last, brought him in England. The irony was that the two main areas of his life, painting and philosophy, were on the hinge of a development that was very substantially inspired by French, rather than English, contacts. He did not always like to reveal publicly the revolutionary change that was occurring. Early in 1951 he spent two crucial months in Paris, but to local reporters who greeted his return to Bristol he gave a deliberately frivolous impression of what he had been doing. His Paris stay, he boasted, was 'a round of receptions, parties, and visits to artists' studios almost every day'. The reporters gathered that 'among the celebrities he met was Humphrey Bogart'.[1] George certainly enjoyed such socializing, but it was almost always with an eye to the main chance. In London he assiduously cultivated the renowned Mrs Emma Tollemache, who, apart from being a poet in her own right, was a rich and distinguished patron of the arts. (She also had the distinction of having seen both her daughters marry Sir Thomas Beecham's sons.) She was a great friend of Sir Francis Rose and had, in fact, in 1948, collaborated with him on a volume of her poetry, *In the Light*. Francis's illustrations were curiously surreal, reminiscent of Cocteau's *Opium* days. Emma Tollemache's poems were intriguing and provoked a storm of critical comment – but mainly because Francis had insisted that the verses should be printed entirely in upper-case type. George hoped that he might jump on this bandwagon. Emma Tollemache had thoughts of building upon her own reputation by creating a salon for the young and talented and he was drawn into the fold – willingly because he and Charmian Deckers were keen to induce La Tollemache to finance and publish a luxury edition of Andrew Marvell's poems, lavishly illustrated by George. This would have been something of a point of departure for him because, although a master of draughtsmanship, he always regarded it as ancillary to his work as a painter. The scheme fell by the wayside, perhaps because of the experience with Francis Rose. George, however, remained friends with Emma Tollemache and was secretly proud when in 1951 she backed his application to join the exclusive Men and Women of Today Club. When the president, Louise Andrée Coury, wrote to inform him of his acceptance in the following terms, his satisfaction was complete: 'I feel that you will like being a member and attending the luncheons. I hope that some of my other members will be useful to you. I shall certainly do my best to make your genius known to my readers. Mrs Tollemache says that you are really brilliant.'[2] Whether or not he did gain publicity from membership is another matter; from his own efforts he was becoming well known and ever more skilful at the not-so-noble art of self-advertisement.

The year 1951 was, in fact, highly productive for George as an artist. The art critic Mervyn Levy used some of his 'page two' feature in the *Bristol Evening Post* to announce: 'One of the most interesting and important painters the West Country has produced during the past half-century is the Bristol artist George Melhuish: he is a master of the expressionist manner, and his work will be prominent in various exhibitions to be held in the city this year.'[3] Levy was also a lecturer at the University of Bristol and at the West of England College of Art and it was in this capacity that he first met George, who had a habit of dropping into the life class to keep in practise. He came to know George and admired his work. Levy also took his part in a long-running 'battle' with the vice-principal, Paul Seyler, who was always laying down the law about the Paris school and about abstraction. This was not at all to George's liking. Levy decided to invite him to give a talk at the Folk Club on the evolution of style and content in his work and he agreed to answer any questions put to him. The local newspaper announced that 'he has promised to tell the whole truth and nothing but the truth. He indicated that perhaps all minds are not prepared to receive all he might feel inclined to say about his own vigorous, many-sided and always unconventional approach to painting.'[4] Little of what George had to say was reported, but Mervyn Levy's words made highly attractive copy next day:[5]

> There would always be room for the creative, unique artist. He was 'someone to pep up the rather drab way in which we live . . .' Mr Levy said he had that element of uniqueness in his work . . . 'He is one of the few artists in this country who is really contributing something fresh.'

The *Bristol Evening Post* informed its readers that three of George's recent works had been on show: '*Greta*, a normal portrait study; *Pont des Arts, Paris*; and *City*, one of a series of works on this theme, completed two weeks ago.' The audience at the Arts Club (which had not been markedly sympathetic to George in the past) heard Mervyn Levy describe him as [6]

> one of the few artists in this country who was presenting the known world to us in a new way. He said there were two main bases on which we could appreciate the best of modern art, the primitive and the instinctive appeal and the aspect of the unique, both of which Mr Melhuish's paintings possessed.
> 'You cannot link George Melhuish with the school of Paris,' he said, 'although he often exhibits there. He is unique in an age where there is very little unique about at all.'
> 'Melhuish as a painter is the salt, pepper and Worcester sauce of living – he produces something which brightens up the humdrum business of life.'

George's old friend and fellow artist, Ellard Hughes, added fuel to this conflagration. He gave a talk to the Bristol Rotary Club on the subject of 'Literature and Art in Bristol'. His main concern was to make the eyebrow-raising claim for the 'forger poet', Thomas Chatterton: 'Had Chatterton lived, his genius and his amazing vitality would have made him a second Shakespeare.'[7] After such a statement Ellard Hughes might have found it a difficult gear-change to go on to say anything very startling about George, but he did his best:[8]

> We have not heard the last of the young Bristol painter. Although some of his pictures have raised violent controversy, I feel he has in him that sense of colour and power which, although he is yet groping,

will one day make his name very well-known not only in this country but throughout the world.

He ended with a faint warning to Bristolians: 'Many people are inclined to slang his works, but time will show what heights he will achieve.'[9]

There was certainly no chance of George's avoiding (or, indeed, wanting to avoid) controversy. Bristol did its best to contribute to the general atmosphere of post-war euphoria and optimism, as epitomized that year by the Festival of Britain. In May 1951 Bristol Art Gallery, building on George's venture in 1949, organized a Festival of Contemporary Painting. Sir Kenneth Clark (one of his old friends) was invited to open the show on 10 May and to give an illustrated lecture on contemporary painting – a rare treat that induced even the Lord Mayor to attend. However, the local art critic was afforded the privilege of previewing the exhibition in a gallery empty of people who otherwise might have been startled by his instant reaction. Everything was wrong in his eyes – at least, almost everything:[10]

> I wonder why Graham Sutherland calls this picture *The Red Tree*? It looks to me like a mixture of a sedan chair and a grand piano, with fountains coming out of it.
>
> Oh look, here's Stanley Spencer, preoccupied with the Bible again. I see lots of housewives with striped jumpers and wings floating about in one of his pictures. I wonder whether he's trying to be profound or merely funny?
>
> Don't look too quickly, but there are some of Henry Moore's hollow women. Wouldn't it be funny if we were really like that?
>
> And there's a big picture of a bridge in London by George Melhuish. Isn't he the Bristol painter that people argue so much about? Anyway, I like the bridge. I can see what it is supposed to be.

With a 'friend' like that George must have wondered: 'Who needs enemies?' He was much more inclined to respect the judgment of Kenneth Clark, who thought his portrait of Vera Apter Smith one of the best items in the exhibition.

All this publicity certainly helped George the following month when he gave a one-man show at the Burrough Gallery at 17 Orchard Street in the heart of Bristol. The exhibition began with the customary private view on Friday, 1 June and ran for two weeks. The local press described him as 'the 31-year-old Bristol born professional artist'. (Had he begun to be coy about his age? He would be thirty-five in two months' time.) But there was no doubt about the youth and vigour of his work:[11]

His portrayals of 'the dynamic moods of streets' are accomplished (his use of primary colours has already brought him distinction at his two Paris exhibitions) and interesting. Typifying this new subject is the Champs Elysées, on wood, in which the street's symmetry, grand architecture, and straight lines are captured.

The exhibition did have one 'casualty'. George decided to exhibit his early study of Deborah Jones, *Toilette*. He had doubts about offering it for sale, not simply because he had exhibited it in the Royal Academy in 1944, but because he was particularly fond of it. Kenneth and Vera Smith overcame his reluctance with some much needed ready cash.

George still had his eye on a much wider public than Bristol could ever provide. In November of that year he mounted a one-man exbibition of twenty-six paintings at the Irving Galleries at 17 Irving Street, just behind the National Gallery. He persuaded Sir Eugen Millington-Drake, the former British ambassador to the Argentine and an acquaintance from his India Club days, to open the exbibition on Tuesday, 6 November. But, even more of a catch, Lord Methuen finally provided him with a few words of introduction for his catalogue. Coming from such a respected source anything that was said was a compliment, but Methuen was genuinely appreciative:[12]

The paintings . . . by Mr George Melhuish strike not only an original note, but one that captivates by its freshness, its rich colour harmonies, and its attractive textures . . . The luminosity of his colour, particularly his architectural subjects, reflects the preoccupation of many young French painters of today in the study of light, and of the luminosity inherent in what they paint. The paintings we see here are a serious and personal contribution to contemporary painting.

(His lordship's skill with the brush compensated for his ineptitude with a pen; both he and George were currently displaying their wares at the Ninety-Ninth Annual Exhibition of the Royal West of England Academy.)

What Methuen had to say brought George some prestige. What the national press thought was much more important. And this was the point at which they responded by noticing that his style was edging away from the purely figurative. The *Manchester Guardian* critic may have been less aware of what was happening:[13]

The technique employed by George Melhuish . . . is so overpowering and appears to be pursued so much as an end in itself that many of his paintings seem to be little more than examples of ornamental brushwork. He is, however, a colourist of distinction and in his more fully realized pictures he is very successful at suggesting the intricacy of city streets.

Art News and Review thought that he displayed a 'sophisticated talent. His work reveals a consciousness of the structural delicacy of line, the interwoven sensitivity of constitution which distinguishes the work of many of the younger French artists.'[14] Echoes of Lord Methuen! The critic was strangely unhappy about George as a portrait painter, although he did commend his study of Jean Cocteau – a curious choice since it might be considered to be an unappealing piece of work. But it was the *New Statesman* critic's comments on his 'multicoloured diffusions or dazzles of light' that hit the mark as he expatiated on the successful execution of his Paris scenes: 'As your eye is led from the perch of a nearby roof, over the gullies of streets, through the mist of colour, to the rim of the horizon, your awareness of the way that a city sticks up through the elements of light and dusk is really sharpened and increased.'[15]

It was the *Scotsman* critic who perceptively talked about George's desire 'to emphasize the evanescence and sense of dissolution' in his paintings and ended with a typically canny comment. He felt that his technique was 'too much influenced by the ephemeral' but that he was 'certainly . . . a tryer.'[16] Yes, perhaps, but why was George interested in the evanescent and the ephemeral? And what was he trying to do? The fact was that he was succeeding in what he was doing and not just trying. Patrick Hughes succinctly explained what was happening:[17]

The beginning of the 1950s saw George Melhuish experimenting with quasi-abstract paintings. Although superficially his change from figurative expressionism to abstract expressionism appeared sudden and abrupt, it was in fact logical. It seemed natural for a painter, brought up to review figurative painting as the occasion for dynamic expression, to go somewhat further by equating the picture's observable figuration.

The early 1950s was, indeed, the point at which George apparently suddenly developed an abstract expressionist style. After the frenetic activity of 1950 and 1951 with all his exhibitions, the year 1952 seems like a desert period, but it was, in fact, a meaningful hiatus in which he reworked and rethought in a definite form his artistic style. One is not, however, suggesting that he 'became' an abstract expressionist in that specific year, since the seeds of this particular development had been planted and were already beginning to sprout as far back as 1948. The evidence for this can be seen in his paintings, particularly in the architectural landscapes that seem to dissolve into studies of form, line, colour and light. Even the most staid of critics recognized this. Curiously enough, if one rereads the articles on architectural landscape painting which he wrote for *The Artist* as early as 1944, his preoccupation with abstract form is even then evident. Perhaps this is not so remarkable when one finds Plato in the *Philebus*, as early as the fourth century BC, stressing the natural and absolute beauty of lines and forms independent of figurative depiction.

The year 1948 is always regarded as the cardinal point in the emergence of abstract expressionism. However, it was a phenomenon that appeared in the first instance to be peculiarly American, or even more particularly New Yorker. Mark Tobey, Jackson Pollock, Mark Rothko, Willem de Kooning, Robert Motherwell and a small handful of others seemingly spontaneously developed, out of a figurative expressionist style, a highly expressive abstract idiom which, once stripped of its specific figurative connotations, invited an unbiased and objective consideration of pure form, line and chromatic juxtaposition. From that point, needless to say, the viewer's response might be to revert in his imagination to the world of figurative forms. But that was not necessarily part of the artist's job, especially in the early, experimental years.

Because the abstract expressionist group was so geographically discrete, in the first instance, it is unlikely that George knew much about them, their ideas and their activities. One thing is certain: apart from the odd black-and-white magazine illustration, he saw no 'live' example of the American abstract expressionists' work until 1954 when he saw paintings by Sam Francis and met the artist at the Galerie Rive Gauche. The meeting was enormously inspiring, even if his own style and technique were different from Francis's, though nearer than to the New York school's style. Frankly the lateness of this encounter with Francis is surprising, since he had been working as an exiled Californian in Paris since 1950 and by that time George was already in contact with the French informalist school and continental *tachistes*. If anything, the influence of Georges Mathieu's work on his development was more marked, although talk of 'influences' on his work may appear to detract from his own originality of thought. Certainly he did not dream up an abstract style in a vacuum, but there are times when one wonders who was influencing whom. For one thing he was older (by six years) than somebody like Mathieu and had infinitely more experience as a painter when they both simultaneously moved towards the abstract.

Certain points must be made about George's abstract style. One thing that he was not doing was rejecting the past. The new style flows naturally out of the old and retains forms and colour patterns that are characteristic of his figurative output throughout the 1940s. At times one detects echoes of the futurism of the early part of the century; a hint of the wartime paintings of forbidding blast furnaces and factories expressed in terms of rhythmic linear patterns recurs; even the jagged lines of some of the blitz canvases find their way excitingly into the spiky lines of the early abstracts. What he did was to impose a form on his compositions by means of a series of sharp linear patterns and weave into them colour blocks and, invariably, some discreet *tachiste* touches achieved by dribbling techniques. Some of his paintings are so visually stunning, the use of line so active and unrestful, the colour schemes so startlingly fresh, that the immediate disorientating effect has to pass off before one can fully appreciate the control and precision of the overall formal contruction of the composition.

George avoided the extremes of the extrovert life-styles of his fellow abstract expressionists. He saw little virtue in the tendency to cock a deliberate snook at society. He was always a complete individualist, resistant to any form of authority, but he was never anarchic in his way of life and, if and when nihilism entered into the matter, it remained at the philosophical level as he strove to comprehend and formulate different concepts of nothingness. This restraint was reflected in the rigorous control of his style. His American counterparts made a virtue of their non-conformity with some of their apparently haphazard methods of applying paint to canvas. The discerning saw this as avant-garde and started buying. He was not inclined to learn more than an odd lesson or two from their activities, some of which were a little too physical for somebody of his character. (Besides, it was not easy in Bristol to find a female model willing to allow herself to be dragged naked and covered with paint across a vast canvas.) He respected classical theories of form and control, and even in later decades, when the linear rhythms have gone, accusations that he was 'throwing a pot of paint in the public's face' are really too undiscerning to be taken seriously. In fact, if one could criticize him at all as he worked to achieve an expressive formal structure for his paintings, it is when in the mid-1950s he experimented with monochrome or extremely simple colour schemes. Compositions in black, white and grey, though telling from the point of view of form and line, lose the benefits of his expertise as a colourist at the very point when this skill was set to achieve its maximum effect in his abstract expressionist style. The monochrome paintings are, quite simply, dull, though useful as exercises in form. He quickly realized this; he sold off some of them and spent the rest of his life periodically giving them away as wedding presents to couples with more important things on their minds.

What his viewers read into the best of his work is intriguing, but only relevant at the personal level. Looking at one of his gouaches in the cellars of the Bristol City Art Gallery, an unusually delicate work with soft lines and colours, including untypical pale blues, it is easy to see it as a lovely picture of a waterfall, whether such an impression was intended to be conveyed or not. One feels that the journalist Max Barnes, in one of his interviews in George's house, let his imagination run riot at the sight of one of his studies: 'H-bomb bursts of vermilion spattered over the canvas. A tortured dragon writhing in a trail of colour.'[18] But he might have come close, at least in spirit, to the mood that George intended to communicate.

Part of the reason for his unusually agonized style was, as he explained to Charmian Deckers, dictated by practical necessity and by a desire to preserve his individuality. She recalled that 'George used to say – and I am sure that he meant it – there is a time, when you start off with an abstract painting, you've got to fill in that great canvas, but it takes over and starts being spontaneous: it comes from God.'[19] One wonders if he was generally anxious to acknowledge the Almighty's role in the process, but he certainly saw his work as inspired from within, in a way which he would never tolerate from any human source. As Charmian Deckers remarked, 'I don't think that he ever went cap in hand – except, as he always said, before his Maker. He always said: "Beside the grave, I shall be cap in hand."'[20] And even that was something that he could not easily accept. He cherished his autonomy as an individual, as he did as an artist, and could not easily reconcile himself to the finite implications of man's material existence. Accompanied by an awareness of departing youth, an apparent inability to achieve intellectually, let alone physically, a personal relationship, and a philosophical preoccupation centred on the very meaning of the Universe itself, George's inner torment found its natural expression in his early abstracts. There is seldom anything tranquil about them. In that respect his move towards abstract painting as an expressive mode meant that he secured for himself an idiom ideally suited to his current state of mind. In the process he also found himself in tune with other individuals whose philosophical attitudes and aspirations were complementary or, at least, close to his own while still at the nascent stage.

TRANSITION AND TRANSFORMATION

The year 1952, when George exhibited practically nothing in important exhibitions, was truly a transitional period, a time of adjustment and settling down in two important aspects of his life. In January his diabetes, which had been diagnosed just over a year previously but seemed initially susceptible to treatment through dietary control, became markedly more problematic. His blood-sugar level was far too high and so his doctor started him on the regular, twice-daily injections of insulin that continued to the last day of his life. His diet was also strictly regimented: high fat and low carbohydrate (nowadays considered to be less than desirable in every respect). But, for a social nonconformist, he was remarkably obedient to his medical adviser's dictates and made great efforts to adapt himself to the strict new regime of diet and injections. The result was that, until he regained his self-confidence, he committed himself to very little in terms of social and professional activities.

But 1952 was also a vital period of settling down for him as an artist. By the end of the year his transformation from a painter wedded to the figurative into an exponent of the abstract had been accomplished. The painting entitled simply *Study*, which was chosen for the hundredth annual exhibition of the Royal West of England Academy that opened on 1 December 1952, pointed the way forward as a transitional work. It also gave a hint of a shift in the media favoured by him. Although one always feels that he was happiest when painting with oil on canvas or board, in the 1950s his works are, more often than not, executed on paper with either gouache or oils. This seemed to increase the speed with which he could attack and complete individual pieces of work.

By 1953 he felt ready to tackle a public beyond the Bristol horizon. He exhibited some paintings in London at the Redfern Gallery and made an unusual departure by showing some special studies in an abstract style for an exhibition entitled 'Paintings into Textiles', at the Institute of Contemporary Arts in Dover Street, just off Piccadilly. Alison Settle explained in the *Manchester Guardian*:[1]

> That finely produced British export magazine, *Ambassador*, which we are unable to buy in this country but which for years campaigned for the textile world to use the work and inspiration of high-ranking artists, such as Graham Sutherland and John Piper, has now put on a show of 'Paintings into Textiles' at the Institute of Contemporary Arts . . . It shows artists' work, some of which has been bought or commissioned, with another score or so of artists whose work the industry could use.
>
> What a revolution such an influence could achieve. Outstanding designs by George Melhuish; James Tower, the potter, here transferring his feeling for form to fabric; Edward Wright and Eileen Agar. But Henry Moore, John Piper, Sutherland and Ivon Hitchens are all represented.

Nothing came of George's 'career' as a textile artist. One suspects that he was uncomfortable with the utilitarian implications of an applied form of art, although the correlation between manufacturing industry and finance may have provided the initial impulse. One thing is certain: he was influenced by his close friend Sir Francis Rose. In the 1940s Francis developed his natural talent for design and made a name for himself as a designer for Roosen Silks. For some years he also did sterling work producing designs for carpets and tapestries for the enterprising Edinburgh Tapestry Company. There was, however, an abrupt parting of the ways when Francis submitted a huge cartoon as a design for a tapestry based on the life of St Francis of Assisi. It was exquisite, but the saint was too obviously modelled on his sailor boyfriend, Pat, to be acceptable to the puritanical Crighton-Stuart family, who owned the company and controlled its artistic policy. George found all this intriguing, but, at the end of the day, even the faintest suggestion that he might end up as an 'employee', working for a commercial enterprise, reminded him of his three unbroken childhood vows – and he beat a strategic retreat.

Much more in tune with his approach to aesthetics was the major two-man exhibition that he gave with the South African artist Edward Wolfe in the colonnade of the open-air patio at the O'Hana Gallery, at 13 Carlos Place in Mayfair. It opened on 12 May 1953 and attracted a flurry of press attention. Edward Wolfe was perhaps an unlikely artist to pair with the new George; his canvases were virtually all of scenes of the pre-package-tour Costa del Sol, Morocco and Ischia and, as the *Studio* critic said, he and George were 'as dissimilar as chalk and green cheese'. He went on to explain what he meant:[2]

> The former has painted landscapes of Spain with a poetic and sensitive simplification such as Dufy and Marquet extracted from nature but with an individuality of his own . . . Mr Melhuish by contrast has numbered his compositions and thus removed any topographical hints to the subject obscured in the zig-zag lines that trace angular graphs across the picture planes in bewildering but exhilarating patterns.

In that case George was presumably the 'green cheese'. He explained to the *Bristol Evening Post* what he hoped to achieve: 'I prefer the viewer to make his own image and have tried to create a more poetic approach to this world – to give an other-worldly impression of towns and cities.' The critic thought that he had succeeded: 'His use of brilliant colour catches the eye, but save for *Toulouse*, *A Gothic House* and *City*, he leaves everything to the imagination, even the titles.'[3] As Patrick Hughes later commented, the O'Hana Gallery exhibition was the occasion when the public first realized that George had 'almost dispensed with an observable subject matter.'[4] The *Manchester Guardian* critic spotted what was happening in his paintings: 'In some . . . architectural themes are vaguely visible in a planned confusion of slashing criss-crossed lines. In others the architecture has disappeared and only the brilliant brushwork remains. They are interesting specimens of technique operating almost entirely in vacuo.'[5]

The surprising thing about George as an abstract painter is that, from the beginning, he attracted little adverse criticism. Granted, traditionalist friends and clients (mainly in Bristol) said that they knew what they liked and that was certainly not abstract art. But press critics appreciated it for the vibrant and thought-provoking breakthrough that in fact it was. Even on home territory, which was never very sympathetic towards him, he elicited sounds of approval. Of the hundreds of paintings hung at the Royal West of England Academy's 101st exhibition that opened on 9 November 1953, the *Bristol Evening Post*'s critic mentioned only a handful of works – George's contribution, entitled simply *Composition*, created a distinct impression on him: 'The predominating tone of the exhibition is quiet and pleasant. There is little abstract painting, but one or two notable exceptions catch the eye. George Melhuish, a Bristol artist, is very abstract – and in a large and highly colourful way. Paul

Seyler, also of Bristol, is abstract in a less violent mood.'[6] The critic then
went on to mention how Lord Methuen had praised the dry-point etchings
of Malcolm Osborne and commented: 'Although he now lives in London,
Bristol should not forget he is one of her gifted sons.' He added an aside: 'I'm
bound to say the same for George Melhuish.' He confessed that what he
enjoyed most was 'the use he has made of colour'.[7] The exhibition was
inaugurated at a private view on Saturday, 7 November, by John Betjeman.
Before declaring it open, he addressed a few words to the invited guests. If
he had anything to say about George's canvas (which was well beyond the
scope of his aesthetic appreciation), nobody cared to record it.

George knew what he was up against with the Bristol public and the type
of people invited to open the academy's exhibitions. But it appealed to his
sense of humour and he took increasing enjoyment in pontificating drily
whenever some controversy involving modern art arose. In April 1954 the
committee of the Bristol Museum and Art Gallery voted on the strength of
the chairman's casting vote to spend £765 on a bronze, *Draped Torso*, by
Henry Moore. The decision was not acclaimed universally. A Mr Kenneth
Bull (aptly named), the chairman of the Bristol Ratepayers' Association,
commented: 'I think it is a flagrant waste of public money and I do not
consider it to be a work of art. If I battered a piece of bronze into the shape of
this object, I don't think I would be paid £765.'[8] It was not even a case of
Bristol ratepayers having to find the whole sum. The Contemporary Art
Society had offered to contribute £100. But therein lay part of the problem
for the worthy citizens of Bristol. The society had made a similar offer when
Manchester City Council considered purchasing the work but turned it
down. The society had been 'perturbed' at a 'rather offensive' remark made
by one Manchester councillor. (Apparently he thought that there were
striking similarities between the shape of the bronze and Marilyn Monroe!)

At this point George's definitive opinion was sought by local reporters
and subtly he poured scorn on the Bristolians' inaestheticism, from which
he himself had long suffered:[9]

My impression is that it is one of Henry Moore's more conservative
works. I think it has sufficient importance to stand alone, without the
name behind it. It certainly has a certain monumental quality that
sculpture should have, but I prefer his more abstract work.

It is probably a good thing that Bristol has bought a Henry Moore. The
thing to do is to regard it as a visual encounter, rather than as a thing of
obvious beauty. I would not say it is without beauty of sorts.

One wonders how many of the *Evening Post*'s readers heeded George's
eminently sensible and positive comments but, none the less, Bristolians

became the joint owners of a bronze that soon would be worth far more than the trifling sum paid for it.

As regards aesthetic atmosphere, George felt more at ease in London. By the 1950s the city's art lovers had become considerably more open-minded than in the immediate post-war years and he was not slow to take advantage of this. He was active in organizing a faintly bizarre exhibition at the gallery of the Institute of Contemporary Arts in Dover Street in December 1954. An impressive list of artists and patrons was persuaded to contribute works to what was called a picture fair. The artists' signatures were all concealed and visitors to the exhibition were invited to buy tickets at the cost of twelve guineas each. Every ticket-holder was entitled to one piece, to be settled by a blind draw at a sherry party at the exhibition's conclusion on 10 December. As the catalogue explained, 'Miss Marjorie Steele, who is starring in *Sabrina Fair*, has graciously consented to officiate at the draw, the purpose of which will be to establish the priority in which ticket owners . . . may choose a picture.'[10] Patrons may have thought twice about risking twelve guineas on the gamble, but the prizes were worth having. A list of illustrious collectors had been persuaded to contribute, among them Sir Kenneth Clark, R.J. Sainsbury, Roland Penrose, Saul Steinberg and the gallery owners Gimpel, Juda and Mayor, and among the artists' work there for the taking were canvases and sculpture by John Piper, Graham Sutherland, Matthew Smith, Julian Trevelyan and George Melhuish. George met an important new friend in the process, a fellow contributor, the up-and-coming young artist Anthony Hill; and it was through George's efforts that the Princess Fahrunissa Zeid el Houssein, by now a friend of years' standing, gave one of her paintings as a prize. Whatever the success of the exhibition in monetary or publicity terms, it paid dividends for George. Once again he found himself drawn into London's glittering society. He had an inordinate love of the glamorous life and relished being invited by the young King of Iraq to one of his parties at the London embassy. Here even alcohol was to be had – but not for long: a few years later, in 1958, King Feisal II and the royal family were massacred in the successful *coup* that initiated the Iraqi Republic. At the time Princess Zeid was in London, far from Baghdad, and consequently escaped the terrible penalty for having royal connections. The art world would have been the loser.

The exhibition had a surprising side-effect. One of those who came to view it was a woman of Greek origin, a writer and an avid collector of modern art, Effie Damoglou. She and George fell into conversation, as one does with strangers at *vernissages*, and, although she was a few years older than him, they soon became firm friends and mutual supporters.

For George it proved to be a productive relationship; for Effie Damoglou probably less satisfactory in the long run. She was apparently quite well-off and highly intelligent, if rather dogmatic in her views. She was unmarried and, therefore, George was seen as a potential suitor. He clearly realized this and rather deviously avoided committing himself – without discouraging her benevolence.

When in London, he was to be seen everywhere with her. They would talk to each other for hours on end. The subject of their conversation was frequently art, but anything under the sun might come under the dissecting-knife of their sharp minds – anything except his work on metaphysics. She was convinced that her pragmatic criticism of his ideas would have been so harsh that it might have proved destructive. She may well have been right. He had still to find his philosophical feet and he never did manage to cope with negative criticism of his ideas once formulated. Nor did they ever discuss business. When she learned about his car-dealing activities, she made it plain that she disapproved of an artist's talents and time being squandered on something so squalid. This, however, gave him an ideal opportunity to plead that even artists must eat to live; and she took him under her protective wing. One feels that he played upon this. It certainly meant that he was not expected to pay for everything like a normal lady's beau. Rather the contrary. Anthony Hill has a distinct recollection of the situation:[11]

> It seemed a very odd relationship because . . . she gave me the impression that she was supporting him – even to the point when she said: 'I gave him some blankets.' I definitely remember this because (you know I didn't then know George very well) I thought he must have really hit hard times if he doesn't have any *blankets*.

George seems to have cultivated the image of the struggling painter and, even in Bristol, the rumour circulated that he was being kept in London by 'a rich widow'.

Although this was not true, he made sure that being 'kept' had no emotional implications. From the outset of their friendship he gave her the distinct impression that he was homosexual – and, therefore, unavailable on the marriage-market. Perhaps she was deceived by his high style, colourful dress-sense and the startling bleached-blond hair that he sported at that period. He compounded the myth by implying that he was passionately involved with Sir Francis Rose. Events soon proved that he was involved with Francis, but not passionately, as he was apparently not Francis's 'type'. Effie insisted that she and George were so close that he could not conceal from her what she assumed was his true sexual orientation. He deliberately cultivated the image. The two were frequently to be seen in Barclays Buttery. Situated near the Hyde Park end of Piccadilly, it had such a reputation for serving good food at reasonable prices that millionaires as well as the less affluent frequented it. This was the last period when George regularly ate in restaurants. His diabetes soon made that impossible. But he certainly made the most of his appearances at the buttery. If Effie was in need of any further proof of her assumptions about him, her public appearances with him were finally convincing. As she remarked, 'Sometimes it was really very strange. When we would go into a restaurant or a gallery, immediately the air was thick with interest from other people round him. He could draw them. He had the knack.'[12] This attention came from men as well as women and apparently at his entrances in the Barclays Buttery heads turned, most notably the male ones. This fact of life even generated its own mythology. The story swept London and Paris (but not Bristol) that an incident had taken place at the Paris Opéra. Effie had taken him to a performance and he had spent the whole time ogling a handsome youth a few seats away on the same row. Her patience finally snapped. Dealing George a resounding slap, she flounced out of the theatre. The details of this alleged incident are certainly false but, like all myths, it tells one something about the complexities of human life.

Quarrels and tantrums did nothing to disrupt their close attachment. This was very much to George's advantage. Effie profoundly admired his art and bought a number of his (generally monochrome) abstract gouaches at high prices. She even bought an earlier work entitled *The Castle*, though it fitted less easily into her private collection dominated, as it was, by her prize possession – a painting by Victor Vasarely. George's work was also favoured by being included in exhibitions that she organized at this point.

Having achieved a 'moderate success' in 1955 with a show entitled 'Aspects of Contemporary French Painting', she mounted a sequel exhibition entitled 'Aspects of Contemporary English Painting' in the Parsons Gallery in January 1956. The Parsons Gallery was, in fact, a paints shop in Grosvenor Street, which Sir Michael Newton of Thomas Parsons Limited had allowed to be transformed into a gallery for the duration of the month-long show. That Effie saw herself as an apostle of modern art comes across clearly in her introduction to the catalogue:[13]

It is my firm belief that there should be more exhibitions of this kind at frequent intervals to enable the public to become more familiar with and so enhance their appreciation of modern painting. We have many good artists in this country, and some very great ones; but it must be stated that much creative talent is slumbering, lulled by the security of official aid in the way of teaching assignments and museum purchases. The public must again become the foremost patron of the artist. Interest in painting is more than a hobby or a means of entertainment. It can be an instrument of great spiritual import.

An apostle indeed – and a born didact. She went on to explain that the exhibits had been grouped into three categories: the first was realistic painting; the third was 'wholly abstract in content and form'; but the second category initially raised an eyebrow: 'trans-realistic painting', which she had the consideration to describe for the ignorant as 'figurative in content but much transformed in the process'.[14] The selected example of George's work, *Composition IV*, fitted unambiguously into the third category, as it nestled cheek by jowl with fifty-nine other pictures by artists of the top rank: Francis Bacon, Louis Le Brocquy, Merlyn Evans, Barbara Hepworth, Patrick Heron, Ivon Hitchens, Henry Moore, Ben Nicholson, John Piper and Graham Sutherland. Effie Damoglou knew the cream of the art world. She could also spot up-and-coming talent. She regarded the 25-year-old Anthony Hill as the next best thing to Vasarely with his constructive geometric art and was happy to have him in her exhibition. Both Anthony Hill and George would continue for some years to have cause to be grateful for Effie's help, even though they found her a difficult woman.

CHAPTER FIFTEEN

FRENCH DIVERSIONS

Effie Damoglou and George shared a love of things French and she encouraged him to develop his contacts in Paris. They made several trips there together in the mid-1950s, but took care to let it be known that they stayed in separate hotels. George's ability to put up with semi-primitive conditions in the Royal Condé was not shared by Effie. Besides he had work to do and people to see who were of no interest to her. Moreover, he did not always want to be associated with any other specific individual in public: that might close certain social avenues to him with the speed of light. Effie, though highly intelligent, had a rather weird cackling laugh that was a guaranteed conversation-stopper. The French thought it very unsophisticated. However, the pair did do the social rounds and, although they apparently never, in fact, went to any operas, Effie persuaded George to break his rule and attend a number of plays. This could produce curious coincidences that he found intriguing.

He had a number of friends in Paris whom he jealously regarded as exclusively his own. Sir Francis Rose continued to mesmerize him, even though George found it increasingly difficult to cope with his eccentricities. In early days when staying with Francis in the flat in the Quai d'Anjou he had become used to Francis's departures in the evening with a warning word: 'If you hear me coming in with somebody, please don't come into the room.'[1] George tried not to be disturbed either in the physical or moral sense. But Francis never ceased to amaze him. One morning two letters for him dropped through the letter-box. One was from his sailor boyfriend, Pat, the other from his wife, Frederica. Francis pounced on Pat's illiterate scrawl first. 'Do you think he loves me?' he asked George. The letter from Frederica was still waiting to be opened.

However fascinated, George was careful not to allow himself to become too seriously caught up in Francis's nocturnal world. He was physically, rather than psychologically, afraid of involvement. When one of Francis's all-male parties threatened to evolve into a mild orgy, George took fright and fled. A pleasant evening might culminate with his standing outside a nightclub notorious for catering for a specialist clientèle and Francis trying to persuade him to come in. George invariably lacked the courage and just as invariably was left to make his way home on his own.

If incidents like this sent George into a state of confusion, Francis made no concessions to his inhibitions. The problem was that Francis's antics illustrated just how conventional the would-be eccentric George was. The case of Luis was just one other example of real eccentricity. In 1952 George was staying at his hotel when Francis invited him to the Quai d'Anjou for a special dinner. Among the guests were two extraordinary women, the Princess Nina Mdivani and the wife of the *Vogue* magnate, Nadia Pacevitch. Another member of the assembly seemed to have been recruited for the occasion as a waiter, even if manifestly clumsy and brusque. George later described what Francis was up to with this youth of around fifteen or sixteen:[2]

> We happened to be away momentarily from the rest of the party, where this boy was putting one or two dishes on the table. And Francis turned to me and said: 'What do you think of him?' And I said: 'He's quite a personable boy.' And he said: 'Interesting boy, I found him in Marseilles.' He said no more . . . and, when we met again, he said: 'You remember Luis, don't you?' I said: 'Yes.' He said: 'Yes, you know, my son.' He'd never given any kind of clue before that he was his son. He was just a boy he'd found.

Luis was, indeed, just a boy whom Francis had picked up, but who had triggered off a psychological reaction in him. By this time Francis was approaching his forty-third birthday, and the prospect of his growing older without the guarantee of some form of human attachment filled him with alarm. His relationship with Luis had been stormy from the start, but it was precisely at the point at which the boy seemed about to leave him that Francis 'discovered' that Luis was a long-lost son; then he went through a legal process of formal adoption, or rather an acknowledgement of him as his child. Francis had apparently convinced himself that his fantasy was fact, even though most of his friends, George included, had serious doubts. But worse was to come.

These puzzling events had the effect of making George feel left behind in the eccentricity stakes. He redoubled his efforts to keep up with his friend's extrovert behaviour. In later years he boasted that he actually shared a mistress with Picasso, although, more likely, his dalliance was with a light-of-love who had long since been discarded. He also claimed to have fallen in love with the wife of a Parisian nightclub owner and to have had an affair with her. The circumstances in which all this took place were so dubious that the woman kept a revolver under her pillow. This alarmed George because he feared that it was intended for his own protection against the vengeance of the deceived husband.

Rather safer was George's attempt to shock (or, at least, surprise) with a public claim that he was the world expert on the subject of women's underwear, and that he was preparing to write the definitive historical study of the subject. If he did ever put pen to paper (which one doubts), nothing of his efforts has survived. But the ripples of speculation about this curious fixation continued for a long time. Even in his final years stolid Bristolians believed that he kept drawers full of exotic lingerie in his house. Truth be told, in Paris he did have a connection with the world of high fashion, but an entirely respectable one in the form of Charmian Deckers.

He had known Charmian since at least 1946. About then she had married a social golden boy, a Belgian called Eugène Deckers. His hobby was bicycling and he had no difficulty in winning the Tour de France in the days when it was still a gentlemanly sport. Deckers subsequently became a film star, taking advantage of his French accent to specialize in 'foreign' character roles. He also enjoyed a reputation as a womanizer, but his friends thought that marriage to the exquisitely elegant and beautiful Charmian might settle him down. And so it seemed for a while. They frequented the best avant-garde circles of London society. It was at a party at the Roses' flat in Flood Street that George was introduced to Eugène (for whom Francis had only recently acted as best man). However, it was his wife Charmian who became one of his closest friends. She was more aesthetic than her husband and played her part in encouraging George as an artist. But their relationship tended to be intermittent and very much dependent upon whether or not their visits to Paris or London coincided. The duties of motherhood, once she had given birth to a lively daughter, Nina, also temporarily kept Charmian out of his life. But soon the little girl was old enough to be brought round to his King's Road studio to have her portrait painted, while Charmian and George gossiped together and old Mrs Melhuish, on one of her periodic visits, sat serenely and listened.

However, it was in Paris in the mid-1950s that Charmian and George became more dependent upon each other through a combination of unforeseen circumstances. Deckers' marriage to Charmian had not cured his wandering eye and a move to Paris had done nothing to help the situation. She decided to retrieve her position by learning a new skill and, studying to be a professional florist, she realized that there was a gap in the French flower market. As she put it,[3]

> I wanted to have a hole in the wall – you know, like some of the shops used to be, minute – because the French, though they have lovely flowers . . . have no idea about the poetry of flowers, none at all. They just go along and buy a dozen of anything on very long stocks and they have no idea.

Perhaps Charmian's judgment was a little harsh, but she was willing to be proved wrong. However, she was deflected from the course of her vocation to bring taste to the French by friends who kept telling her that she looked so wonderful that she should become a model. Much against her will she found herself in one of the city's top modelling jobs as a mannequin for Balenciaga. George thought this the height of glamour. Charmian hated her work and bitterly regretted taking her friends' advice. Her unhappiness became associated with the city and the more the expatriate community went around saying how wonderful Paris life was, the more she turned against it. George, though totally in his element in the French capital, was a sure source of understanding and comfort for her. She soon repaid him for his concern.

In the meantime his life in Paris was not all crisis and pleasure. While he was asserting himself in London and Bristol as an abstract expressionist who could not be ignored, he continued to regard Parisian acclaim as the ultimate in achievement for a painter. In May 1953, he dragged himself away from work on his various English shows to exhibit his paintings at the Galerie Rive Droite. By now he found that he could accomplish fairly major pieces even in the cramped Parisian conditions. In November 1954 he received what was for him the ultimate accolade. The Bristol press reported with some pride:[4]

> Offering two pictures for the first time to the Salon d'Automne, the biggest annual art show in Paris, George Melhuish, the Bristol artist, has had both of them accepted.
>
> Each is a large canvas, 60 in by 40 in. They were painted in a fortnight in the Paris hotel where he was staying, and he framed them himself. They are abstract paintings of the kind that George is exhibiting at the Royal West of England Academy's 102nd show.
>
> George told me today (writes F.W.B.) that his two acceptances for the Paris show will give him a good deal of help towards attracting more attention to his pictures when he holds his forthcoming one-man show in Paris.

The two paintings, *Composition* and *L'Ampoule*, certainly created an impression, although this did not lead as quickly as George suggested to another one-man show in Paris. But in July 1955 he was considered sufficiently part of the Parisian élite of abstract painters to have his work included in a large and highly prestigious exhibition held at the Musée d'Art Moderne. The organizing committee of the society that held this Salon des Réalités Nouvelles published a very glossy periodical called *Réalités Nouvelles*, combining the function of an exhibition catalogue with a journal containing scholarly articles and a comprehensive series of illustrations of the works singled out for the Parisian public's delectation. George's contribution appeared on page 30.

His one-man show finally did take place at the chic Galerie Barbizon at 71 rue des Saints-Pères. The *vernissage* was on 5 April 1956 and the show ran for two weeks – a short time, but long enough to attract a great deal of attention. A short notice in *Peinture* described it as an 'attractive exhibition by the English abstract painter who has a penchant for compositions on a black and red flat plain, whose animated contrast is a pretty rare phenomenon'.[5] In the *New York Herald Tribune* Yvonne Hagen wrote a complimentary, if curious, review. She began by informing her public that 'George Melhuish had entirely abandoned the figurative since his last show in Paris in 1950 . . . His work shows a strangely personal approach.'[6] But having said that, she went on to describe his paintings in terms of figurative allusions: 'He uses stark black swathes, through which mountains and rocks of colour can be seen. Within this technique, he has found interesting variety. In one canvas, the blacks fly over the background blues as though they were bats, and the effect is strong in movement and contrast.'[7]

The critic from the influential magazine *Arts* echoed some of these sentiments. He described George as 'a young English painter who specializes in abstract art with virtuosity and occasionally even delicacy. His angular, explosive compositions, in deep blacks on coloured bases, combining violence and style, are as good as any French abstracts.'[8] George could have wished for no higher praise and he must have enjoyed a certain frisson at the writer's quoting the formula of a fashionable academic critic: 'Organization of space, articulate draughtsmanship, chromatic saturation.' This, he declared, perfectly described 'this scholarly painter'.[9] The writer clearly meant this as a high compliment and went on to mention his personal preferences. He liked his paintings on paper in which 'the accentuated subtlety of the parallel strokes have a delicate charm'. And he ended by saying: 'It is also interesting to realize on viewing these pictures, how certain characteristics, the linear coldness, the literary aspect of the subjects, explain the present-day taste for abstract art in the Anglo–Saxon world.'[10] An odd line of thought, but the critic had succeeded in honouring him as an abstract artist of international standing.

After such unusually universal praise George felt that his fellow Bristolians should be made aware of his triumph. He wrote a letter to the art critic of the *Bristol Evening Post* describing the success of his opening:[11]

> There was a considerable number of people of the Paris art world there . . . including some of the well-known critics of today.
>
> Almost everyone said they were surprised that the paintings were English, as the Frenchman's view of English art is something rather without colour and quite traditional!
>
> A one-man show by an English artist is quite a rare thing, as few of our artists of today seem to have exhibited in Paris since the war.

George's triumph had scarcely faded to a warm glow when a hideous crisis broke – at least he regarded it as hideous, although at a distance its comic aspects are more obvious. The wartime hero of pioneering frogmanship, Commander Lionel ('Buster') Crabb, disappeared while apparently engaged in underwater reconnaissance. The attempts on the part of the government and the Admiralty to allay suspicion and gloss over the bizarre anomalies of the case only seemed to fuel speculation. On 18 April 1956 the Soviet cruiser *Ordzhonikidze*, bearing the Russian leaders Bulganin and Khrushchev on their historic visit to the United Kingdom, had docked in Portsmouth harbour. It did not take the mind of a genius to work out that Crabb had been reconnoitering the Soviet ship and had met a mysterious end – mysterious because his body was not found for another year (and it was headless) and because nobody dared speculate on who had disposed of the hapless frogman (assuming that one so experienced had not met with an accident). Opinion as to the truth depended upon one's ideological leanings, but by mid-May the British government was having to make abject public apologies to their Soviet counterparts for Crabb's apparently official temerity. Many considered that the Russian secret service had done the deed. Some even thought that Crabb had been in the pay of American agents. Controversy raged for weeks in the international press. *Pravda* and *Izvestia* had a field day.

George was blissfully unconcerned about the whole incident. He was having a good time in Paris and he had a delightful companion in the form of one of his neighbours, Mrs Clare Jenkins. She was the lively widow who, during the war, had rented her top-floor flat to Barbara

Addison. Her big house at 75 Cotham Brow had been a homely centre of happy occasions as friends and lodgers would gather in the drawing-room for drinks and music-making. In his lonely moments George would drop in for a chat and frequently found himself engaged for hours in philosophic discussions with Brian, the younger Jenkins son. Disapproving comments by neighbours about her son's eccentric artistic friend only made her shrug her shoulders. She was as much his friend as her son – and a tolerant friend. For a time George latched on to her as a willing typist, there to put up with his idiosyncratic methods of working. When his one-man exhibition materialized, he persuaded Clare Jenkins to come over to Paris as his travelling companion. She fitted with a natural ease into the colourful artistic circles frequented by him. She was particularly taken with Francis Rose, who was in Paris at the time, living in a Bohemian little attic flat next door to his original one on the Quai d'Anjou. Francis seemed in a calm and jovial mood and Clare Jenkins left for England bearing with her a store of happy memories. George stayed behind to take care of the exhibition's aftermath and he was still there in mid-June when Francis suddenly had a crisis.

The problem was that Buster Crabb had been one of his closest friends and Francis had received a letter from him, posted on the day before his disappearance. When Crabb's fate came to light, the letter took on a new significance. For one thing it had mentioned that the perpetually indigent frogman was now suspiciously awash with funds and able to repay a debt owed to him. However, by this time an intruder had broken into Francis's flat and, ignoring the Graham Sutherland, Henry Moore and Christian Bérard originals on the walls, had taken only Crabb's letter. Francis was convinced that something sinister was afoot and that he was at the centre of an international conspiracy involving the major powers' secret services, including the French ones. What compounded this apparent fact was the arrest of his 'son' Luis and his detention without charge in the prison at Saint Quentin. In fact his legal status was so ambiguous that he had been held because of visa irregularities. (Nobody could decide if he was a French or Spanish citizen or if, in the former case, he was avoiding national service.) Francis saw the matter in a more sinister light and convinced himself that Luis was being held as a means of bringing pressure to bear on himself. He scuttled off to the British Embassy where the Ambassador, Sir Gladwyn Jebb, patiently listened to the whole story. The international press were fascinated by this odd twist to the Crabb affair and Francis's wilder statements were reported widely enough to reach the columns of *Pravda*. French plain-clothes policemen were assigned to watch his flat. George was one of his few English friends to whom he could turn in his 'hour of need'. Years later he recalled the situation:[12]

Francis . . . extrapolated from the fact that he knew Crabb fairly well
to the point that, if they'd done away with Crabb, they would do
away with him. I told him that this was quite silly and it was possibly
an accident in any case, but he'd got this terrible feeling by then. He
said: 'My own life is in danger because they will come for me.' I
remember his coming to the hotel where I was living at the time,
saying that he felt that Russians were tracking him all along the way to
my hotel, but I doubt if it was really true.

George tried his best to calm Francis down, but by this time fantasy
and paranoia had him so completely in their grip that nothing short of
drastic action could solve the problem. George contacted Francis's wife
Frederica, who by now was living on a shoestring, virtually separated
from him, in distant Ajaccio. Newspaper men flocked to her Corsican
door. In *Le Monde* she was reported as dismissing Francis's fears as the
product of an over-fertile imagination. He was acting out a detective
novel. But that only exacerbated Francis's condition. The hitherto calm
George apparently lost his nerve and collapsed in terror. Frederica took
command. Scraping together some money, she came to Paris and took
Francis, figuratively, by the scruff of the neck back to England. It was
not an easy journey as he spent the whole time on boats and trains
haranguing the other travellers about the Crabb affair and his own
involvement in it. Frederica deposited him in the psychiatric unit of a
National Health hospital in Virginia Water and a few weeks saw him
restored to a calmer frame of mind – and, some said, to sanity. She
returned alone to Corsica feeling George had failed her when she most
needed his help. He had, but he was scarcely to blame.
The stresses of the preceding few weeks precipitated a crisis in his
health. His diabetes went completely out of control and he collapsed.
Fortunately, Charmian Deckers was to hand. The June weather was
proving to be very hot and George had arranged to take her out to dinner
in the cool of the evening. Instead he rang her at the Hôtel Montalembert
and told her that he was not feeling well. She knew him well enough to
be alarmed. She arrived at his hotel to find him lying in bed looking
distinctly green. She called a doctor. George was duly examined and
Charmian accompanied the medic to the lift. He winked and, by way of
explanation, suggested that George had been drinking too much wine.
Charmian dismissed him as a fool and rushed to telephone a second
doctor, who instantly realized that he was suffering from acute hypo-
glycaemia and severe dehydration. She watched with almost superstitious
alarm as he was carried out feet first and taken to a clinic specializing in the
treatment of diabetes. An array of drips in his arm slowly but surely

restored his metabolic balance. He eventually returned to his hotel, but it was clear that he was still not completely well. Charmian had to write to his mother in Bristol to explain his delay in returning. 'He is rather worried about you,' she wrote, 'and hopes that you will be alright.'[13]

Once on his feet again, George immediately returned to Bristol and Charmian moved back to London, where they met up again. She commented on his restored health and renewed zest for life:[14]

> He made a remarkable recovery. When he got back to England, he was so pleased to be alive – dear George – that he went straight to the man in Barclay Square who specializes in Rolls Royces and bought the very biggest Rolls Royce that they had. Huge it was, body-wise. It had thirty-two cylinders. It was the biggest one they made.

The limousine was intended as a token of gratitude to Charmian since he himself could not drive it. She was fascinated and not a little puzzled. His laconic comment, 'Oh, I've always loved cars and to play around with them. I buy them and sell them,' intrigued her.[15] But she had to wait a little time before she fully understood what he meant.

The irony of Charmian's letter to George's mother was that soon he would be restored to some semblance of health, whereas Elsie's own health now began rapidly to deteriorate. She had not been well for years. She had endured the constant excruciating pain of her arthritic condition, abscesses on her knees and the operation to fix her knee joints with great stoicism. She never complained, never ceased to radiate sweetness and light to all around her. But as 1956 turned into 1957 George realized that her condition was worsening. He could no longer cope with her on his own and sought professional help. She was taken to Snowdon Road Hospital in Fishponds where it soon transpired that nothing could be done except to make her comfortable. He was so distressed that he could scarcely bring himself to visit her. Faithful friends had more courage and did their best to comfort both mother and son.

Elsie Melhuish finally died on 30 October 1957 at the age of sixty-seven. Her death represented a considerable loss for George in the purely physical sense; at the age of forty-one he had scarcely known what life was like without his mother's supportive presence. He had also lost one of the most important psychological props of his life. Thereafter he would unconsciously seek out mother-substitutes, only to encounter disappointment and sorrow time and again.

PART FIVE

1957–1967

TOWARDS THE PARADOXICAL UNIVERSE

Charmian Deckers arrived in Bristol just in time to attend Elsie Melhuish's interment. She remembered noting that it was, appropriately, All Souls' Day, 2 November 1957. By this time her marriage to Eugène Deckers was all but over and she had decided to leave Paris, with all its unhappy associations. She returned to London with her daughter Nina. However, as she admitted, 'I had absolutely nothing at the time. No money, no prospects, I couldn't get back into my house in Chelsea because I'd let it.'[1] She made a final trip back to Paris to sell her car and various odds and ends and returned to London to discover an urgent request from George to come down to Bristol. Even during his mother's stay in hospital he had begun to realize how horrific the prospect of life on his own would be. He set out to persuade Charmian to share the house in Springfield Road with him. She took one look at the place, which, if it had any modern facilities, was concealing them very well, and thought: 'My God, I can't stay here.'[2] But she did.

George's friends and neighbours speculated wildly about his new friend. She was tall, beautiful and incredibly elegant; her furs and exquisite couture clothes made them wonder if he had been more successful in Paris than even he had made out. But their speculation was idle. What he and Charmian got from each other was companionship and mutual support at a time when both were in need of it. She was never his 'girlfriend' in any sense of the word, she was too even-keeled, intelligent and practical.

Charmian and Nina settled down and stayed for what proved to be a highly productive period for George. As Dorian Mogg remarked, 'she was the biggest influence for change in his lifestyle in the middle of his life'.[3] The transitional settling-down process was not easy. George found it very strange to have a little girl staying in the same house as himself – and such a little girl! Nina was one of those clever, hyperactive children with which some adults have difficulty coping. Little Nina reciprocated the feelings of the adult world. She stood for no nonsense, even from those in authority, and soon found herself expelled from her private school for 'cheeking' her schoolmistresses. But her distinctive qualities were already beginning to show through. She excelled at art. She developed a fine appreciation of the subject and subsequently became one of the most devoted admirers of George's later abstract style. In the meantime she became pony-mad and needed little persuasion to have a portrait of her painted in an antique riding habit and hat. It was more stylish than the image depicted in George's portrait of one of her new-found friends, Percy Edgell's young daughter Rosemary. The Edgells proved to be well worth cultivating. When George and Charmian wanted to go off on trips together, it was very convenient to leave Nina with them; the family home was relaxed and friendly and the two girls were ideal companions.

George was a less than ideal companion. Quite simply he had no idea of what other people found acceptable in domestic terms. His careful approach to money often just seemed like meanness. 'Really old light bulbs had to be treated like gold as modern ones did not last as long!'[4] Moreover, he could be seen periodically trotting down the road to the local shops to buy food for himself, but not for Charmian and Nina. Presumably he felt that their dietary requirements were different from his own and outside the scope of his concern. But from Charmian's point of view her sojourn in Bristol, though difficult at times, was a useful period of re-adjustment. She symbolically shook the dust from her feet by advertising for sale her collection of clothes from Paris. She had taken a dislike to them because they reminded her of her past life: 'I had a lot of clothes when I came back from Paris – awful clothes mostly, dreadful they were! . . . Anyway, some woman came along and had the lot. It was so mysterious. She just took them away in her car.'[5]

Charmian's entrepreneurial skills were not lost on George. She found his car-dealing activities fascinating, once all was revealed, and aided and abetted him with gusto. Quite apart from her role as the 'lady going abroad', she was a driver of considerable skill. The cautious Percy Edgell had his moments of doubt. George 'got Charmian to drive his motor cars around and do demonstration runs. She was very much a driver in the French style, full of panache. George admired this sort of driving – but it frightened him to death.'[6] However, both he and Charmian were shrewd enough to realize that the market for the clapped-out luxury-type of car in which he specialized was shrinking in a period when the nation had 'never had it so good' and could afford to buy newer, more utilitarian saloons for their wives and regulation two children. He was also a little at a loss because his mother had always 'kept the books' and made sure that he made no serious financial blunders. Charmian helped him with business-like advice and it was she who induced him to switch from second-hand cars to property.

He had inherited a very small sum from his mother, but this proved to be more than enough to club together with Charmian and buy a rather run-down house in Richmond Terrace, Clifton. He quickly realized that property could be had at knock-down prices; even latterly he never paid more than £3,000 or £4,000; more often £700 was sufficient to secure something with a roof over it. To begin with he had been nervous about the risks involved and picked the brains of Clare Jenkins' younger son, Brian. His mother's experience in renting out part of her own house to tenants provided useful insights into the landlord's world (as if a Melhuish needed much advice on that subject!) and Brian himself, with his experience in accountancy and things mechanical, was able to give valuable advice – which George did not always take. Brian later recalled his experience with a second property, in Freemantle Road:[7]

> He was a bit concerned . . . about the financing of it, but I was very much in favour from the experiences that I had had or was beginning to have with property, and so he bought this one and I know it was in a pretty bad condition, but . . . he didn't seem to look at it with eyes of concern about the property, whereas I, with my accountancy background and being a bit of a perfectionist, I would notice almost immediately if there was a bit of dry-rot or woodworm. He would call me about these things in it . . . but obviously, in explaining it to me, he wasn't concerned about it. I should have been worried. He obviously wasn't worried about it.

Some time passed before Brian Jenkins had another chance to compare notes with George and he was surprised at how his property business had expanded out of its unpromising beginnings. He was amazed to learn that in five years he had accumulated six properties. He himself had only two and found that they occupied more than enough of his time. He surmised that George was not a landlord who paid much attention to the fabric. It was also clear that he had discovered that students made quite malleable tenants. He did not like long-stay tenants who might prove difficult to move if troublesome and, besides, student tenants did not come under the aegis of the increasingly strict legislation designed to protect tenants' rights. He also learned another early lesson: with the occasional disastrous exception, he only let to female tenants, since they were less troublesome and, so he claimed, easier on the eye than men. Brian Jenkins had to admire his style:[8]

> He possibly had qualities that I had not recognized because tenants are quite difficult people, but perhaps he was able to deal with them in a way that was quite adequate and all right. Either that or he employed somebody or got somebody to do it for him, because one of the things that I found about George was that he was very good at persuading people to do things for him.

Any of George's friends who had skills as interior (and indeed, as exterior) decorators were in serious danger of being inveigled into giving his properties a coat or two of emulsion paint, not always a wholly welcome experience; as time progressed into the lurid sixties, George tended to choose extremely bright, extrovert colours for the walls. This was partly in order to compensate for the dowdy, second-hand furniture and carpets with which the houses were furnished; he learned an early lesson that respectable furnishings suffered more than a fair amount of wear and tear, and electrical goods, such as refrigerators, had a tendency to vanish into thin air at the end of tenancies. But what George's friends slowly began to realize was that, as he accumulated up to seventeen properties in Clifton by the time that the rock-bottom prices began to soar and the area became 'desirable', he was sitting on a small property empire. The wisdom of his investment was now obvious. Barbara Thorne had acquired a few properties of her own and played a game of friendly rivalry with him. She used to drive him round the city and he would say:[9]

> 'Come and see this house of mine.' And I would say: 'Well, let's go and see this one of mine . . .' And I remember we went into this top floor in St John's Road and it had a couple of beds in it and he bounced up and down on one of them. He said to me: 'Barbara, we own half of Clifton between us!'

In the early years he quite enjoyed being a landlord. When out collecting rents he never refused an invitation from student tenants to come in for a cup of coffee and a chat. At any time, he liked intelligent conversation, but he took a particular delight in testing out some of his current philosophical ideas on clever young minds: their reactions were not coloured by any compulsion to be tactfully uncritical. The fact was that the 1957–8 period saw the culmination of his years of work on metaphysics. In an interview with Max Barnes in 1961 George supplied details of the process of writing his first book, *The Paradoxical Universe*, which was finally published in 1959. Barnes described it as[10]

> a study in psychology . . . It took him five years to write. For although painting comes easily to him, the written word is a more tedious medium . . . Writing is something done laboriously in long-hand from notes. The script must be patiently rephrased and polished. His first book was rewritten from start to finish no less than three times before he was satisfied.

Truth be told, the work had taken George a lot longer than five years. *The Paradoxical Universe* was, in fact, a vast elaboration of the draft monograph which he confidently expected to materialize as a book in 1945. He wisely thought better of this and spent the next fourteen years developing and refining his ideas. He also allowed himself to be exposed to new sources of inspiration and criticism of whose existence he was previously unaware. As it is, the evolution of his thought and the sources that influenced him are not easy to determine. He apparently bypasses the ideas of philosophers who do not fit into his intellectual system. In the introduction to his second book, *The Paradoxical Nature of Reality* (1973), he purports to make a quick sketch of the history of idealist metaphysics and counter-opinion, but between Nicholas of Cusa and Kant he manages to skip very lightly over almost all the great names of the early modern period and seldom, if at all, mentions them in his works. Descartes earns only odd passing references. John Locke, a materialist 'enemy', is disdainfully ignored. George Berkeley, a typical idealist, merits no mention. David Hume does receive a word, but only as a source of provocation for Kant and, by extension, Hegel. Karl Marx, perhaps understandably, is passed over in silence. More surprising, Søren Kierkegaard might never have existed. Prior to the twentieth century and its intellectual achievements, Comte and Nietzsche alone merit references, but only in George's later work. These deliberate or inadvertent omissions only make sense when one considers his attitude towards his own work. He was not overconcerned about the usual 'academic' habit of fitting one's ideas into the structure of a recognizable tradition and then extending it. He felt that there was something unique about his work or, at least, about his ultimate conclusions. After George's death his close intellectual associate, Dom Sylvester Houédard, thought long and seriously about this question:[11]

Though no one to my knowledge applied GM's ideas to *logic* before he did, his ideas were not exactly 'new', though he came to them independently and expressed them independently – but he was always interested in the parallels I brought up, especially Ibn Arabi and Eckhart (who respectively overlapped in the first and last fifteen years of Aquinas, whose work GM did know though only in part) and Karl Rahner (whom we discussed frequently though never exhaustively).

However, George was profoundly influenced by a most intriguing philosopher by the name of Stéphane Lupasco and was happy to acknowledge his debt to him. One might romantically wonder if George's first encounter with Lupasco's work came during a performance of Eugène Ionesco's 'pseudo-drama' *Victimes du devoir*, when one of the characters, Nicolas d'Eu, as the piece reaches its climax, gives utterance to some fascinating ideas:[12]

> Inspiring me with a different logic and a different psychology, I should introduce contradiction where there is no contradiction, and no contradiction where there is what common-sense usually calls contradiction . . . We'll get rid of the principle of identity and unity of character and let movement and dynamic psychology take its place . . . We are not ourselves . . . Personality doesn't exist. Within us there are only forces that are either contradictory or not contradictory . . . By the way, you'd be interested to read *Logic and Contradiction*, that excellent book by Lupasco.

The play, however, was written not long before its first production at the Théâtre du Quartier Latin in February 1953, by which time George had already run Lupasco to earth. Patrick Hughes later described what happened, presenting it as a coincidental development in the life of the artist and the philosopher:[13]

> Melhuish's change from figurative expressionism to abstract expressionism was coincidental with the artist's immersion in problems of philosophy. It was after George Melhuish had finished the first draft of his book *The Paradoxical Universe* that he discussed it with the French aesthete and philosopher Michel Tapié. Noting a direct correspondence between the philosophical ideas developed by the Englishman and those of the French avant-garde philosopher Stéphane Lupasco, although at the time Melhuish had never heard of Lupasco, Tapié introduced Melhuish to him; they became friends and, when Melhuish's book was published in 1959, Lupasco gave it enthusiastic support.

Michel Tapié, 'the most important entrepreneur of the new abstract expressionism', what Marcel Duchamp had been to Dada, was certainly generous in his introductions and through him George met Lupasco as early as 1949.

In certain circles Lupasco already had a formidable reputation. Since 1935 he had published (in both France and his native Romania) a string of philosophic works on contradiction within logic, and had been granted a prestigious stipend from the French government to enable him to continue to devote his time to research and publication. George was unabashed by his eminence and quickly discovered what a kindly and stimulating friend he had made. (Anthony Hill later approached Lupasco with infinitely more trepidation, but met with an equally warm reception.) What Lupasco did for George was to help him gear into the twentieth-century tradition that insisted that 'the principle of contradictory complimentarity ought to replace the principle of non-contradiction, as the foundation of logic'.[14] As Lupasco went on to explain, 'The new method will thus consist in investigating, when confronted with some specific phenomenon, firstly, what its contradictory phenomenon is, and, secondly, to what extent it virtualizes it or is virtualized by it.'[15]

Lupasco apparently introduced George to theories in sub-atomic physics that had been applied as early as the 1920s to the field of philosophy by the Danish physicist Niels Bohr. In 1927 in a statement known as the Copenhagen Option, Bohr [16]

gave the name of complimentarity to denote a factor not previously encountered by the physicist. By this Bohr meant to indicate the peculiarity that the same physical phenomena (e.g. light of a definite colour) behave so differently in different experimental situations that in the description one has to refer to completely different concepts and ideas.

Bohr was, in fact, 'the first to realize that quantum theory applied to *matter* as well as *radiation*. He maintained that quantum fuzziness is inherent in nature and irreducible'.[17] This was not quite relativity as Einstein had defined it a decade earlier, but it did set the cat among the pigeons of the traditional physicists:[18]

In classical physics such complimentarity would inevitably indicate the presence of an unacceptable discrepancy. Light cannot be both a particle and a spatial phenomenon. According to classical physics' presupposition of the objective existence of physical phenomena . . . light must be either one thing or another – either a particle or a wave.

From some philosophers' point of view, Bohr's statement came as a welcome confirmation:[19]

> Complimentarity is well-known in other fields of experience. Individual human beings, for example, cannot be under the influence of an emotion such as anger or merriment and simultaneously observe the emotion. When a man is filled with emotion by, for instance, looking at himself in a mirror, it would so drastically interfere with the situation that it would become completely different from the situation existing before the idea of examining himself arose.

In 1935 Albert Einstein (and his colleagues Boris Podolsky and Nathan Rosen) produced a paper in *The Physical Review*. This amounted to the 'most cogent formulation of the paradoxical nature of quantum physics, since the position and momentum of a particle cannot be determined at the same time'.[20] Einstein proposed an experiment in which, at a certain moment, two particles come together and the momentum of the second can be calculated from that of the first. Bohr rejected this use of 'an accomplice particle' as a form of 'cheating', but there is no doubt about the seminal effect upon metaphysics of both Bohr's work and Einstein's.

On the philosophical side of the fence George was introduced to the work of two writers of major significance. They were both eccentric in their own ways and inaccessible. Luitzen Brouwer, a Dutch mathematician with a truly great mind, had by the time George came across him attracted accusations of collaboration during the occupation of the Netherlands and had retired in a reclusive huff. (One of the few who succeeded in penetrating his defences was an intrepid young Anthony Hill.) The second influence was the Polish Count Alfred Korzybski, who had by now settled in the United States. But George got to know their work and found a lot in it that was sympathetic to his own evolving point of view. They both 'produced some claims regarding modification or abrogation of basic laws of logic'. As early as 1908, Brouwer had 'attacked orthodox mathematical logic with a paper claiming the abnegation of the law of the excluded middle'. And around 1930, 'in outlining his non-Aristotelian foundations, Korzybski claimed that he had abrogated the law of identity'.[21] Korzybski had the hectoring faith of a philosophic apostle. He founded his own anti-Aristotelian society and published a number of large and impressive works (most notably *Science and Sanity*) that, along with Brouwer, repudiated the classical logic of the law of identity. They provided a point of departure for George, but with Lupasco he felt instantly at ease. Lupasco's earlier works of the 1930s were a form of prelude to *L'Expérience microphysique et la pensée humaine*, published in 1941 in occupied Paris. George was excited by Lupasco's demonstration of 'a more complete modification of orthodox logic with the introduction of his "logic of contradiction"'. He was impressed by the apparent fact that 'no one, save for Lupasco has been able or willing to carry logical modification or abrogation to a point where both empirical and non-empirical reality is rendered consistently in real antithesis'.[22]

However, between his first meeting with Lupasco and the publication of *The Paradoxical Universe* in 1959, George had to go through the agonizing process of consolidating and synthesizing his analysis in a coherent form. The publication of Lupasco's *Le Principe d'antagonisme et la logique de l'énergie* in 1951, soon after their meeting, provided George with yet another force for an intellectual breakthrough. But serious problems still had to be tackled and the agony was suffered by his friends as much as by George himself. Quite apart from his succession of long-suffering typists, who gallantly coped with his dictation made direct onto the machine, he discussed his ideas with and showed his draft text to close associates. They almost all reacted against his use of language, which was so weighed down with a specially evolved jargon that it seemed more like an abuse of language. The more scientifically inclined came immediately unstuck. Peter Tiley's eyes alighted on the sentence:[23]

> It is not the impotence of rigid self-contradiction which is the principle, but a basic energetic operation, an operation that deals with that which is antithetical both with regard to facts and meanings, and which erects and maintains reality through a paradoxical state crossing and condensing in energetic relationship: so supplying every concept with free ground to avoid a statically simple truth-condition.

The word 'energetic' was the stumbling-block: he was not sure if George meant 'dynamic' when using it.

At a more mundane level his use of language was problematic. His prose style and command of syntax left something to be desired. Charmian Deckers spent hundreds of man-hours discussing his work and helping to rephrase what he had written. And Effie Damoglou, who had no sympathy whatsoever for his philosophical inclinations, with her customary assurance, asserted: 'The first volume – I don't want to denigrate his mind in any way – he didn't really write it. He had it ghost-written. Somebody put it together. Now, I met that man because he came to my gallery once and he talked about Melhuish and he revealed to me that really he was the writer of the book.'[24] That man was, in fact,

Michael Langley-Webb, a fellow Bristolian, a schoolmaster who had failed to achieve his ambition as a painter. In the late 1950s George frequently allowed him to stay at his King's Road studio and he ruthlessly extracted his pound of flesh by getting him to correct and even rephrase his prose right up to the last moment. But Langley-Webb was no philosopher and George was not embarrassed about having availed himself of his help. At the beginning of *The Paradoxical Universe* he lavishly acknowledged his (and the long-suffering Percy Edgell's) 'considerable help with the proofs'. In 1958 Percy tried to help George by recording him reading from the nearly finished final draft, and more amendments were made. The process of honing went on until the last possible moment. George's publishers, Rankin Brothers, had to cope with so many costly last-minute proof-changes that they effectively put up their shutters after the experience. So did Michael Langley-Webb. Compared with George's creative achievements he had little to his credit (not even a career as a ghost-writer) and he slipped more and more into a hopeless state of alcoholic dependence that led to his suicide a decade later.

Langley-Webb's presumptuous claim recedes towards the realms of absurdity when one examines even what George claimed to have achieved in his work. He explained the purpose of his book in a way in which no hack writer could:[25]

Recent discoveries in science, psychology and philosophy have disrupted the traditional place of metaphysics to a point where a crisis has been brought about in the nature of thought itself. Through a reappraisal of the basic laws of thought, so universally accepted from Plato and Aristotle onwards, the author throws new light on many problems and dilemmas that continue to tantalize man's curiosity; these range from difficulties in mathematics and physics to the human predicaments posed by birth and death, love and jealousy, immortality and dreams. *The Paradoxical Universe* has a two-fold purpose: it is both a revision of the significance that arises from certain fundamental laws of thought and a justification of this revision through bringing to bear various circumstances drawn from the world of experience.

George had, after all, found a prose style capable of communicating his ideas and he ended his proclamation with a final assertion:[26]

An entirely new significance is given to the state of paradox. It is demonstrated that the long period, in which paradox has been looked upon with the greatest suspicion must now be superseded by the realization that particular situations are only permitted to be what they are by their participation in a universe that is itself intrinsically paradoxical.

To George, what he was doing was very simple: readers of the *Times Literary Supplement* learned that 'this book is possibly the first to attempt, at a logical level, an attack upon the foundations of our whole system of knowledge. Instead of accepting that truth implies something in particular, the author demonstrates that truth signifies a paradoxical balance.'[27]

Having made such a huge claim on the eve of *The Paradoxical Universe*'s publication, George, like all authors new to the game, suddenly realized how vulnerable he was. He had put his neck on the line and now he could only wait to see what happened.

REACTIONS AND COUNTERACTIONS

George clearly believed that his years of toil on his monograph would attract instant acclaim for the metaphysical breakthrough that he believed it to be. Truth be told, he was not mistaken in his estimation of his own worth. The only problem was finding people prepared to take the time necessary to absorb his complete thesis. Since chapter 4 of *The Paradoxical Universe* touched on the subject of art, Anthony Hill wrote a review that was published in *Art News and Review* on 4 July 1959. As an artist and philosopher in his own right, he could instantly see the problems that fellow artists might have either with the philosophy itself or with their expectation of being presented with a new philosophy of art. While revealing George's background as 'a *tachiste* painter', Anthony Hill felt that an honest warning was necessary: 'By raising the question of art Melhuish introduces a topic philosophers take to least of all and one wonders how many artists are so prepared to beard the philosophers and cap the logic-choppers.'[1] But while warning potential readers that they would find the style difficult, he recommended the book as a 'well-wrought organum offering a key to the universe and a new light in which to view and evaluate our experience.'[2] What Anthony Hill's review did do was to fit George firmly into a distinct philosophical tradition, citing Brouwer, Korzybski, Bridgeman and Lupasco, and thereby displayed his own expertise in the subject. In fact, between them George and Anthony did more than anybody else to introduce Lupasco to an English public almost entirely ignorant of the contribution that he had made to metaphysics over a quarter of a century, with his principle of antagonism and the logic of energy.

Anthony Hill's efforts on George's behalf did not stop there. He sent a

copy of the book to Brouwer and put his mind to having it reviewed in
Encounter by somebody such as Sir Alfred Ayer. In the event Mike Smith
wrote a perceptive piece on it. He too warned the English-reading
public, but this time because George, much better known as an artist on
the Continent than in Britain, had a 'very continental' way with words
that might cause difficulties. But he then went on to state that, whereas
paradoxes had previously been regarded as flaws in the system, inter-
fering with man's ability to think clearly,[3]

> Mr Melhuish has taken the novel position that paradoxes arise *because
> they correspond to reality*, that the Universe is intrinsically paradoxical.
> This then leads to a reappraisal of accepted logical assumptions (e.g.
> the Laws of Identity, Contradiction and The Excluded Middle) and to
> the introduction not of a dialectic but an 'energetic-logic'.

Before summing up, Mike Smith uttered another word of warning for
those who might think that George was just playing with words: 'In
common with the existentialists, Mr Melhuish is fond of ad hoc technical
phrases and the result of their interaction is what Wittgenstein might call
"language free-wheeling".'[4] George may have taken that as a
compliment as, indeed, his final paragraph was:[5]

> The book has one great commendation; it is, in some sense, a return to
> the old meaning of philosophy – a way of looking at experience as a
> whole. If it is the first sign of a renaissance in this country of creative
> rather than destructive philosophical thinking, then its appearance is
> more than welcome.

Self-advertisement was nothing new to George and he let no opportunity slip by unexploited. Later in 1959, while arranging an exhibition,
he made sure that the press representatives of *To-Morrow's News* received
a 'plug' for his book. *The Paradoxical Universe* was recommended to
'those who find abstract pictures difficult to appreciate and want to know
more about them'.[6] His explanation of 'Art and Non-Art' was high-
lighted for special attention and his words were used to back up his
contentions: 'Were art an exact replica of the world of natural phenomena it would contain no class of difference from the world of natural
phenomena . . . To paint as well as Rembrandt in a style exactly the
same as Rembrandt would amount to no more than a feat of technique
today.'[7] However, in order to avoid giving the impression that the work
was primarily designed for seekers after the truth about abstract art, it
was made clear that 'the book . . . attempts to introduce a certain

revolution in thought, and is a work to be studied for its philosophic interest, quite apart from any connection with the author's work as an artist'.[8]

An old acquaintance of George's, Jasia Reichardt of *Art News and Review*, also tackled the question of his duality of occupation:[9]

As a painter he fulfils his need for self expression, as a philosopher he re-examines the phemomena of reasoning and deduction in order to establish some concrete truth . . . Unexpectedly perhaps his paintings are free of logical reasoning and analytical approach; they represent rather, in the painter's life, the emotional search for a significant statement. If this final statement happens to apply to George Melhuish's intellectual definition of what the functions of art are in his philosophical writing, one must stress that the original idea behind the painting is simply an intuitive one.

Had Jasia Reichardt, in fact, got hold of the wrong end of the stick? No matter, her article was still good publicity.

Though addressing a much narrower public, a review by N. Sri Ram in *Theosophical News and Notes* did succeed in coming to grips with George's philosophy and began by informing readers that 'modern philosophy is making advances comparable to, and as revolutionary as those taking place in science'.[10] George was then presented as part of a French school of thought at home with 'the Lupasco symbolic notation' and as the re-appraiser of 'the traditional laws of thought so universally accepted from Plato and Aristotle'.[11] For obvious reasons the reviewer took delight in quoting passages from his section entitled 'Mortality and Immortality':[12]

The indestructibility of life or experience appears as fully sanctioned as any religious dogma has ever made it . . . Immortality arises when experience is seen to be at one with the paradoxical consequences of reality itself . . . To experience existence is to touch hands with the basic operational force of reality.

The reviewer threw in a final telling passage:[13]

The notion of the particular body or mind, as some especially selective stronghold or giver of the status of 'experiencing', is rendered illegitimate, as the vehicle itself is seen to be no longer a contingent entity (of a selective nature), but an epistemological relationship involving the alternation of mere presence and mere absence.

After that N. Sri Ram felt confident enough to recommend the work: 'Students of Theosophy will find much in this book a welcome improvement on the sterile approach of the logical positivists.'[14]

These comments were gratifying, but of marginal importance. George was much more eager for the seal of approval of the philosophical and academic establishment. That was not quite so forthcoming, for the purely practical reason that busy scholars have little time to spend on complex works that unexpectedly land on their desks. He did not appreciate their situation nor their hesitancy about committing themselves through excessive enthusiasm. But why he should have sent a copy to England's current *enfant terrible*, John Osborne, is hard to say. His secretary kindly informed George that 'Mr Osborne is at present on tour with his musical, *The World of Paul Slickey*, but I shall place your book on his desk so that he will find it whenever he returns to London.'[15] George wrote offering a copy to J.J. Good of the Admiralty Research Laboratory at Teddington and received a puzzled reply: 'I cannot tell from your letter whether I should be interested in your book since I cannot understand your terminology. I can only say that I find the terminology intriguing and I am curious to see the book.'[16] The Astronomer Royal was even more self-deprecating: 'Thank you for writing to me about your logical problem on the interpretation of the physical universe. I am myself a very practical astronomer and doubt whether I can say anything useful about your discussion.'[17] Luminaries such as Professor H.B. Acton of the Royal Institute of Philosophy, J.O. Wisdom of the London School of Economics, C.P. Snow and Arnold Toynbee of the Royal Institute of International Affairs all wrote appreciating the gift of copies of his book, but there is no record of their following it up with detailed critiques. J.O. Wisdom did, however, reciprocate with an off-print of his paper on 'Esoterism', which apparently 'stimulated [George] to further thought'.[18] Professor the Reverend Canon Ian Ramsey of Oriel College, Oxford (the 'Mini-Ramsey', later Bishop of Durham) made a similar response: 'Already, from glancing at it, I am encouraged to look at it more closely. Oddly enough, I am hoping to talk about "Paradox in Religion" to the Joint Session of the Mind and Aristotelian Societies at St Andrews in July, and . . . I will gladly send you an off-print as soon as I have done one.'[19]

George wrote to the illustrious Karl Popper of the London School of Economics. In his reply he did not waste time with elaborate British courtesies:[20]

Thank you for your letter of April 1st. I must confess that I did not understand it. I realize, of course, that one can do without, say, the law of the excluded middle, or even the law of (excluded) contradiction; in fact, I have myself published various formal systems of interference, about ten years ago, in which these laws were (to use your phrase) 'abrogated'. But still I fail to see the fruitfulness of such abrogation.

Sir Russell Brain was more enthusiastic: 'I found it most stimulating. I am now going to read it again and perhaps, after that, I may send you some comments, or perhaps questions.'[21] Richard Wollheim of University College, London, modestly told George that his 'opinion on these matters is definitely an outsider's'. And he added: 'Mr Michael Dummett of All Souls has been working on this problem, and his opinion would be of more value than mine. But it is hard ever to extract a letter from him.'[22] George did not succeed, but he did gain in Richard Wollheim a valuable acquaintance who, years later, gave him practical advice on endowing post-graduate scholarships.

His French contacts were considerably more uninhibited in their enthusiasm. Stéphane Lupasco expressed himself excited at the prospect of reading his book and sent him an annotated list of journals that might review it. He also mentioned interested individuals, including, obviously, Georges Mathieu and, less obviously, the Duchesse de La Rochefoucauld. But Lupasco added a word of caution: 'I am not recommending to you my colleagues at the Sorbonne . . . because they don't command any general audience and are extremely conventional, academic and old-fashioned; you would be needlessly wasting your copies of the book.'[23] Lupasco did, however, later recommend one colleague, R. Poirier, Professor of Logic, but it was his own comments that George wanted and they were almost unrestrainedly enthusiastic.

In England George also met with some reactions that flattered his vanity and gave him positive food for future thought. A fellow philosopher and artist, Frank Avray Wilson, read *The Paradoxical Universe* from cover to cover and wrote to him:[24]

Straightway let me say that it is one of the most remarkable and revealing books I have read, and it comes to me at a most opportune and significant moment. For some time, I have been turning over what has seemed to me a fundamental aspect of creativity, namely, the oscillation between fixed form and dynamic energized form, and I have sensed that there was here a relationship to some basic property of reality. The Heisenberg Principle, for example, had been teasing at me, among other things, and I know from personal creative experience that there is not and cannot be a final solution, a precise ideal delimination of art form and content - the actual isolation . . . of the individual work of art being merely conditioned by multiple imminent existential factors.

Avray Wilson then picked up another point from George's discussion of existentialism:[25]

I am most interested to read what you say about Heidegger and Sartre . . . I have always felt . . . that they were touching upon some fundamental but elusive property, and you have now brilliantly related them. (I wonder if you would not partially exclude Kierkegaard and Jaspers?) . . . I see you mention two books I have also just read, Smythies and Brain's, but yours is the breakthrough. Do you know C.G. Jung's little work on synchronicity (*The Interpretation of Nature and the Psyche*), a related view from purely psychological angles, very interesting?

The reaction that George received from close friends was unpredictable. Most were adulatory. One of them, a leading collector of modern art, James Bomford, wrote saying that he was 'struggling' with the work: 'I think the set up in general is good and, of course, I wish you all success.'[26] But a few weeks later he wrote him a letter in an entirely different tone:[27]

I feel you have such enormous possibilities in front of you in the visual arts that I want to say to you very definitely chuck up your delight in this pin-pricking philosophy and get on with your real job. I understand very well the excitement of a success in a new expression but in the end it will engulf you. Though miles above my head in philosophy, you are still an amateur, I personally think your expression is in . . . visual interpretation and through that you should be able to get your ideas over.

Bomford, in so few words, had succeeded in saying everything that George had no desire to hear. One suspects that his feelings for him suddenly cooled, but that it did steel his resolve to continue on his chosen path.

As old friends became former friends, George replaced them with new contacts. Colin Wilson, famous as the author of *The Outsider*, wrote at length and confessed his frank puzzlement. He was impressed by how 'formidably professional' *The Paradoxical Universe* was. Then he continued:[28]

But when I come to your concepts, they're so extraordinarily unprofessional that I hardly know how to reconcile the two! I am left with the feeling that your book may be either a revolutionary work that compares with the *Principia* or *Origin of Species*, or a piece of brilliant reasoning with a few defects which I am not clever enough to discern.

However, he did go on to utter sentiments that were as music to George's ears:[29]

> For many years now, one of my ambitions has been to devise some method that will overthrow positivism and materialism from the bottom. [And he added that he felt that] a positivist is rather like a timid bank clerk who spends a lifetime in the same job because any attempt at change would 'obviously' lead to an increase in life's uncertainty . . . One can only reply that his preference for 'stability' is not a matter of logic, but of *temperamental instability*. So I am naturally cheered to see someone with your intellectual equipment setting out to plead for a broadening of limits.

Though critical in places, Colin Wilson's words were encouraging. He and George kept in touch and, indeed, it was through Wilson that his interest in composition briefly revived in the early 1960s. The abstract possibilities of dodecaphonic music suddenly seemed a most obvious intellectual avenue to explore.

An advertisement for *The Paradoxical Universe* in the *New Statesman* attracted the attention of a nineteen-year-old budding artist and writer, Patrick Hughes. He bought the book, read it and then wrote to George what he later described as 'a silly, juvenile letter saying how much I liked it and saying what other things I was interested in. And he wrote back a very serious letter.'[30] The letter was, in fact, neither silly nor juvenile: it was colourful and effervesced with enthusiasm; it showed a grasp of the subject and a degree of lateral thinking that George instantly appreciated. But what had attracted him to George's work? His imagination had first been stirred when the play *Victimes du devoir* drew the parallel between Ionesco's thinking and Lupasco's. He was working on a student thesis and was delighted to discover that George was one of Lupasco's allies and, as he added with characteristic modesty, he 'thought it would be good to have some sort of philosophy'.[31] The possibilities of George's logic of contradiction stimulated his imagination. He had just read Foss's *Symbol and Metaphor in Human Experience*, but had disliked its flippancy on the subject of paradox. However, he told George, he did find it an 'adequate introduction', even though it was 'a less perfect work than your own'.[32] Patrick Hughes rehearsed Foss's argument that[33]

> the symbol, because of its exclusiveness, is a form less useful than the metaphor, in which the referrals are equal. But the symbol has the

advantage that makes it obvious that it is referring to dual concepts; a metaphor has a less conscious aim. Perhaps this explains the glory of the cliché, which being metaphorical, has attained a symbolic significance in the terms in which it has been referred to so often.

What perhaps attracted George to Patrick, quite apart from his obvious clarity of mind, was his ability to fix on homely images to illustrate serious philosophical points. Again with genuine but uncalled-for modesty, he explained:[34]

Since I am unlearned, I have only been able to refer, until I read your book, to the paradoxes which I have found in the visual arts – one should see the Grant's Stand Fast advertisement in the *Daily Express*, and know that abstraction is an attempt to portray a total referral.

Already we have a hint of the Patrick Hughes of the future with his brilliant (and often highly entertaining) work as an artist and writer, with a mission to popularize the visual and literary manifestations of life's paradoxes. And in George he had found a staunch supporter, as well as a lifelong friend.

CHAPTER EIGHTEEN

EXHIBITIONS AND EXHIBITIONISM

If some of George's friends were afraid that his philosophical inclinations would subsume his creativity as a painter, they were wrong. He left them in no doubt about that within a few months of the publication of *The Paradoxical Universe*. Effie Damoglou, who was one of his detractors as a philosopher, made sure of that. By this time she had acquired a small basement gallery in an attractive Nash house at 1 Albany Terrace, near Regent's Park. She called it the Paris Gallery because of the city's artistic associations, but it was her own ancestral origins that dictated its visual appearance: 'The owner is of Greek descent and . . . she has attempted to recapture in London the famous light of Greece by painting the walls of her gallery in pure and dazzling white.'[1] She welcomed George back to the artistic fold by including him in an exhibition entitled 'Abstract Variations'. Thirty-eight artists of distinction were represented, including Hans Hartung, Ben Nicholson and Victor Vasarely. It opened for a private view on Friday, 29 May 1959, and was considered important enough for the public to be given two months in which to visit it. Later that year, in November, Effie put on a parallel exhibition entitled 'Figure Variations'. This time George was not invited to contribute, for the simple reason that he was still maintaining his exclusive image as an abstract painter.

However, immediately preceding this exhibition, Effie had given him a show all to himself. It ran from 21 October to 10 November 1959 and left his public in no doubt that, even when absorbed in philosophy, his painterly energies remained undiminished. All the twenty-three canvases (except three earlier ones from Effie's own collection) were painted in the 1958–9 period. Jasia Reichardt in her article on George in *Art News and*

Review certainly saw him as a painter among art's front-runners, while twining together the philosophical thread with that of his art. She explained to her readers:[2]

> The development of George Melhuish from the time he first began to paint till now has been a steady one from naturalism to impressionism to romantic expressionism, but the consciousness of the present has made him move forward uncompromisingly to a way of painting which, in a great measure, is an experiment. He feels that in art there is no room for moderation if the final personality of the picture is to assert itself. Often he sees a mental image of the painting he is going to work on, but the image becomes concrete only as it takes its shape on canvas, board or paper, the first idea is sufficiently indefinite so that the outcome may even be a surprise to the artist.

She ended by summing up his approach to art by stating that 'one quality has been persistently present in the work of George Melhuish and that is the light and versatile romantic vision.'[3]

One of his old friends, Maurice Carpenter, up from Marlborough, dropped into the Paris Gallery to see George and his pictures. Later he wrote to him:[4]

> It was good to see you again, as young and enthusiastic and busy as ever. You must be Dorian Gray . . . I was interested in your new developments. I suggest it is a voyage of discovery in paint. What is fortuitous or accidental is made use of – as is the puzzled reaction of the public. You make a good cloud of words appropriate to the occasion. I suppose the revolt from the Subject, from the Natural and Objective world, will go on as long as Society is in such flux.

Effie Damoglou continued to have a turnover of exhibitions as well as operating a press. She produced some attractive, hand-printed exhibition catalogues in addition to a limited edition of her own poems. Between 14 June and 2 July 1960 she mounted a show entitled 'My Private Collection'. It consisted of fifty-eight works of art from the 1953–8 period, five of them by George. They were all (except for five, including one by George, *The Louvre, Paris* (1953)) offered for sale to the public. Since it seemed like such a personal sacrifice, friends wondered if Effie's attention had gone off in another direction, or perhaps if she were gradually winding up one phase in her life. As it transpired, both assumptions were true. One suspects that, as a form of unconscious rivalry with George, she had developed philosophical yearnings. She began talking of an essay that she wanted to write. George became irritated by the endless talk and no action. He turned round and said: 'I'm getting tired of this. Why don't you write it?' So Effie did. She closed her doors and in three weeks had produced a work entitled *The Three Stages of Love, or l'Education d'Amour* (1960). It sold quite well because, as she remarked dryly, people 'thought that it had something to do with bed-love. It wasn't anything like that. It really was a very serious work.'[5] One wonders. It was only eight pages long and the fact that she had it bound in velvet might have suggested that it was less than scholarly.

Another essay followed three years later, *Art and Ideas and their Relation to Life*, and, if anybody were still in the dark as to her philosophical approach, now there could be no doubt. Contrary to what the title suggested, her piece was more concerned with archaeology and evolution than with high art. At the outset she placed her cards on the table: 'Art is the quest for Truth, the Absolute, the Universal Law. That quest is part of man, his search for self-discovery, seeking to understand the meaning of his existence and of his destiny.'[6] In a way George was engaged in the same quest, but Effie's almost totally materialistic approach to the subject was virtually the opposite of his metaphysical focus. They both went their own separate ways. She gave up the Paris Gallery and, for the next two decades, lived in France and Spain as she wrote a massive, 'definitive' work on her theory of evolution. She and George saw each other again only once – and very briefly.

By this time he had made adjustments to his way of life. He became largely Bristol-centred in his activities. His Paris contacts faded and, when his studio at 45 King's Road was bought over his head and the whole building demolished to make way for a supermarket, he ceased to have the London base that he had had for two decades. His property business demanded his constant attention (and presence) in Bristol, all the more so since it was beginning to secure him a steady income. But, otherwise, his life lacked a degree of stability. As Effie drifted off, so too did Charmian Deckers. She had not intended to stay long with him. Their arrangement was convenient as a short-term measure, but she felt that they both had their lives to lead and so, stung by the property-buying bug, she bought a cottage for herself and Nina in Kingsdown. Although Charmian and George kept constantly in touch, always dependent upon each other for advice, he was dramatically disorientated by her departure. For one thing he hated being on his own in the Springfield Road house. He turned to his old friend, the vivacious widow Clare Jenkins, and, since she still took lodgers in her house on Clifton Brow, he asked her if he could stay in one of her spare rooms. Her son Brian recalled what subsequently happened:[7]

He came and stayed at my mother's house for a period. He came as a friend . . . who'd come to stay. And my mother assumed that it would only be for a few days. And I can remember my mother, after about three weeks, saying that she was a bit concerned. I don't think that she necessarily cooked or did a lot for him, but I think that she felt that to some extent George had taken over . . . There was no reference to what he was going to do or when he was going.

Mrs Jenkins had to devise the most tactful way of suggesting that he was staying longer than expected. He took the hint (but with the worst possible grace) and moved back round the corner to his own house. The problem was that, from this point onwards, he floundered emotionally. His compulsive need for a female companion as a mother-substitute was doomed to disappointment because of the unresolvable paradox innate in the situation.

Another disconcerting fact came into play. George had long had problems with his urinary system. From as early as 1944 he had periodically had stones in the bladder. Though unpleasant, he found that he could pass them without any need for surgery. However, by the late 1950s and early 1960s he had begun to experience additional discomfort and prostatitis was diagnosed. He was admitted to the hospital in Frenchay and on 2 August 1961, within weeks of his forty-fifth birthday, he went into surgery to have a Wilson–Heye, transvesical prostatectomy. He liked to talk about 'his operation' in later years. He boasted that, because of his delicate metabolic state, he had to be attended by a 'top consultant physician' as well as his consultant surgeon, Mr Butler. Yet he carefully guarded as a close secret the nature of his operation. The point was that, although this procedure would technically not result in actual sterility, if orgasm were achieved at all, it would involve retrograde ejaculation and, in effect, amount to a form of sterility. One thing is certain: from this point onwards he knew that he would never be able to father any children. And worse, the psychological effect of his operation almost certainly resulted in a more or less permanent state of impotence. For somebody of his relatively young years (not to mention somebody of his temperament) the experience was traumatic in all senses of the word.

One of the more positive results of this episode was that he consciously tried to assert that he was still vigorous and in the prime of his creative life. The writing of *The Paradoxical Universe* had taken a great deal out of him; he had achieved a form of success, but he knew that it would be a long time before a second volume could be completed and published. He, therefore, redoubled his efforts as an artist. There was an immediate result:[8]

The early sixties saw a new series of oils on paper which introduced a new graphic quality which re-instated specific pictorial organization and even a kind of subject matter but now the confrontation with subject matter occurred at the level of suspended identity. There is something of a paradoxical balance between the objects indicated in the painting and the art of the picture as an object.

But he also tried to combine the image of the *enfant terrible* with that of the *grand seigneur*. He had always been rather pontifical in his manner. Now Bristol was deliberately made aware that he was a man of substance as well as a creative writer and artist. Max Barnes' article on him in the *Bristol Week-End* on Friday, 13 October 1961, was designed to put over this image:[9]

He was a small man lost in the deep recesses of his favourite armchair. A man with clean-cut aesthetic features, smooth fair hair and an arresting personality. George Melhuish, artist, author and individualist, has spent a lifetime swimming defiantly against the stream of convention. A little of it shows in his mode of dress. Bow tie with a thread of gold, mustard waistcoat and chisel toe shoes with gold studs.

However, other than giving an insight into the man in the setting of his unconventional home, the interviewer was clearly meant to record things designed to surprise his readers. George deliberately pointed out some of his recent and most provocative works of art:[10]

I was taken to inspect two of the most extraordinary art 'treasures' in the country. One was a slab of scrap iron. He found it rusting away on some waste ground, brought it home, shaped it a trifle, named it *The Fish*, and mounted it on a wall.

The other was called *The Plaice*, and was a plaque painted in exotic sea colours. On closer inspection it turned out to be – a battered enamel bowl.

No, these are not gimmicks for giggles. They are proof of a search for beauty in the unusual by a most unusual man.

George had, in fact, been experimenting with collage techniques. Some of his efforts, such as his scrap-iron compositions, were successful and even witty; others, using more fragile materials like cardboard and paper, too soon turned into greying dust-traps.

He also took advantage of the Barnes interview to remind his public of his work as a philosopher. His current obsession was calculated to stimulate curiosity as well as respect:[11]

He is engaged on probing the fantasy world of dreams. He is writing a book on dreams and their significance . . . a new adventure in psychology – exploring the uncharted world of dreams. He is trying to school himself to retain an image of his dreams on waking. He feels he has a facility for this, one that has been heightened during a recent illness . . . He believes that the secret world of dreams holds the key to many mysteries of psychology and personality. They all have some meaning . . . however strange and disconnected.

None of this was particularly surprising to anybody who knew the man, but what did raise an eyebrow was the statement that, because of this preoccupation, he had 'laid aside his brush and his disturbing canvases for a time'.[12] This was far from the truth, as he soon proved.

For an artist who never had himself elected to the Royal West of England Academy, he continued to have remarkable success in having canvases regularly chosen for the annual exhibitions. Then, in May 1962, he was given a whole exhibition to himself. It was designed to be a retrospective show and it certainly was: the paintings in the Sharples Gallery were from the 1941–53 period and most had been lent by old friends such as Charmian Deckers, Percy Edgell, Kenneth Smith and Leslie Urquhart-White; but the works in the Winterstoke Gallery came from the year 1954 right up to 1962 itself. George, in other words, may have put aside his brushes in 1961, as he claimed in the Barnes article, but only temporarily. Nonetheless, he did not let slip an opportunity to blow his philosophical trumpet. The introduction to the catalogue only lightly sketched in his career as an artist and primarily dwelt on his publication of *The Paradoxical Universe*; it then announced that 'he is now working on a second philosophical work, *The Ambiguous Universe*, which he hopes will be published shortly'.[13]

But that was not the only trumpet that was being blown. The BBC broadcast a review by the art critic Vivian Ogilvie on its *Round-Up* programme on 10 May 1962. After sailing easily through the earlier, figurative currents of George's art, he approached his abstracts with some trepidation:[14]

To be frank, I wasn't exactly looking forward to this part of the show. I'm getting a little tired of abstracts, especially as so many artists are turning out abstracts that are monotonously similar and very often dull to look at. I'm happy to say that I cheered up at once when I saw Mr Melhuish's. They have plenty of variety and are extremely colourful. And also what is there is obviously intended: I'm old-fashioned enough to prefer that a mind should be at work choosing the colours and where they go.

Even George's scrap-metal constructions came in for interested comment. Ogilvie thought that one composed of 'a bit of an old field mower and a set of rusted gas burners' was very odd, but rather likeable.[15]

The following day Valerie Roach in *Nonesuch News* allowed George to monopolize her column to introduce his exhibition by forcefully expounding his views on abstract art. He began with a truism: 'Of all the arts, the art of painting is most often appreciated for the wrong reasons.' He had advice for both painter and public. The artist should attempt 'to give his picture an air of distinction'; he should be a 'serious experimenter'. On the other hand he believed that 'the averagely civilized man should be "at one with visual art". He should be educated by being given a chance to see original works. Why are public galleries always closed during the only times the working man has to visit them?'[16] Then George tackled the central problem:[17]

> The common man has inherited the idea that the visual world is perfect, hence his hostility to abstract forms which appear to differ from nature – the visual arts are in fact often more abstract than we think they are. Anyone uneducated in the appreciation of painting will glean his pleasure from association of ideas, and because of this many popular pictures have been created by artists not worthy of the name.

Three days later, on 14 May, an old art-critic friend of George's, F. W. Brown, wrote 'a personal memoir' in the *Western Daily Press*. He had always been fascinated by him as an artist; now the writer had intriguingly emerged. 'When he starts talking about art, you have to listen hard and think fast to catch up. Few artists are vocal; George is eloquent.' And Brown considered that his eloquence extended to his creation consisting of 'a lump of mowing machine and gas burners and that the Gas Board has missed a selling-point of which they would never have thought'.[18] Brown enthused about him as an avant-garde artist: 'Show George a convention and he lands it a straight left and puts something more interesting in its place. He is the only artist that I know who has painted an impression of the H-bomb. Well, it's a vermilion something, and it made a bomb-burst impression on me.'[19]

But his writings also made an impression on him. Apparently George had once agonized to him about how much more difficult it was to write prose than to paint. Brown recalled:[20]

> The only comfort I could give him was to tell him to suspect the thing that comes easily. He took that to heart. He polishes and polishes and gets a good, taut, meaty prose. There's always something in a Melhuish sentence as there is in one of his brush strokes. Even if the

design is entirely abstract, there is something satisfying about the confident swing of the line.

He ended by speculating on what George might do next. Very likely even he himself did not know, but one could guarantee that, whatever it was, it would be stimulating.

But on 23 May he allowed himself to take a more passive role. He had just had a gossipy 'coffee and cake' session with a new friend Richard Blake Brown and found himself invited to a fashion show at the Colston Hall presented by the current top dress designer, Norman Hartnell. Blake Brown pressed him: '*Do* bring all your lady-lodgers to see the lovely dresses of my old Cambridge friend on the 23rd. I'm sure you'd all appreciate his gorgeous colours.'[21] Whether or not George took a bevy of beauties with him is another matter, although in such an ambiguous atmosphere he might have regarded them as useful protection. The show itself was too good to miss and his scruples were easily overcome by his love of glamour and public personalities; he also fancied himself as a connoisseur and designer of exotic female attire.

However, there was nothing particularly original about his next essay in public display. He gave the *Bristol Week-End* newspaper an interview with a heavy emphasis on the originality of his house at 75 Springfield Road, which, although from the outside an apparently ordinary dwelling, contained such an extraordinary contrasting mixture of antique furniture, richly patterned wallpapers and avant-garde art that it left the visitor wondering about the owner's intentions. The reporter concluded: 'You never know what you will find behind the most ordinary door, do you?'[22] Indeed not: one thing that the interview did reveal was that George had once tried his hand at sculpture: 'As you enter the house, next to the abstract in the porch is the stone carving of a woman's head. Another of Mr Melhuish's works. But at one and a half cwt scarcely portable enough to show at exhibitions.'[23] One suspects that that was not the real reason. The newspaper photograph revealed a rather unsophisticated effort. George's friends knew only too well that he could never be comfortable with a medium that demanded so much physical effort and time.

In the early 1960s another medium with which he flirted was musical composition, but it too demanded so much effort, especially since the task of producing anything worthy of public attention would have been well-nigh impossible for an amateur like himself. Yet a sheaf of manuscript has survived from this period. It contains a number of unfinished sketches that on the surface look rather fantastic, uncontrolled and clearly derivative, but they turn out to be exercises in twelve-tone technique. Even if he was unable to sustain his effort through more than a couple of dozen bars of an unscored piano concerto, one is impressed by his grasp of the underlying principles of what he saw as an essential abstract art form.

George begrudged none of the effort that went into his painting, and 'effort' had begun to be the operative word. He had started to paint much larger canvases than before and that involved him in undreamt-of logistical problems. On 12 November 1963 'Blackboy's Diary' in the *Bristol Evening Post* did a short piece on him as he was working on a series of paintings that he called his 'Mood Pictures'. At least one of them, entitled *Blue Mood: Night Figures*, made the interviewer stop to look again; quite apart from the fact that it seemed 'to conjure up half-seen figures including one of a nun', it was so large (all five-foot square of it) that it would present an exhibitor with serious transport problems. In this instance the problem was particularly acute since, George revealed, he intended the result of his beaver-like activity to be shown as a one-man exhibition in Paris the following spring. But *Blue Mood*, he had already decided, was not going, for purely practical reasons:[24]

> Its size has prevented its chances of being exhibited . . . For although the Customs people were quite co-operative about its shipment to France, the problems of its transit were too much for him. 'It would cost £15 to send this one canvas to Paris . . . And that would only see it as far as the Gare du Nord. Then there would be the nightmare of trying to take a large painting across Paris from the railway station to the galleries. I know from experience what a job that is.'

Blue Mood may have been destined to stay in Bristol, but other paintings would be going over, with pride of place being taken by one canvas entitled *Spring Mood*, 'dappled with green and striking just the right note for Paris in the spring'.[25]

However, there is no evidence that even *Spring Mood* got as far as the Gare du Nord. The effort and cost clearly daunted him so much that even the prestige of having another Paris exhibition to his name had to be foregone. Thereafter, he made no further serious efforts to have his work exhibited in Paris, although as late as December 1968 he was in correspondence with François de Vallombreuse of the chic Galerie Mouffe, at 67 rue Mouffetard. George may have been tempted, but by then he had become cautious about taking risks that he would have taken in his stride two decades before. Besides, in the 1960s, George as philosopher was again in the ascendant. Moreover, as he approached his half century in 1966, he was becoming more, not less, preoccupied with distracting problems of a personal nature.

CHAPTER NINETEEN

LOVE AND FRIENDSHIP

In the spring of 1963 George received a telephone call in reponse to an advertisement in the *Bristol Evening Post*. He had a bed-sitting-room to let and a painfully shy 24-year-old girl, newly returned to Bristol, needed a place to stay. And so it was that Victoria Malins came into his life. She moved into the room for a number of months, during which she and George came to know each other. She later moved to share the house at 75 Springfield Road with him. For the next four years she was the closest domestic companion that he had in his entire life.

Vicky was the daughter of Edward Malins, a schoolmaster and writer (with works on Yeats and Samuel Palmer to his credit). Her mother, a vibrant American heiress, the kind of person who excels at everything to which she puts her mind, was clearly psychologically overwhelming for such a sensitive soul. A sister who was regarded as a paragon completed the perspective of early influences. Even life as a boarder at Badminton School in Bristol did not help much to bring the girl out of her shell. However, when she left school, she chose an adventurous enough course of action. She studied art in London and then went to New York to continue her studies. While in the United States, urged by a humanistic desire to do something 'useful', she tried her hand at nursing. This was not a good idea. She found it upsetting and the experience made her more introvert than before. She returned to the United Kingdom, back to more familiar surroundings, but she later recalled: 'I . . . still found it hard to get on with my family and friends. It seemed that I had no real friends or job and I thought I'd live alone in Bristol and get a job and make friends. And then George came into my life through a fragile decision to 'phone him for a place to live.'[1]

Once she had given up the bed-sitting-room and gone to live in Springfield Road, she settled down to a routine of life with him, even though the faintly primitive conditions that he did not seem to notice surprised and occasionally irked her. But then, if one were used to better, the fact that his electric kettle was the cheapest that Woolworth sold was noticeable. But life with him had its compensations. He coaxed her out of herself and taught her a great deal about the finer things of life, about art, antiques, opera and abstract philosophy, as well as about personal relations. What he did was to help restore her self-confidence and eventually, through a process of counter-argument, he inadvertently helped her regain her Christian faith. But all this emerged in time as the by-product of a *modus vivendi* that had about it a general air of contentment. She later wrote a note about their life together:[2]

> He was sensitive and kind and not difficult to live with. He was very serious and didn't laugh a lot but he was happy with me. Sometimes he showed it by sort of singing or humming in the kitchen and rubbing his hands. I liked to hear him then. He hardly drank and never smoked. It seemed strange and out of character to see him after drinking. He lost his spirit and real presence. He was eccentric. I liked this about him. He'd leave his shoes outside his bedroom door as though he expected them to be cleaned in the night.

Life did, indeed, follow a basic routine,[3]

> George doing the shopping in the morning. We'd have lunch and talk for hours. Then maybe he'd want to be alone to write his book and after supper he might have a typist to copy his work . . . Sometimes at the weekend we'd be driven somewhere. A car or a taxi often left us in the country near the suspension bridge . . . He didn't like the country. He felt the country was sad. It seemed strange as he was an artist. We would walk in the Leigh Woods . . . He would be quiet and somehow out of place.

He was happier in an urban setting, even though in Bristol he and Vicky did not socialize a great deal. He retained his love of London and, when he lost his King's Road studio, he obtained a flat at 56 Harley Street. Despite the allure of the address and the convenience of the location, Vicky thought it 'rather crummy'.[4] She felt that now he was becoming richer, he could easily have afforded a place in Cheyne Walk. But he would not begrudge the expense of taking her to the city's more up-market bars, at the Hilton and Dorchester, rather than go to ordinary London pubs, which he viewed with suspicious, sanitized eyes. Otherwise, his great indulgence was to visit Christie's and Sotheby's, where he acquired (usually when the serious dealers were out of town) bits and pieces of antique furniture to add to his existing eclectic collection. Some of the items were attractive in themselves, but his taste occasionally deserted him; a chandelier that was given pride of place in his property at St Vincent's Priory really did look as if it had been acquired at Woolworth along with the electric kettle.

In London there were old friends to visit. Barbara and Barrie Thorne were back from the United States and were living in grand style in Hertford Street. Vicky was impressed by the sight of Vasarely's paintings on the walls. She was impressed by the closeness of the friendship between Barbara and George. And, if anything, she thought that her hospitality was almost too generous: he could end up, uncharacteristically, the worse for wear.

Another renewed contact in London was Effie Damoglou. She came to call at the Harley Street flat and George introduced Vicky to her as his 'wife'. Vicky was clearly as much taken back aback as Effie was and she withdrew to the bedroom to listen to the radio while George and Effie chatted. She left without enticing Vicky out to say goodbye. Effie and George never met again nor did they have any other form of contact. The question of what these two women in his life thought on the subject of marriage was kept firmly in the background. He was quite happy with things as they were.

With Vicky he took more holidays than he had since childhood. She was, however, surprised at what he liked to do. He was rich enough to take her to Venice or New York; he talked constantly about going to Paris with her, but he never did. Instead they found themselves in second-rate hotels in English cities at precisely the time when the inhabitants were deserting them for seaside resorts. Vicky also found it difficult to come to terms with with his catering arrangements. Whether for reasons of diet or economy, he seldom went to restaurants and 'on holiday', she recalled, 'we would eat out of tins in the hotel room and heat our coffee on a camping burner'.[5] He seemed to prefer this to anything more stylish. Vicky was used to life's comforts, but she was happy enough to go along with his eccentricities. For his part he seems to have been remarkably content with the arrangement, even though the intellectual intensity of his work deprived him of natural sleep and he found it difficult to sleep in the same room as somebody else, and well-nigh impossible in the same bed. In the 1960s he got into the habit of taking far more sleeping pills than he was prescribed and he was one of the first and most faithful of the new generation of tranquillizer consumers.

Their relationship drifted on for more than four contented years but, since he was emotionally non-committal, Vicky began to feel more and more psychologically insecure. She wanted them to marry, if only as a form of assurance. She would periodically go off to stay with her parents in the hope that the thought of her leaving him permanently might stimulate him into action. Tackled on the subject, he said: 'It's not as though I'll never marry you.'[6] But he would have found it difficult to adjust to a broken vow of celibacy. She (one thinks mistakenly) took this as indicating that he did not love her, and suddenly one hot summer in London she packed her bags and left to make a new life for herself.

One thing that Vicky did note about the 1963–8 period, during which she knew him, was that George devoted very little time to his art. But she did recall his painting 'some excellent abstracts on paper. I think these ones satisfied him. They were complex, some rather oriental looking with hard black lines and subtle colours.'[7] Otherwise, she recalled his painting an 'official' portrait of the sheriff of Bristol. He also painted a striking portrait of herself, full-face and looking uncommonly like Jacqueline Kennedy, to whom she bore more than a passing resemblance. However, the truth was that for George his philosophy was in the ascendant again. One of the reasons for this was that the publication of *The Paradoxical Universe* had gained him a number of new friends whose enthusiasm encouraged him. If anything, it brought him closer to Anthony Hill; and Patrick Hughes was in constant touch by letter and telephone, although it was not until 1967 that they met face to face. Eric Toms, a lecturer in philosophy at Glasgow University, responded with dry enthusiasm to George's work. They too kept usefully in touch by letter and telephone and finally met at a joint session of Mind and the Aristotelian Society in Bedford College, London, in 1966. All these contacts proved enduring and highly encouraging. George Ward-Jackson, however, entered George's life with meteoric suddenness and, after a few years, left it with equal abruptness.

Early in 1963, Ward-Jackson, a great browser round London bookshops and a member of the London Library, quite by chance stumbled upon a copy of *The Paradoxical Universe*. He devoured it and immediately concluded that it was 'a work of genius and a work of tremendous and piercing imagination and originality'.[8] Ward-Jackson was a gentleman of leisure whose life had been spent in the vigorous pursuit of intellectual awareness. Born in 1900 and a midshipman who saw service in the First World War by the age of sixteen, at the end of hostilities he realized that the navy could never again match the Grand Fleet that he had seen in review as a boy in 1912, and so he left to read history at Christ Church under Professor Namier. At this point his uncle, the Bishop of Newcastle, died and left him enough money not to have to work; and, indeed, except for a spell in naval intelligence during the Second World War, he never had a paid job. As his wife Muriel later remarked, 'many people in that position . . . would just slip into laziness, but he was one of the most energetic men I ever knew and, whatever interest he took up, he followed it with tremendous enthusiasm and energy'.[9] Philosophy was his main passion, every branch, even its most complicated mathematical off-shoots. Psychology attracted him, particularly the theories of Freud and Jung, and for a time in the late 1930s he worked as a voluntary psychiatric counsellor. But it was the pursuit of self-knowledge that motivated his life. In the 1930s he had been powerfully attracted to the more heterodox groups of intellectuals in France. He was close to Ford Madox Ford in Paris and he stayed with Romain Rolland for a period. But, ultimately, it was with Eastern philosophy that he felt most at home. He went off to India to stay at the ashram of the great guru of the period, Sri Maharshi. The effect of his teaching profoundly moulded his thinking for the rest of his life, and so it was that, even from the first glance through *The Paradoxical Universe*, he could feel sympathetic vibrations. The section on dreams particularly claimed his attention. The author's statement that 'it may be said that the philosophical significance of dreams has remained a very neglected study'[10] was itself almost an understatement. However, while this is true of Western philosophy, this was not true of Eastern philosophy – whether George Melhuish was aware of it at the time or not. But he and Ward-Jackson quite independently had come to believe in dreams as a valid part of human experience. In the latter's case he had almost scriptural authority behind him: 'In *Advaita Vedanta*, waking, dreaming and sleeping (the Three States) are given equal importance (or unimportance) and it is only after penetrating these three states that consciousness emerges.'[11] By a strange coincidence the subject of dreams had just become the obsessional focal point of George Melhuish's philosophical attention at precisely the point when Ward-Jackson stumbled across his work.

Ward-Jackson and his wife Muriel (an intellectual powerhouse with a successful civil service career behind her and currently a director of the John Lewis Partnership) kept a flat at 45 Connaught Square, but they had just bought an early nineteenth-century cottage, Beacon Hill, deep in the Wiltshire countryside at Heddington, near Calne. When he realized that George lived in Bristol, he wrote explaining his feelings about (and difficulties with) *The Paradoxical Universe*, suggesting a meeting. He was impressed by George's 'incredible feat of setting forth [his] general thesis in non-technical language', but he longed to seek his personal clarification of his paragraphs 'on the basic matrix referring to presence and absence'.[12] He quoted a key passage: 'Therefore no conceptual image as a subject-affirmation-denial can be entrusted to assert for a mere given absence without an antithetical crossing in meanings with its perceptual image of a mere given absence.'[13]

George invited Ward-Jackson over to lunch at Springfield Road, but immediately the obvious problem arose: what kind of image does one gain of an author and his lifestyle simply from reading his work? Ward-Jackson preconceived of George as a man of means and something of a bon viveur, possibly a wine-buff like himself, and, anticipating his visit, he wrote: 'I hope that you will allow me to pay token homage to your unique achievement by bringing to our lunch a unique achievement of the vintner's art in the shape of a bottle of Krug (1955)!'[14] This did not cause George to alter his planned menu: when Ward-Jackson arrived in his large Citroën DS (that 'looked like a shark') bearing the bottle of Krug, he found himself served with a Spam salad. Neither man was in the least disconcerted: to Ward-Jackson, a virtual vegetarian, life was about higher things. He continued to visit George in Bristol. However, on one occasion he had just arrived when George glanced out of the window. 'Your car's moving,' he exclaimed. In a flash Ward-Jackson was out of the house in hot pursuit to apply the foot brakes before it reached the steep hill at the end of the street. After that he found it safer to come over to Bristol, pick up George and transport him down to Beacon Hill for a day of untroubled discussions. But now it was George who had to do the adapting – to country life. Muriel Ward-Jackson recalled the sight of him daintily stepping out of the car in fashionable (but impractical) winkle-picker shoes. He looked extremely dapper with his city suit and bow tie, but the copy of the *Daily Mirror* under his arm involuntarily raised an eyebrow.

For at least five years the two Georges met regularly. Each time they would plunge into long hours of philosophical discussion of such intensity that they got into the habit of taping their conversations and playing them back afterwards. Ward-Jackson regarded his 'discovery' of George as something of a spiritual revelation. In one letter to him he wrote: 'Please allow me once more to say how unique an utterance *The Paradoxical Universe* is: from the personal angle it is as if I had suffered a whole life-time of blurred vision and neuralgic headache due to eye-strain and then been given the perfect ophthalmic prescription.'[15] Muriel Ward-Jackson added an intriguing comment by suggesting that both men fitted into the Sufist tradition:[16]

There can be Sufis in every religion, although it is identified in some people's minds with Islam. There is no reason for it to be so, but many of the early Sufis were Persians and the like. But Sufis themselves say that there are Sufis in every religion and that a Sufi nearly always recognises another Sufi. I think probably that Sufis are the people with the purest form of religion . . . They are really the mystics of every religion; and there is something about each of them that one recognises in another . . . I think that the point of Sufism is that every Sufi regards the only point of life is to travel towards the centre and they, therefore, recognise others who are travelling in the same direction. And in a way one could say that there was a trace of this in George Melhuish which caused my George and him to recognise one another.

Their relationship was a unique phenomenon in both their lives, each benefiting enormously from his dialogue with the other. Sometimes Vicky Malins would come along with George, but she made no pretence about her displeasure at being excluded from George's discussions and sulked. Muriel Ward-Jackson and a frequent visitor in the form of a friend and fellow enthusiast for mystical philosophies, Elizabeth Clough, were perceptive enough to leave the men to themselves. Elizabeth Clough even felt guilty at an 'obtrusion' into their exalted philosophizing when she cooked hake for lunch one day and burdened them with a distracting obstacle course in the form of its ubiquitous bones. But George and Elizabeth Clough liked and appreciated each other. On one visit to Bristol she bought from him one of his most stunning abstracts.

The Ward-Jacksons and Elizabeth Clough did not cease to wonder about George's sensitivity. Just before acquiring his Harley Street flat he came to visit them and was put up in a hotel just round the corner from Connaught Square. After only one night he was in a state of acute agitation: a grandfather clock on the landing outside his bedroom had ticked away any possibility of sleep. He had to be transferred to a room where the passage of time took place less noisily. On the other hand, he had a worldly side to him with which Ward-Jackson could not cope and eventually gave up trying. George Melhuish adored gossip of the kind that could be gleaned from the social pages of newspapers like the *Daily Mirror* and the *Daily Express*. He found the activities of Europe's royal families and the vagaries of the nobility endlessly fascinating and, once the serious business of their philosophical discussions was over for the day, he would relax over the latest piece of social chit-chat. Ward-Jackson seemed incapable of conveying to him the extent to which he disapproved of a philosopher whom he admired lowering himself with an interest in such trivia. But at the end of the day it was over George's ambitions as an author that Ward-Jackson felt that he had to make the break.

He honestly believed that George had said all that was necessary in *The Paradoxical Universe* and that it should provide the basis for intelligent discussions such as they had enjoyed together. George, however, was determined to elaborate his ideas in the form of a second volume that would take his public by storm. Ward-Jackson did not approve of such worldly ambition and quite suddenly in May 1968, after one of George's visits to Beacon Hill, he wrote him a letter expressing his feelings in as abrupt terms as he ever employed:[17]

> I find that I am unable to continue assisting (in however slight a degree) with the finalization of your book. In case this disappoints . . . I offer the excuse that I never pretended to have any enthusiasm for the book as such, but only for the clarification by necessary elaboration for the subject. Thus I have frequently and often avowedly felt a certain frustration in submitting to the considerations inevitably involved in such a project.

And although he admitted to looking forward to reading George's final published version, he insisted that there should be no acknowledgement of his own help. The friendship ended, symbolically, with one of Ward-Jackson's obliging neighbours bringing the files of their discussions back to George on a visit to Bristol.

He was taken aback and offended by the suddenness of Ward-Jackson's decision. Vicky Malins knew how much the friendship had meant to him and did her best to bring about a *rapprochement*, but neither George would consider compromising his position. The result of this severing of ties for George Melhuish could have been disastrous, had it not been for the fact that (although his book *The Paradoxical Nature of Reality* was still five years away from publication) the main bulk of his project had been completed. Ward-Jackson's letter indicated that, apart from a preface and some bridge passages, it required little more in the way of reworking. However, given George's nervous state and his preoccupation with personal problems, one feels that Ward-Jackson's abandoning him could quite easily have scuttled the whole project, if it had not been for the support and encouragement of a faithful group of friends whose advice he valued: Anthony Hill, Dom Sylvester Houédard and Patrick Hughes. George's own self-confessed arrogance was the final deciding factor encouraging him to continue regardless.

CHAPTER TWENTY

FADS AND PHILOSOPHIES

George Ward-Jackson had good reason to be critical of George Melhuish's worldly attitude towards life. It was riddled with contradictions that did not worry him or even impinge upon his consciousness. He could be wildly extravagant in matters such as dress: if anything his wardrobe became more and more exotic and colourful; velvets and rich brocades were the order of the day. He used more make-up as his features faded with age and ill-health. He was totally unabashed if, for example, one of his lady drivers found on the car seat a box of rouge that had fallen out of his pocket. Increasingly he doused himself with popular brands of scent invariably designed for female skin. He seldom used masculine colognes. And as the 1960s progressed he became obsessed with the image of some of his heroes. He easily saw himself as the Nietzschean superman. (His mother had started him on that messianic track as a child.) He saw himself in certain moods in the image of his favourite composer, Giacomo Puccini. He called him 'the Master', as much for his worldliness as for his music. But it was Richard Wagner who was his great model, even to the extent of emulating his physical appearance. Frock coats, top hats and canes were all accessories worthy of the genius of Bayreuth. The unfortunate thing was that, while he took himself only half-seriously, after Vicky Malins some of his women friends were sucked into the fantasy and seriously saw themselves as latter-day Cosimas.

This appealed to a slightly sinister, mocking sense of humour that was as much a product of his dissatisfaction with the emotional and physical card that life had dealt him as with his innate sense of superiority. Often his women friends had physical peculiarities to which he drew attention with perverse delight. One was overweight, a too obvious point in the age of the mini-skirt. Another had a slight deformity in one arm; this fascinated him. And yet another had peculiar bodily proportions to which he did everything possible to draw attention.

The truth was that Vicky Malins's departure (which was as much his 'fault' as hers) precipitated him into a state of melancholia that took many of his friends by surprise. Kenneth and Vera Smith, who by that time were fairly distant from him, were horrified by how dejected he had become. The fact that he also suffered his first heart attack (albeit mild) in 1968 contributed to his feelings of depression and impotence. The apparent moral openness of the 'swinging sixties' only made it more obvious that age, ill-health and lack of opportunity had robbed him of life's more sensual satisfactions. In conjunction with some of his less intelligent women friends, George the voyeur went through a fortunately brief phase that can only be described as pornographic. He allowed this to affect his art. One or two sketches and a handful of photographs of women posed in unusually provocative positions survived the depradations perpetrated upon his estate after his death. But one large canvas of mind-boggling crudity could not be easily done away with. This depicts a woman, naked except for a pair of green shoes, lying on her back with her legs up in the air. Apart from the surprisingly poor technical quality of its execution, the painting can only be described as gynaecological. However, though in the worst possible taste, it does provide a fascinating psychological insight into a tortured soul that bitterly mocked what he was incapable of possessing and now had very little real desire to possess.

In a way he compensated for the problems of his profoundly ambiguous sexual orientation by achieving greater success in his business activities. Having accumulated about seventeen properties, most of which he still let to students, he was the landlord to up to one hundred tenants at any one time and, until he started to encounter problems from troublesome tenants and troublesome housing legislation in the 1970s, he enjoyed a steady and substantial income from rents. The image of George as the businessman touring his properties with his wallet bulging with cash is not far from the truth. A great number of his transactions were done in cash. To make matter worse he kept very little in the way of files and he was averse to paying his bills until absolutely necessary. 'Why should I?' he would ask. 'I might die first.' Was this his practical example of logical contradiction? Perhaps, but his delaying tactics had a habit of catching up with him. Periodically an accumulated rates bill of enormous dimensions would land on his door-step and he was to be seen trotting off to the municipal finance offices to plead poverty and beg the privilege of paying off the outstanding sum in easy instalments.

His satisfaction in his work as a landlord continued to be compounded by his fascination with the student life that he himself had never enjoyed. He relished his tenants' invitations to coffee and an accompanying chat. He even derived a certain satisfaction from tenants and neighbours with different professional interests. As the St Paul's district, bordering on Springfield Road, began to experience social problems, far from being alarmed, he loved to observe (often with the aid of a pair of binoculars) the comings and goings of prostitutes, pimps and drug pushers. Vicky Malins even recalls that he got on well with some of the friendly ladies of the night and even accepted invitations to their parties. She remembers one given by two prostitutes. 'We had our drinks our of jam jars.'[1]

But even the voyeur in George could not conceal the fact that, hovering on the fringes of such society, he could well have come to grief. He almost did when it transpired that one of his properties in Victoria Place was let to a dentist who had been running a syndicate of high-class call-girls. Some of the girls' docility was guaranteed by their addiction to cocaine. Two of them committed suicide. At that point the police intervened as the 'ring-master' fled with his considerable ill-gotten gains to the financial haven of the Channel Islands, and it was George who was subjected to formal interrogation. However, although he was well enough aware of what had been going on, he was not directly involved and no charges were preferred. Perhaps his mind wandered momentarily back to the early 1960s when he had had a close relationship with a pleasant, kind-hearted girl called Yvonne. She had only been sixteen-years-old at the time and subsequently went on to make her living on the streets. George, as in the 'dentist' case, seems to have suffered no qualms of conscience about his own involvement.

This contact with the seamier side of life seems incongruous beside his obsession with health, his fear of contagion and his faddiness about food above and beyond even the dictates of a diabetic's diet. He was also incredibly pusillanimous about the most laughable of matters. Even in the hottest of weather he would never allow any of his drivers to keep the car windows open: he was afraid that a bee might get in and sting him. Nearer the end of his life planned trips to Wales were always cancelled well in advance because he was afraid that Welsh extremists might blow up the Severn Bridge as he was passing over it. He was unable to cope with the thought of dying in pain, however instantaneous. At a more mundane level he was terrified of catching infection, even the common cold. Friends and visitors with the slightest hint of nasal congestion were left on the door-step as he reeled back in hypochondriacal horror. Part of this health anxiety stemmed from his diabetic condition, but he took his feeding peculiarities to absurd lengths. He seldom ate foods with sauces (and one could find oneself having to eat plain unadorned pasta). He ate no bread or ice-cream until deciding to 'experiment' with them at the very end of his life. Elizabeth Clough distinctly remembers him telling her how much he disliked lamb. Charmian Deckers recalled his revulsion at the smell of cooking bacon and, as for lemons, he refused to have them in the house. It made social life slightly problematic. At the marriage of one of his faithful typists, Margaret Granger, he refused the wedding breakfast provided and produced his own snack of crackers and cheese. In fact, his digestive system was so wayward that, in order to counteract intestinal spasm, he became positively addicted to a patent medicine by the name of Collis Brown Chlorodyne. This aromatic and pleasant mixture of treacle and molasses was so heavily laced with an opiate that its potential for abuse, in the hands of somebody as self-indulgent as George, was considerable, and was even worse when taken in conjunction with sleeping pills and tranquillizers. The surprising thing is that, with all this wayward medication, he was latterly able to achieve as much as he did.

But achieve he did and this was in no small part due to stimulation and encouragement by a small band of fellow travellers in philosophy. The interest shown by Eric Toms was particularly helpful. In 1964 he had stumbled across *The Paradoxical Universe* and began a correspondence with George:[2]

> The idea underlying what you say, and underlying the idea of an 'energetic operation', is I think that of the universe in the sense of the ultimate whole of everything. This idea seems to me of the utmost importance and I regard your book as important because it derives so much from this idea. Unfortunately this sort of thing is scarcely noticeable in most modern philosophy, but with the appearance of fundamental paradox in metaphysics it ought to be.

The two men continued to write to one another, but mainly kept in touch by telephone. It was one of those fruitful associations that had little need of actual face-to-face contact and, in fact, George and Eric Toms (with his effervescent wife and fellow philosopher, Joanne) only met once, at the Mind and Aristotelian Society conference in 1966. Toms admired George. He described him as 'a real philosopher', even if not an academic (a barrier that George always had to overcome). But he was not uncritical of his work. With *The Paradoxical Universe*, though impressed, he openly pointed out its flaws, which, in a way, he helped him to eliminate in his second book *The Paradoxical Nature of Reality* (1973). He wondered how comprehensive his reading round the subject had been:

'In that respect his second book was all right, but not the first book as far as I was concerned. His references in his first book were rather crude. I think that he misunderstood things. But the references in the second book show that he got things together much better.'[3]

But even in the 1960s Toms did respect George for his grasp of scientific and mathematical concepts and, unlike almost all George's readers, he had little difficulty in coping with his distinctive use of language. However, he made no bones about the fact that he felt that he had approached the question of contradiction from the wrong angle. With remarkable clarity he explained:[4]

> It seems to me that there is a logical fault in George's work and that is that he has not studied properly the logic of his position of allowing contradiction . . . There are two ways of accepting paradox or paradoxes. One way is to say that a contradiction is true – as he did. And another way is to say – well, really it is almost the opposite – that a contradiction does not happen, to show how the paradox avoids contradiction. Suppose you had two propositions forming a paradox opposite to one another. You can deal with that opposition in two ways. You can say straightforwardly: 'It *is* a contradiction.' Or else you can say that the one side does not negate the other. Then it is not a contradiction. If you can show that one side does not negate the other, then it is not a contradiction . . . George took the bull by the horns, I suppose as an artist is inclined to, and said that contradiction was true. And I don't think that this position is feasible.

While he encouraged George with his attempts to resolve this problem, he more positively helped him with a certain sympathy for his attitude towards the law of identity: 'He says that nothing can stay put as it were. There is no determinate state of affairs ever. It is always indeterminate. It is never what it is . . . the law of identity. He calls it non-tautological logic.'[5] Toms was also sympathetic to George's venturing into the area of dreams and his consideration of the validity of dream-conditions. He thought that in his views George was fundamentally sound: 'People too readily take the wakeful state as a test of reality. I don't think that this is right. I agree with George there.'[6] All this added fuel to George's imagination as he struggled to finalize his next metaphysical venture.

He could look to another source of encouragement for his views on paradox. After eight years of letters and telephone calls he finally met Patrick Hughes on 24 November 1967, when he and his wife came to stay at Springfield Road as they passed through Bristol on their way to

Exeter for the Festival of Surrealism. George instantly liked the tall, imposing young man with his John Lennon looks. He appreciated the wit with which he managed to cross-fertilize his art with his philosophical interest in paradox. George himself was not the wittiest person in the world, but he did recognize that he and Patrick were a complementary pair. He even went so far as to have themselves photographed together by John Timbers. He clearly intended these extravagant compositions to form the basis for a double portrait study. Unfortunately, only a skilful sketch on canvas survives from the project.

Anthony Hill also remained a supportive friend. In 1968 he edited an impressive anthology, entitled *Data. Directions in Art, Theory and Aesthetics*, an exploration in art and philosophy of problems similar to those that preoccupied George and Patrick Hughes. It was, in part, the happy result of Anthony's remarkable success in penetrating the paranoid defences of Luitzen Brouwer. While even his technical disciples, researching their theses on him, were denied access to the recluse, Anthony was not regarded as a professional rival and on several occasions was allowed to meet the great philosopher and mathematician, who turned out to be a very polite and charming man, just a little amused to meet somebody from the outside world. Anthony reciprocated the compliment by publishing in his anthology 'an abstract of one of his more readable things'.[7] Entitled 'Consciousness, philosophy and mathematics', it was given pride of place before the other distinguished contributions. Unfortunately, Brouwer died before it came out, so he had no opportunity to savour the honour paid him.

At this juncture Dom Sylvester Houédard came into George's life. A scholarly Benedictine monk from Prinknash Abbey high in the hills behind Gloucester, he had a wide-ranging interest in comparative religion and philosophy. He introduced George to areas of Eastern (particularly Buddhist) thought that seemed to accord remarkably with his gestating concepts of nothingness. Whether or not that side of his influence was a force for good has been disputed, but there is no doubt that, at the practical level, Dom Sylvester helped George considerably to organize his thoughts in the years up to his death.

Dom Sylvester floated into George's ken through one of life's coincidences. Sir Francis Rose suddenly reappeared as a factor in the equation. Since the Crabb affair, George and he had lost touch. Francis thought that George had let him down. George was nervous about Francis' apparent psychological instability. Ironically, through his friendship with George Ward-Jackson he was reminded of his erstwhile friend: Francis and he had known each other decades ago, before 1939, and, indeed, in the early war years they had shared a distant refuge at Ruan

Minor on the south Cornish coast. But after that they had lost touch. However, the knowledge of this shared friendship did not tempt George to revive his contact with Francis. In June 1966 it was Francis who took the trouble to get in touch. He telephoned George from Brighton. He had just had a large and successful retrospective exhibition in Camberwell and it had now moved to the south coast town. Francis wanted him to come and see it; and he added another piece of information designed to pique his curiosity: 'I'd love you to meet this very, very charming and beautiful woman, whom I may marry.'[8] Knowing Francis of old, George had his doubts about the wisdom of this scheme, quite apart from the fact that Francis was still technically married to his estranged wife, Frederica. But George was intrigued enough to go to the exhibition, as much to see the new woman as to see the pictures. Beryl Montefiore Davis was, indeed, an attractive widow, rich with the proceeds of her first marriage. It was obvious that Francis saw in her a financial safety net. Unlike Frederica, Beryl was not a woman of any particular aestheticism. For George this was summed up when Francis took him to her Park Lane flat. As he opened the drawing-room door he said: 'It's very terrible in here, George. It's all reproduction furniture.'[9] Both men bridled at the sight. It was Frederica Rose who proved to be most helpful and sympathetic. Thinking only of Francis' potential security and contentment, from distant Corsica she arranged for a divorce, followed by an annulment, and Francis did, indeed, marry his new bride on 7 February 1967. Soon George's worst fears about the advisability of the match were fulfilled. In the meantime, his revived friendship with Francis had a more fruitful side-effect. Under the twinkling gaze of Francis' paintings of happy clowns at the Brighton exhibition, George was introduced to Dom Sylvester Houédard, artist, concrete poet, theologian and, more significantly, philosopher of remarkable sympathy with his own way of thinking.

1967–1985

CHAPTER TWENTY-ONE

ARCHITECTURAL AND HUMAN FOLLIES

In March 1967, Barbara Thorne, as a property owner of discrimination, received a telephone call from an estate agent. 'Mrs Thorne, I've got a house that's going very, very cheap in Clifton, if you're interested. It's St Vincent's Priory, opposite the Avon Gorge.' Barbara and her husband Barrie went over to Sion Hill to have a look at the property. Their reaction was instantaneous. It was truly dreadful. They would not have it, even as a gift. However, Barbara surmised: 'I suppose they got their second string out – old George.' Next day George telephoned her: 'I've bought another house.' She said: 'Don't tell me – St Vincent's Priory!' He said: 'Yes. Why?' Barbara exclaimed: 'George, it's an absolutely terrible house.'[1] However, in time she agreed that somehow it suited his image, since unlike all his other properties he saw this one as a potential home eccentric enough to match his own extravagant style. On 21 March he put down a deposit of £350 and on 9 May the purchase was completed for a total sum of £3,495.

The problem about the Priory was that, although it commanded a stunning view of the Clifton Suspension Bridge (of particular attractiveness at sunset), it was one of the most hideous mock-Gothic buildings ever created. Moreover, as a dwelling, it was completely impractical as it rose elongated for two storeys (plus attic rooms) above a substantial basement and ground floor, but it was so narrow that effectively it had only one substantial room per floor, each adjoined by a tiny, irregular-shaped room facing out to the back. The various floors were connected by stairs so narrow and precarious that no family with young children would have risked living there. Externally this lighthouse of a building was typical of a Gothic folly of the early nineteenth century. Even the rather anodyne description in George's official guide to the Priory hints at some of its aesthetic problems:[2]

> The façade is noteworthy for its many bays and numerous sculptures. The lower ground floor window is set in a stone bay and is really the light for the high basement room. The upper ground floor's traditionally Gothic windows are crowned with four sculptured stone caryatid figures. These strange cavorting figures are similar to some small carvings at the church of St Mary Redcliffe; they support the largest of the bays. In contrast to the Gothic bays the first floor is strictly Classical in form. The second floor balustrade has ornamental iron work with a spear and serpent motif . . . The second floor bay is crowned by four small sculptured wood figures of somewhat grotesque appearance, above which is the small window of the top floor, the only one that is not in the form of a bay. Gables above the roof support elaborate crosses on the centre of the side wall of the house and on the façade.

The fact that one is dealing with a jumble of styles and second-rate craftsmanship cannot be concealed even by the building's most mentally blind admirer. A glance at the interior reveals that, far from the Gothic theme being followed through with any consistency, a classical mood prevails. In the upper ground floor reception room (which George eventually used as his study) an attractive fireplace in green and white marble, with 'a relief sculpture representing David with the head of Goliath', is matched in the *piano nobile* drawing-room (the Music Room), where George spent a great deal of time removing layers of brown oil paint from the fireplace and restoring the remarkable frieze. He surmised that it had been 'modelled in relief from Pompeian murals, now in the Vatican. The *Nozze Aldobrandini* is easily recognisable among other Classical and Romanesque [sic] scenes.'[3] He had the walls of the Music Room painted in an attractive terracotta colour and generally his choice of hard colours was quite successful (except in the bathroom where the overwhelming fir-green tones were depressing). Apart from an occasional lick of paint and the original restoration of ornamental features, he did nothing more for the house, although its fabric suffered from every conceivable problem. In some cases they constituted a serious hazard to life and limb, but they had to wait until after his death for proper attention. He seemed to imagine that it was sufficient to cram the place with the random collection of more or less genuine antique furniture and ornaments that he had accumulated over the years. The problem was that, again, there was a total lack of consistency of style about everything. Strangely, the haphazard visual effect was made almost exciting by his hanging all the walls with his own paintings, his spiky abstracts contrasting remarkably well with some of the Louis-Seize and early Victorian furniture.

However, the Priory, despite its ecclesiastical name, despite George's claim that it had been built on subterranean caves used by early Christians, despite the ornamental crosses surmounting its external façade, was a building pervaded by the most sinister of atmospheres. One is surprised how time and again independent 'witnesses', who had visited or lived in the Priory, spoke about their involuntary reaction of unease and even fear. Even Anthony Hill, that most vociferous critic of all superstition, religious or otherwise, remarked: 'I found the Priory rather a creepy place. I don't really like it very much.'[4] Whether George himself was sensitive to the house's emanations or not he never revealed. He saw it as the ideal setting for himself in his combined role as eccentric and *grand seigneur*. But two things are certain. It took him well over two years finally to move into the Priory from Springfield Road, and the period of sixteen years of his actual residence in the building were ones marked by depression and a decrease in creative activity.

In the meantime he became involved in a property deal of quite another kind. Sir Francis Rose's marriage took a very short time to collapse in ruins. His unsuspecting but unsatisfied wife returned early from a weekend trip alone and found Francis in bed with a personable youth. The young man fled clutching his trousers in his hand. The subsequent year was one of crisis for the Roses, with Beryl making vain attempts to cope with the situation and Francis resolutely refusing to leave. Finally, in the autumn of 1968, she obtained a committal order on Francis and, one afternoon, sitting peacefully in the flat, he found that two men in white coats had entered the drawing-room. They bundled him off to a psychiatric institution. It soon became apparent that, despite his drink problem and his mildly psychotic behaviour, he was not a paranoid schizophrenic. Francis' old-world charm quickly re-asserted itself and soon doctors and nurses were eating out of his hand. Indeed, after his release one of the male nurses was noble (and foolish) enough to allow him to stay temporarily at his house. But it was George who came to the rescue. Summoned by a telephone call from the hospital, he found himself taking command of the situation.

After the departure of Vicky Malins he had given up the lease of the Harley Street flat but, after a quarter of a century with a place in London, he felt lost without a *pied à terre* in the capital. He decided to take a lease on a basement flat in Chapel Street, just off Belgrave Square, as a base for Francis and himself. Francis immediately entered into the spirit of the place. Chapel Street was still redolent with the atmosphere of the Beatles era (only a couple of doors away Brian Epstein had died a few years before) and Francis became a giver of extravagant parties, to which pop stars were invited and often came. The ambience was relaxed, facilitated by drink and surreptitious drug-taking. There were even suspicions about Francis' ageless cat, Miss Orpheus Rose (always known as 'Pussy Balloo' or 'Boo Boo'), perched tenaciously on his arm in a trance-like state. The hippy atmosphere was helped along by such characters as the extrovert, if ageing, Indian poet Tambimutu. Joss-sticks and records of Indian music completed the scene. George took to this tinsel world with caution. He liked to arrive from Bristol to be told that the last person to sit on a certain stool was Yoko Ono. But he was terrified of situations that might get out of hand (and with Francis they often did). George had seen the flat as providing his last chance to be a man-about-town and he did enjoy being invited to lunch by the likes of Cecil Beaton. However, with a wildly self-indulgent character like Francis Rose calling the social shots, George was put distinctly in the shade.

The situation resolved itself in an alarming way. George suddenly found himself with a summons from the owner for non-payment of rent over a period of months. He had been foolishly trusting: he had been giving his share of the flat's rent and expenses to Francis who, instead of adding his own contribution, had been spending the proceeds. As George recalled, this was the one occasion on which he became really nasty with Francis. Francis shrugged his shoulders and revealed that Cecil Beaton had been lecturing him on the same subject. Francis added: 'All that I can say for both of you is that you are being merely middle-class. A man of my position would know how to handle this and not pay.'[5] And handle it he did. He tackled the landlord who, though a barrister by profession, was a central European strangely unfamiliar with the English establishment; he seemed unduly alarmed by Francis' explosion on the subject of his kinship with the Queen Mother (though the connection was only by marriage) and he agreed to drop the summons on the settlement of the debt and a promise that Francis would be out of the flat within a few weeks.

One would have thought that George had learned his lesson by then. On the contrary, he allowed Francis to come down to Bristol for extended visits. What was worse, Boo Boo came too.

George, who had lost his childhood love of cats – indeed, of all animals – found Boo Boo a particularly neurotic and at times vicious feline. If not clinging to Francis' person, she would mysteriously disappear. One night George found himself rushing down Sion Hill in search of the wretched creature. When he reached the bottom, he spotted a cat in the

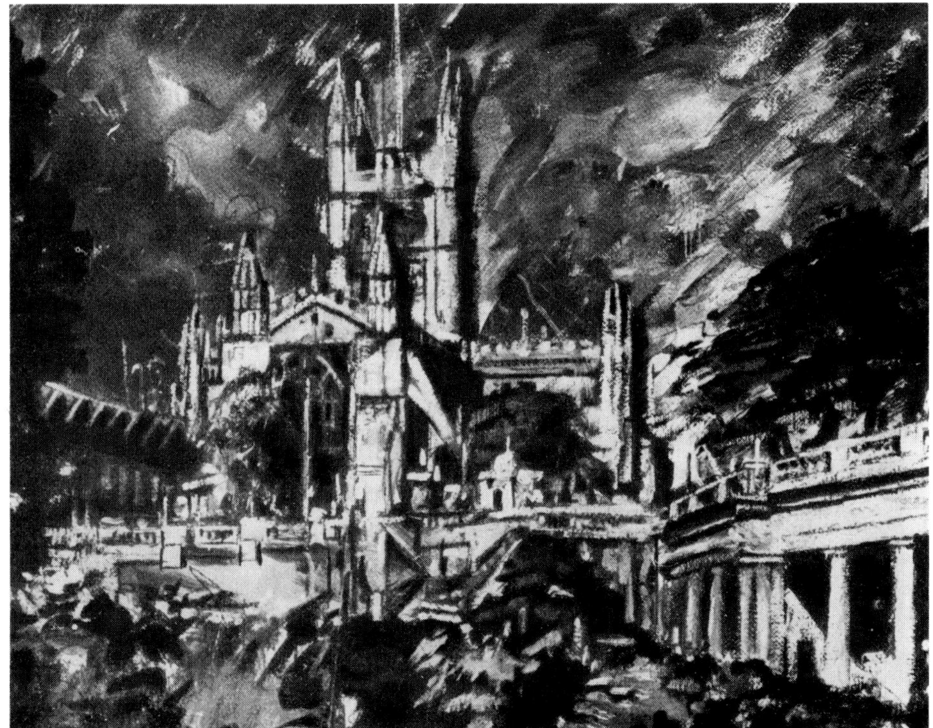
14.   *Bath Abbey after the Blitz, c.* 1942

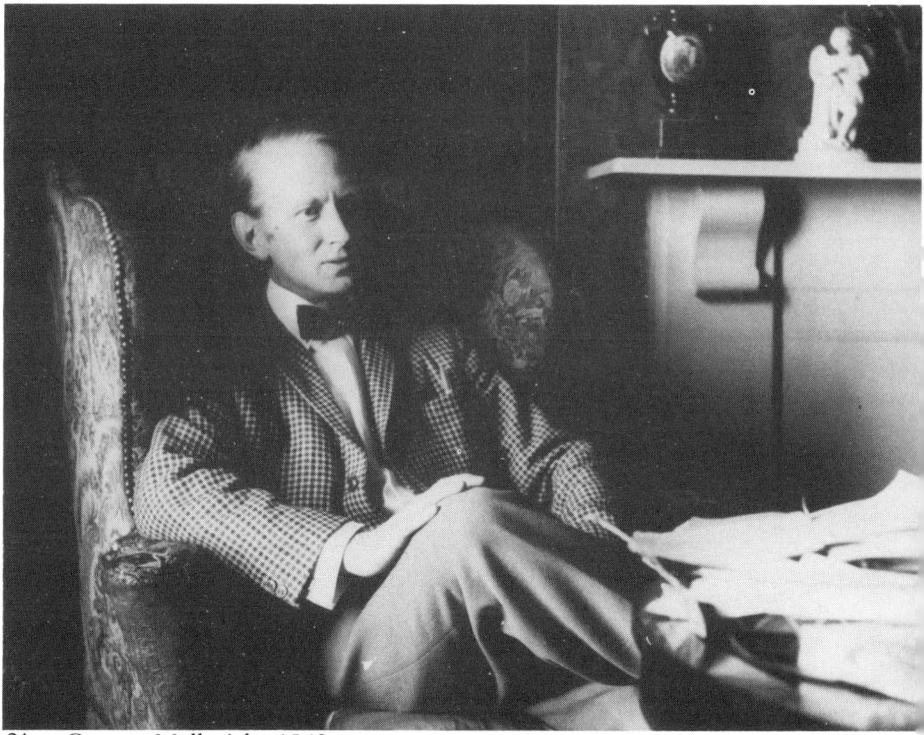

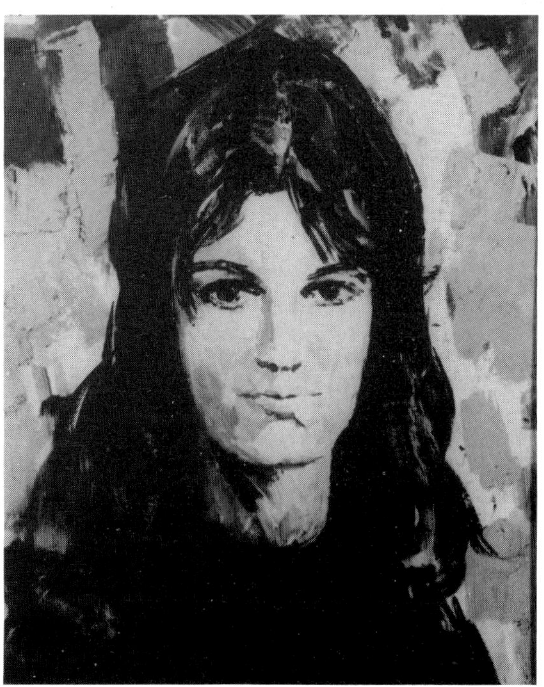

21.   George Melhuish, 1962

22.   *Portrait of Vicky Malins,*
      c. 1965

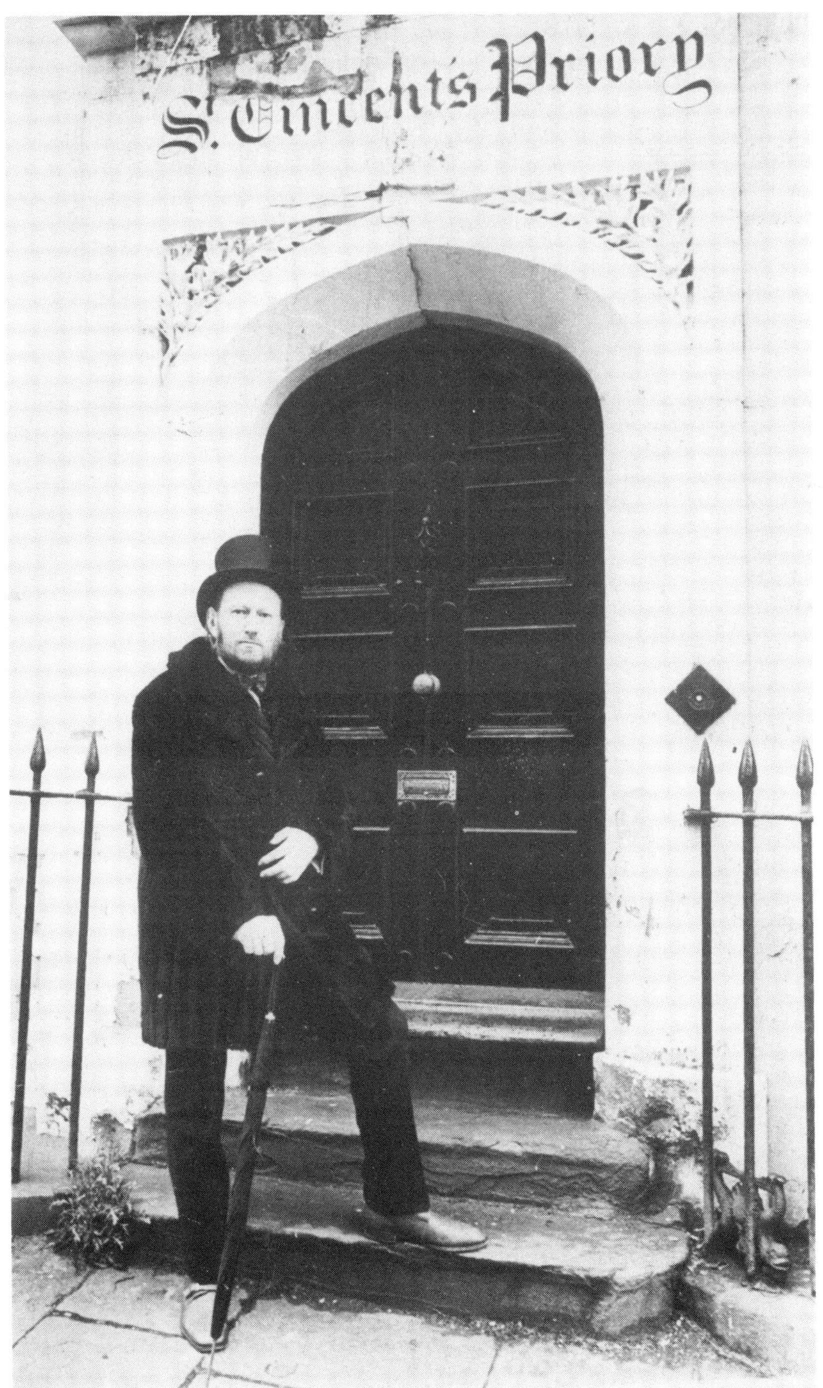

25.   George Melhuish in top hat and coat at the door of St Vincent's
       Priory, 1968

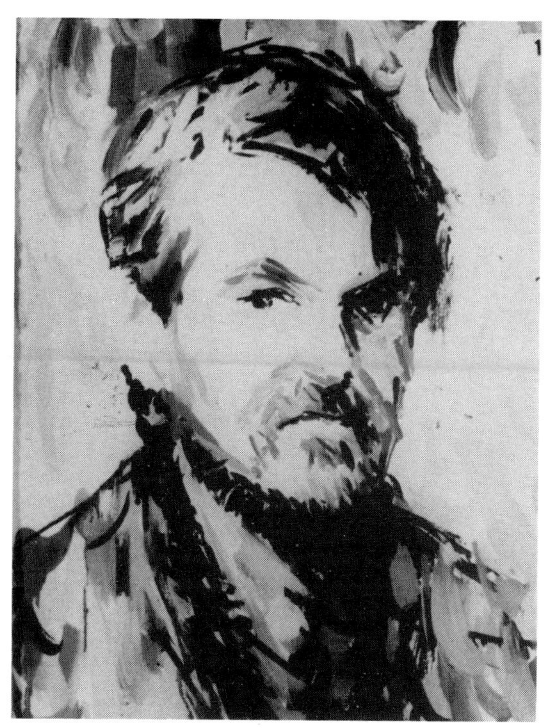

23. *Portrait of Viscount Weymouth, 1973*

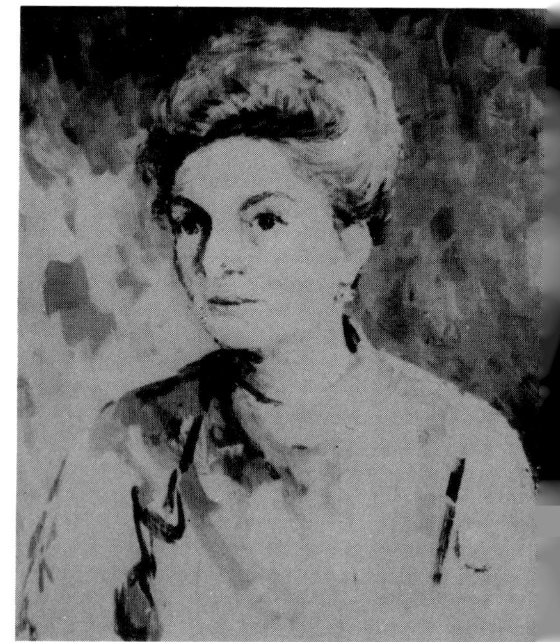

24. *Portrait of Dorian Mogg, 1977*

Paragon and proceeded to stuff it into Boo Boo's cat-box. A formidable woman started to berate him: 'What are you doing with my cat?' Boo Boo, it transpired, had all the time been hiding in an attic cupboard in the Priory. The cat's master was just as bad. George affected a pose as a connoisseur of cognac. Francis was less discriminating about drink, just as long as it was alcoholic and plentiful (which it never was in George's house). George exploded with rage when he realized that Francis had been helping himself from the brandy bottle and topping up the level with water. One wonders if his anger stemmed from a faint inferiority complex that Francis engendered in him. Did he perhaps think that George was not discerning enough to notice that the cognac had been watered? Certainly George put up with more from Francis than from anybody else, although, truth be told, he quite enjoyed having him to stay. He liked the way in which his friends were duly impressed by his title and his charming manner. He enjoyed taking him on motor-car trips to see the sunset at Portishead or to look at the maritime and industrial activities at Avonmouth. Francis always felt relaxed in working-class situations in a way in which George would not allow himself to be.

But the final crisis inevitably came. Francis assiduously curried favour with George and solemnly made out a will entirely in his favour. George was impressed, even though his solicitor, Arthur White, did append a note to the document stating that, since Sir Francis was still under the Court of Protection, having been sectionalized as mentally ill, he was not competent to make such a will. George finally gave up the struggle when Francis became friendly with the 'underground' film director Kenneth Anger. Francis persuaded him to come down to Bristol with their mutual friend, the artist Michael Wishart. One night at George's, when the boredom became too intense to conceal, Francis decided to telephone his old friend Stephen Tennant at Wilsden Manor in nearby Wiltshire. The information that, as a boy, Kenneth Anger had appeared in a film with Shirley Temple was enough to set this Hollywood addict's heart a–flutter and the three men rushed off in response to his instant invitation to stay. George was left behind, puzzled and not a little annoyed. But curiously enough Kenneth Anger did condescend to return to the Priory without Michael Wishart (who found George rather too 'homespun' for his taste). But to George's alarm Francis began to behave very peculiarly; he seemed half-crazed and, when he attempted to 'fly' out of the drawing-room window, it was time to call a doctor. The medic was suspicious and asked if he had been taking hallucinogenic drugs. George confessed a genuine ignorance. Francis was, in fact, seriously ill, but gradually responded to treatment (although to this day his name evokes ripples of alarm in the Montpellier Health Centre where he was treated).

However, this was the end for George. Francis was no longer invited to Bristol. There was some correspondence between the two old friends; and Dom Sylvester Houédard kept George informed of his sorry rake's progress (including a spell in gaol for hitting a priest round the ears with a walking stick). But they did not set eyes on each other again. George had little time to reflect upon the matter as he plunged blindly into yet another crisis.

He rather enjoyed hearing about his friends' domestic vagaries. His new driver, the strikingly beautiful Mrs Marjorie King, would regale him with interesting titbits as she ferried him round in her Jaguar twice a week. A kindly friend, Margaret Walker, who selflessly painted and decorated most of his properties (always with a cigarette in her mouth), had a difficult time of it with her boyfriend, a relaxed jack-of-all-trades from Birmingham (and always known as 'Brummy'). George loved their hippy ways. He enjoyed his smutty conversations with Brummy and probably envied his sexual prowess and inventiveness, but after the couple's marriage they disappeared from the scene in the direction of Wales; not even the bait of the small legacy that he left Margaret in his will tempted them out of obscurity again.

George felt lost as friends successively passed out of his life, and he was prompted to sail blindly into a relationship with a girl still in her late teens. He had first encountered her when she answered one of his advertisements for an 'artist's assistant'. She was never one of George's models because her proportions were not right (as one of her rivals bitchily pointed out, only drawing attention to the fact that the same – and worse – could be said of herself). The girl was there to help him at the easel, but she had no particular talent as an artist. She did, however, have a strikingly powerful singing voice and she happened to come on the scene at precisely the point when he was discovering more and more consolation in music, particularly in opera. He not only caught her up in his fantasies about his composer-heroes, Puccini and Wagner (she quickly adapted herself to the part of his Cosima), but he also encouraged her aspiration to become an opera singer. He paid for her to have lessons with artistes from the Welsh National Opera in Cardiff. But it soon became apparent that, though adequate in decibels, her voice would take years to train. She was a product of the instant-success mentality of the pop era and expected to become a prima donna overnight. She was severely disappointed and took her resentment out on George. In a short time, he realized that she was psychologically unstable, but it did not stop him from parading her around as his current companion at social functions. She was there at his side at the opening of exhibitions. She was taken to luncheon at Longleat with Lord Weymouth (and even he expressed surprise at her habit of bursting unprompted into operatic arias). George took her up to London to stay in Cheyne Walk with his old friend Edna Macdonald, who was faced with the daunting task of catering for his peculiar dietary requirements and rescuing his girlfriend from boredom by spending hours at the piano accompanying her ear-splitting vocalizing. Edna Macdonald, whom she regarded as a rival from the past, was shrewd enough to spot the fundamental problem. The girl was desperate to arouse George. He would not, or rather could not respond, while making the matter worse by using his skills to work her up into a state of excitement. It is difficult to decide which of the two was more to blame for what subsequently happened. Edna Macdonald could see trouble on the horizon and categorically forbade George to bring her to visit again.

George and the girl staggered from one argument to the next, but the relationship survived for about four years until, eventually, in the autumn of 1974, it collapsed. George had to be taken to stay at the house of John James and his wife Mary in Northumbria Drive, Henleaze. Once there, his metabolism proved to be so badly affected by the emotional stress that he became seriously ill. The Jameses imagined that a couple of weeks would see him on his feet again and be sufficient time to let the girl realize that attempts to make contact were futile. But George stayed on throughout the winter months, his hosts struggling to keep him supplied with the special foodstuffs and luxury fruit that he demanded, while he paid them only the merest pittance for his board. Finally George was persuaded to return to the Priory in the spring of 1975, chastened by his experience but none the wiser for it, as his subsequent friendships proved. What is remarkable is that through this stormy episode of his life, as he was approaching the age of sixty and in delicate health, he was in top creative form both as an artist and as a philosopher.

CHAPTER TWENTY-TWO

THE NATURE OF ABSTRACTS AND REALITY

Some of George's friends felt that his life as an artist diminished during the late 1960s and early 1970s. His philosophical and emotional involvements were distracting; his business activities were more lucrative than hard graft at the easel. But the assumption was only partly true. He continued to paint; indeed he began to produce larger canvases than ever before, and he was still keen to have his work exhibited, although he now had no need of the income from sales. In 1968 his thoughts had strayed again in the direction of Paris and a show at the Galerie Mouffe. Instead he contented himself with exhibiting regularly at the Royal West of England Academy's annual exhibition. Between 1965 and 1973 he only missed the opportunity once – in 1969 – to exhibit one or more pictures. However, in 1971, he decided to relaunch himself spectacularly on the artistic public with a one-man exhibition.

Though still not a member of the Academy, he persuaded the committee to mount a show. The fact that the ground floor of the building was given over to a separate exhibition by the young New Zealand sculptor John Panting did not make George's show any less of a solo effort. Indeed, a friend, the fine-art dealer David Cross, who did his framing for him, was amused by George's comment that there was such an amount of wall space that he would have to paint some more large canvases – which he promptly did, working with extraordinary vigour, despite the fact that he was 'really quite frail'.[1] The only significant help that he enlisted was from Patrick Hughes, who wrote a fine introduction to a well-produced catalogue. This subtly combined a biographical and analytical discussion of George as both artist and philosopher. If the Bristol public still failed to appreciate his achievements, they now had no excuse for ignorance. The exhibition's opening took place on 22 April 1971 and attracted a curiously mixed assembly of guests. Old friends, like Percy Edgell, with his daughter Rosemary, Edna Macdonald, the incongruous 'girl' and her friends; establishment figures like Robert Cook, the eminent surgeon and father of the local MP Robin Cook; and Patrick Hughes with his new wife, the eye-catching novelist with so many *succès de scandale* to her credit, Molly Parkin. The only problem was that few of the groups knew each other and even the party held afterwards at the Priory would have been a more relaxed affair if George had served more than just thimble-size glasses of ordinary wine.

The show itself was so impressive that it could not fail to be successful. The distinguished art critic, James Belsey, wrote about it in the *Bristol Evening Post*. Explaining how George had overcome technical problems through his adoption of a favourite Edwardian table knife as a palette knife, he indicated that the result was 'a series of very large energetic pictures'[2] painted over the period from 1965 until the moment that the show opened its doors in April 1971. Belsey explained:[3]

> The knife has given a great deal of freedom with big slabs of oil paint in clear, uncluttered compositions. Melhuish has only recently taken the plunge into using these very large canvases and it's been a completely successful venture. His colours are interesting and bright and he has found a simplicity which his earlier works lacked.

There were earlier, small, more intricately-worked canvases in the show and they were 'well-made and certainly worth seeing, but the new pictures are definitely the best in the show'.[4] One agrees with Belsey. George's big canvases composed of large planes of subtle colours in effective combinations represented his splendid lingering sunset as an abstract artist. This was possibly more generally prophetic of the end of a rich period of pure abstraction.

The Bristol show made such an impression that a selection of canvases was shown as a separate exhibition between 5 February and 11 March 1972 in Gloucester. This was not as simple a matter as might be supposed, if only from the logistical point of view. 'Blackboy' in the *Bristol Evening Post* published a little piece whose title told all: 'Art by the acre'. The writer explained: 'Some of the largest pictures ever painted by Bristol artist George Melhuish have just been carried into the Gloucester City Museum and Art Gallery. Quite a chore this for the removal men,

since some of the canvases measure eight feet by six feet.'[5] One wonders
if that were the only hazard for the removal men. Apparently he had
completed a few of the paintings only two weeks beforehand. Was the
paint dry? Perhaps so. As he explained to the local newspaper, *The
Citizen*, he had employed a specially developed oil-wash technique
involving oils thinned down to the texture of water-colours. Then he
would set to with his famous palette knife in order to give his paintings 'a
very marked depth and texture'.[6] It was a style that he had discovered
years back during the heyday of his architectural painting.

Highly necessary for an audience perhaps unfamiliar with abstract art
was *The Citizen*'s explanation of the correlation between the process of
execution and the titles of George's work:[7]

> Melhuish will start with a very rough theme; develop it and eventually
> arrive at a title, though as he says, the title is not meant to influence the
> observer's interpretation. He believes the technical qualities of all his
> works should become apparent on closer inspection. 'Paintings can be
> no more impressive than the quality of paint used.'

And the art-loving citizens of Gloucester were given five weeks in which
to make up their own minds.

This was effectively the end of his public career as an artist. Later that
year he had one of his works exhibited at the Royal West of England
Academy and a year later, in October 1973, he made one final submission to the annual exhibition, *Orange and Black*. Although he continued
to paint sporadically, he made no more efforts to show the results in
public, except when visitors came to the Priory and could appreciate
them in a domestic setting. The reason was simple: apart from finding
the physical effort of painting difficult to sustain, he was largely
preoccupied with his philosophical work.

His second book, *The Paradoxical Nature of Reality*, was finished in draft
by the end of 1968 but, because of difficulties in interesting main-line
commercial publishers in what was an immensely scholarly and intellectually taxing work, the problem of how and where it should be
published was considerable. He turned to Patrick Hughes for advice.
Hughes suggested that, in order to avoid further delays and the distinct
danger of his ideas being purloined in the meantime, he should have it
published in Bristol. There were considerable advantages to being one's
own master. Patrick warned him against paying any attention to the
snob-value attached to securing 'a respectable imprint'. He added:
'Publishing your book yourself is not an act of indulgent egoism on the
part of a lady nature poet; it's what you have to do considering the

climate of opinion.'[8] However, although it was a simple task to create the St Vincent's Press and engage the Stonebridge Press as printers, the whole process of editing, typesetting and (inevitably) amending proofs took a surprisingly long time until final publication in December 1973. Even then, what he would have done without the long-suffering Percy Edgell as his proof-reader and the equally faithful Margaret Granger as his typist is hard to imagine.

The book was a handsome piece of production work. George felt justifiably proud of it and confident about launching it upon the public. As a publicist he remarkably managed to boil down his ideas sufficiently to convince potential readers that his work was 'the definitive book of a revolutionary metaphysics'.[9] He started from the claim that 'reality is at base energetic and paradoxical'. This had been put forward by Heraclitus and later by Hegel. However, he claimed, 'despite obvious relevance to contemporary scientific investigation, modern philosophy has lacked a philosophy of change'.[10] His work was designed to rectify this omission. His aim was to repudiate the static central position of standard logic. He was concerned about the way in which many people ordinarily operated on the basis of a series of imperatives: 'Whenever we . . . define things particularly at dogmatic level we use identity and so bring into play the tautological system.'[11] He was determined to demonstrate something different:[12]

> The innate flux of the experiential moment demands that we disclose the non-tautological system of logic. Paradoxically energetic process is used as the basis for the non-tautological foundations . . . The aim of the new metaphysics is not to offer a facility for further dogmatic illustration of the world, but to render interim and paradoxical all dogmatic ideas and selective truths made available by orthodox tautological logic.

What George was intent on doing was describing 'an entirely novel cosmology' introducing the 'idea of universe in virtue of never less than a double significance; incorporating the finite world of the universe that is selective with the infinite world of the universe which is non-selective'.[13] He argued that a fundamental philosophical and empirical error of cosmology had been made in inferring that, 'since the universe comprises particular constituents, it itself is something particular'. He was concerned to turn attention away from 'dogmatic cosmology to a discipline wherein each representation of the circumscribed world implies actuality only in consequence of the uncircumscribed world.' And he concluded his argument: 'The selective universe is necessary because it contains only some things, but the non-selective universe is necessary *because of there being nothing which it does not contain.*'[14]

George stimulated interest by announcing that the final section of his book was devoted to 'an original representation of experiential immortality'. He drew attention to 'a surprising complimentarity regarding experience, whereby its individuation and mortality are ever opposed by its non-individuation. The pulsation of the experiential matrix involves always some subject-matter but pulsation itself is never reliant for its initial force upon any one particular category of subject-matter and this implies that no one category of subject-matter interferes with, or modifies, the energetic basis of the experiential continuum.'[15]

John Walker was quick off the mark in penning a substantial review for the March 1974 number of *Studio International*. He explained for the reader that George, though fascinated by the Hegelian dialectic, rejects any concept of a final category: he 'argues that we should accept the paradox of the law of identity and the rest of orthodox logic (which he calls the Tautological System) being extended to include the non-static anti-identity logical order of his Non-Tautological System'.[16] It was the synthesis of these apparently contradictory systems, the Tautological and the Non-Tautological, that produced what George called the 'Paradoxically Energetic State'. 'His logic of change is completed by a similar analysis of time into the Particular Time of sequence and the Basic Time of the primordial flux.'[17] What readers might find intriguing was George's culminating section on 'dreams and hallucinatory states'. They are 'considered as phenomena of the non-selective universe and finally a concept of immortality is outlined on the basis of a dissolution of the dogmatically unambiguous view of personal identity'.[18]

As an international journal of modern art, *Studio* was addressed to a predominently artistic audience, and John Walker made a perceptive observation:[19]

Without denying his originality, it is strange that, although in relation to current British philosophy Melhuish seems to be an outsider, in relation to twentieth-century art, even to British art of the post-war period, his viewpoint appears much less unorthodox, since paradox and ambiguity are commonplace in art and literature of the modern movement.

But, he warned potential readers, although George did briefly deal with art in his earlier book, *The Paradoxical Universe*, the new work did not. However, Walker did point out that 'the present work acknowledges the enthusiasm of Patrick Hughes for the ideas expressed, and the hard-edged ambiguities of that painter's work parallel Melhuish's attempt to define the indeterminate in logical terms'.[20]

The Paradoxical Nature of Reality attracted much attention in the French scholarly press and Alain de Benoist, an old acquaintance of George's mentioned him and his work in an article on Stéphane Lupasco in *Valeurs Actuelles* in September 1974. But it was the review by Robert Blanché that appeared in the prestigious *Revue Philosophique* in June 1975 that was something of an accolade. Again he explained George's basic thesis and his rejection of the orthodox principles of logic with the assertion that 'in order to define the pure change inherent in the continuum of experience, we need both to confirm and to abrogate the standard principles of logic and in doing so *we create new logical principles*'.[21] His central aim was to demonstrate that 'the Tautological System can never cover more than half of the logic that we need to take into account, and it is my aim to show the other half of the logical coin may be developed only in virtue of an entirely novel logical matrix'.[22] Blanché's review was on the whole sympathetic, but some of George's conclusions clearly left him puzzled: 'With respect to cosmological antinomies, he declares that one must admit at one and the same time that the universe is finite and that it is infinite, but he also says that in these two propositions the word universe ought not to be understood in the same sense: is it then paradox, or contradiction?'[23]

Eric Toms's review of George's book in *Leonardo, the International Journal of the Contemporary Artist* did not appear until the spring of 1975, but it was worth waiting for. Toms provided the usual sketch introduction to the three stages of George's argument through his consideration of Zeno's paradox of motion towards the conclusion that 'motion and change are of such a nature as to elude the tautological system'. Second, George showed that 'an unchanging experience is unintelligible . . . Experience, like change, cannot be understood in terms of the tautological system.' And George's final conclusion was that 'the non–tautological system is needed for understanding experience'.[24]

Eric Toms showed a particular critical interest in his views on the individual in relation to survival. He explained on his behalf:[25]

Experience cannot finally depend for its existence upon an individual entity (e.g. the brain). There can be no final allotment of experience to individual persons. All negation of individuals by death inevitably falls within experience as a whole. Again it is not through the survival of any individual through an infinite future that immortality is feasible but only through the nature of unindividualized experience itself. Experience is undivided and eternal.

Toms did, however, pose an apposite question: 'But does the argument about survival apply when one takes into account the possibility of an individual's unlimited power of growth and adaption?'[26]

In case anybody happened to gain the impression that he was criticizing George's basic thesis, Toms ended with what, for a highly restrained and careful scholar, was an enthusiastic endorsement:[27]

> In my opinion this is a work of great originality and force, opening the way to fascinating investigations for the future. The author has convincingly supported the thesis that a paradoxical reality underlies experience and has developed the conception of energetic paradox with remarkable power. I am left with a strong desire to pursue the analysis of paradox further and to seek explanations of further aspects of human experience in terms of paradox.

Eric Toms' approval was important because, although with this work George had learned from the earlier lesson of casting too wide a net in the direction of prominent individuals likely to be sympathetic to his thesis, he did send out a limited number of copies to potentially interested individuals. But, again, friends and strangers alike tended to confess to problems of comprehension. William McRea had recently published an article in *Cosmology Now*. It had attracted George's attention and prompted him to send a copy of his book to him at the Astronomy Centre of the University of Sussex. Professor McRea pleaded that he was not a professional philosopher and simply did not know the language: 'When your book arrived, I tried to understand it without much success. Now I have tried again, with no better success.'[28] However, the fact he commented that 'some philosophers go astray by assuming that there is logic where logic is non-existent'[29] might indicate that he was not far from some form of appreciation of George's position.

From a farming community in Monmouthshire, Philip Toynbee wrote to say that he was having 'to concentrate ferociously on books with titles like *Goat Husbandry*, leaving the philosophy to look after itself for the time being'.[30] However, he had clearly made enough of an effort to tackle the book to confess that he often found it very hard going. But, he added, 'what did get through to me made me feel that you have written a very remarkable work; and one to which due attention will one day be paid'. He suggested that George should not be discouraged if the critics neglected him. He added: 'I feel sure that this marks an important stage in the coming revolt against the whole positivist tradition, at least in its present narrow form.'[31]

However, experience had also taught George that, despite his over-whelming desire for instant success and recognition, some of the most valuable appreciation of his work came from individuals who just happened to stumble across it by chance. And, indeed, over the next decade he received letters of genuine enthusiasm from discerning readers from the four corners of the earth. This convinced him that he must forge ahead with his plans for the ultimate exposition of his thesis in the form of another book, already endowed with the descriptive title of *Death and the Double Meaning of Nothingness.*

CHAPTER TWENTY-THREE

THE SEIGNEUR AND THE SAGE

The ultimate manifestation of George's illusions of grandeur was his opening St Vincent's Priory to the public as if it were a miniature stately home. He had already tried to project the house's image as a unique piece of Bristol architecture. As early as February 1969, Sir Francis Rose obliged him by penning an article, published in *Art and Antiques Weekly*, in which the glories of the building and its furnishings were extolled. (One wonders what Francis really thought about it because, despite his down-at-the-heel existence, he had a highly developed sense of aesthetics.) When in 1973 Bristol decided to celebrate the 600th anniversary of the granting of its charter, George added a guided tour of the Priory to the city's list of celebratory events. He did the thing in style. He had a glossy guide published. (After all, ordinary visitors being charged twenty-five pence expected to be told what they were there to appreciate.) He had posters printed announcing that the Priory would stay open between 2 and 14 July. He launched the venture by giving two parties, on 3 and 10 July, for guests specially selected for their closeness or their prettiness. The press seemed constantly on hand to recórd George's doings, not always with the most elegant of results. Miss Nikki Barrett was photographed sitting, her legs tucked up under her on George's favourite chair (once upon a time the Duke of Wellington's favourite chair). Alas, the photograph in the *Bristol Evening Post* on 7 July showed little of the Priory and massive amounts of Miss Barrett's exposed thighs. As a one-off event the opening of the Priory was seen as a quaint gesture of civic pride. But when, two years later, George decided to open the building each summer to stray visitors, many of his oldest friends thought it bordering on the outrageous, and even more so since he invariably fanfared each new season with assiduously curried publicity. In July 1975 Charles Lines produced an article in the smart social magazine *Gloucestershire and Avon Life*, quite a prestigious achievement despite the fact that the author confessed to having made a truistic gaffe as soon as he arrived to see the house: ' "It's like a lighthouse!" I exclaimed, not realizing that this was about the most unoriginal remark I had made in my life, for I gather that every other visitor says precisely the same thing.'[1] His repentance did not restrain him from giving his article the title 'Clifton's "Upstairs-Downstairs" House'.

In the *Western Daily Press* on 30 July 1975, Harry Smith mentioned his teasing George by suggesting that he was 'trying to get his foot in the door of the stately homes business'. He laughed deprecatingly, but relished it as a compliment and revealed that he did 'take some pride in the fact that his is possibly the smallest private house in the country open to the public'.[2]

Whether the experience left visitors impressed, bemused or shuddering, George himself found that he had attracted some valuable new acquaintances. One of the more significant contacted him in October 1973, having missed the brief 'open season' in July, and was invited for a private view. Andrew Rogers, an art student from Weston-super-Mare and later an artist's model employed by the County of Avon's educational department, achieved an instant rapport with George. Like him, Andrew had a passionate interest in art, antiques and history. They both enjoyed biographies – and social gossip. Andrew kept George supplied with mountains of the kind of newspaper that had a regular page devoted to regaling readers with the choicest titbits of current society scandal. The sort of thing that had made George Ward-Jackson shudder with disapproval, George Melhuish relished it as if vicariously participating. Very soon he became dependent upon Andrew for other forms of help. He developed the routine of visiting the Priory at least twice and sometimes three times a week, often during his lunch break while modelling in Bristol. Since George refused to employ a daily cleaning woman (not because he could not afford one, but because he had no desire for an 'alien' presence in the house), Andrew found himself doing the basic housework, washing, cleaning and vacuuming – with an antiquated and ineffective Hoover that George refused to replace. And, soon after their first meeting, when George fell seriously ill, Andrew found himself cast in the role of nurse while he returned slowly to health. Andrew was uncomplaining in shouldering what was a considerable physical burden of work, to the extent of doing handyman jobs around the Priory, as well as painting and decorating its interior and those of many of George's other properties in Clifton.

Andrew Rogers had another 'hobby'. He was a passionate genealogist and monarchist and had the habit of corresponding with the noble and famous. Now that the Priory was part of his everyday existence, he set about publicizing it in exalted circles. Lord Weymouth, Yehudi Menuhin and Lord Snowdon found themselves presented with information about the building. They all responded courteously and in Weymouth's case the correspondence continued. As a painter of great originality, and something of a philosopher in his own right as founder of the Wessex Party, the highly colourful viscount, with his eye-catching clothes and his spectacular head of pleated hair, recognized a fellow eccentric in the form of George and responded to the suggestion that he might paint his portrait. He was duly invited to lunch at his genuine stately home at Longleat and immediately a bantering friendship grew up between them. George did, indeed, do preliminary work for a portrait study and, after another sitting, finished off at his own leisure a striking expressionistic study of Weymouth, his hair in a pony-tail and a ferocious look in his eye. It is a fine piece of work but, strangely, an oil sketch that George did of him, with his hair flowing free and his face turned slightly to reveal his stunning profile, is almost better as a work of art.

A number of invitations to Longleat followed. In the summer of 1974 Lord and Lady Weymouth gave a huge, lavish and glittering party to celebrate the 'baptism' of their two children. George was invited and arrived with Andrew Rogers and the 'girl' in a car driven by the faithful John James. George was in a grand, affected mood and told James that, as the driver, he must stay with the car. James was taken aback and, as he watched his trio of passengers disappear in the direction of the house, he made a bee-line for the marquee which, he discovered, was groaning with a lush buffet, awash with champagne and knee-deep in familiar personalities from the world of the arts and show business. James had a wonderful, sociable time and thought no more about George and his entourage. A few hours had passed when he spotted them again, huddled in the corner of the tent and looking very miserable. George announced that he wanted to go home. James was surprised because it was only about three o'clock in the afternoon and the party was scheduled to continue well into the night. James explained that, since he had had a few drinks, it would not be safe for him to drive for at least a couple of hours. He had assumed that they would stay a lot longer and he would have adequate time for his alcohol level to drop. George just grunted. He was clearly annoyed at the inconvenience, but was even more upset at the thought of being driven thirty miles back to Bristol by an over-the-limit driver. James shrugged his shoulders: for once he was in command and George could do nothing about it.

The incident is very revealing of George's character. He was seldom comfortable at social gatherings where he was not the absolute centre of attention or where he was not calling the shots. In fact, he much preferred situations where he could enjoy the company of friends face to face. The astonishing thing is that in his final years he attracted to the Priory a series of regular guests, old friends and new. Invariably they had their own regular visiting times: Deborah Jones, Barbara Thorne, Percy Edgell, his neighbours Jack and Esmé White, his curious friend Norman from his distant pacifist past and a number of others including regular visitors who came to work for him. Marjorie King had a regular arrangement and Alec Hodges, a highly practical businessman, tacitly drove for him and gave him invaluable help with his properties. However, the amazing thing is that George was expert at contriving to keep this constant stream of visitors apart. They seldom, if ever, met each other. He also had a habit of keeping his friends to himself by avoiding alluding to them by name and, if so, invariably in some circumlocutory fashion: Andrew Rogers was always referred to as 'my friend from Weston-super-Mare', joining Sir A.J. Ayer whom he (this time affectedly) insisted upon calling 'dear old Freddy'. George was certainly proprietorial in his attitude towards his friends. The only unfortunate thing was that the less discerning of them imagined that they were the sole focal point of his existence and that, as he (or rather she) floated in to see him perhaps one or two evenings a week, George had been aching with loneliness waiting to enjoy his (or rather her) company. It was all part of his manipulative approach to other people. Alas, it proved to have its tragic side when certain individuals convinced themselves that theirs was a special relationship. Nothing could be further from the truth. Lord Weymouth had a shrewder eye than most for George's game of friendship, mainly because, apart from one visit to the Priory when he risked George's providing lunch, he was always in charge as host at Longleat. He enjoyed these private visits and responded well to his inevitable philosophical expositions. He felt a certain sympathy with his ideas on paradox and contradiction. But he was perceptive enough to realize that his philosophical theories were so highly worked out before being allowed a public airing that no dialectical argument (and still less a casual discussion) stood any chance of altering his position.

Apart from Anthony Hill, Patrick Hughes was the one person who could tease out George's ideas in a constructive way. Otherwise George simply pontificated. Patrick also did more than most to propagandize his work. Quite apart from seeing that *The Paradoxical Nature of Reality* was reviewed in *Studio*, he encouraged George to construct an interview with him. Originally this was intended for publication in *Studio*. The dialogue was designed to introduce his ideas, in as simple a fashion as possible, to an audience with an intellectual interest in modern art. Even then it proved to be over-ambitious, but it does remain as a valuable exploration of George's ideas. He explained his fundamental position, outlining the historical basis for his theories of paradox, and then continued, explaining his philosophy of change:[3]

> Ever since the significance of change presented itself to me as a real problem, I found myself considering it in relation to the totally surprising evanescence of our perceptual moment. Investigation of the logical difficulties involved in outlining the state of change caused me early to realize that flux and movement had never received adequate logical definition. At first, the paradox involved in defining change seemed obscure, but I was soon persuaded that my notion regarding *energetic* paradox was the central key to our philosophical understanding.

For an audience of art lovers the basic claim of such a thesis might, at first glance, have hinted at problems. The medium of art (except perhaps in its more adventurous mobile form) tends to freeze the perceived moment and, therefore, arrests objects in motion. However, most would have realized that human perception had a vital part to play: one never looks at the same picture in exactly the same way twice, just as one cannot step twice into Heraclitus' river. And this was precisely the direction in which Patrick led the interview, since he himself, as an artist, was heavily preoccupied with the representation of the philosophy of flux in visual terms. The work of Magritte and Duchamp automatically came to mind. Patrick suggested that they[4]

> both have a high degree of contradiction in their work, and it seems to me that an art of paradox could only be achieved through the use of figuration. I also understood that splashing the colours about in a state of flux was not necessarily the best way to propose a philosophy of flux. Magritte's careful representation of metamorphoses, of states of change, seem to me more successful.

The interview, one feels, was a by-product not only of George's recently published book, but also of Patrick's work with the Cologne-based American artist, George Brecht, on literary and artistic paradoxes. Published in London in 1976 under their joint-authorship, *Vicious Circles and Infinity. A Panoply of Paradoxes* explained their purpose. They had 'no particular axe to grind'. They wanted others to share their own enjoyment of verbal and visual paradoxes. And they certainly succeeded in illustrating that 'one of the bonds between the authors of this book is a sense of humour; perhaps paradoxes should be seen in this light'.[5] Their starting point was a quotation from Samuel Butler: 'There is only one thing certain; and therefore it is not certain that we can have nothing certain.'[6] The whole book is so sparkling with the wit of paradox that one is slightly taken aback by its final pages where the authors talk about the tradition of philosophers who had embraced paradox, and a serious note of scholarly meditation followed hard on the heels of the outrageous Alfred Jarry's explanation of 'pataphysics' or the laws governing exceptions. Quotations from Nicholas of Cusa's *De Docta Ignorantia* of 1444 were rounded off by a six-page piece specially written for *Vicious Circles* by George. Although his submission lacks any of the humour of the rest of the book, it is clear that, through judicious encouragement, he was becoming more adept at communicating his ideas to a public wider than just specialist *cognoscenti*. He explained his position:[7]

> In order to define the innate flux of things, it is necessary to state a fundamental paradox and to say that what is the same as itself is in self-modification, whereby it is not the same as itself, for any less paradoxical operation will commit us to the acceptance of a merely static identity and this will imply that different things will not need to be in a state of change in order not to be the same . . . In fact we must break completely with the long-standing logical tradition based upon the unambiguous nature of identity and its legislation by the law of non-contradiction.

And it was George Brecht who took the matter further. He was already a fan of George's work and George had become used to his Brechtian mode of expression. In June 1975 a postcard arrived at the Priory: 'I am still dreaming on your book. In revery [sic] I have considered mixing all ashes with all dreams, dissolving them in aqua pure and (re)-distilling them.'[8] He clearly did more than dream about George's book because the following month he began writing a letter full of highly detailed and learned observations on paradox. Brecht's erudition showed through in the sources to which he almost casually alluded: Heisenberg and Gödel, Aquinas, Jung and Koestler, with a bit of Taoist thought for good measure. Brecht did not finish the letter until February 1976, by which time he felt it necessary to enclose it in a second letter and to reiterate his admiration for George: 'You have encouraged me very much. George – the spirit of Zeno, Heraclitus, Nicholas of Cusa, is not dead – and I thank you for it.'[9] He followed up his compliment by having the piece that George wrote for *Vicious Circles* republished in 1976 in an avant-garde anthology of art, poetry and philosophy in Malmö in Sweden. And two years later, when he was tempted over to visit George at the Priory, he seemed intent on encouraging Vieweg Verlag, the German publishers of *Vicious Circles*, to publish *The Paradoxical Nature of Reality* in German. Nothing seems to have come of the suggestion, but George was clearly delighted by this form of international recognition. He was already attracting considerable attention from individuals, invariably strangers who wrote to him out of the blue.

As early as December 1973, Macmillan Educational Corporation wrote to him saying that, in the 1974 edition of *Collier's Encyclopedia* they were considering including 'a section of "the new metaphysics", referring to the anti-positivistic, anti-linguistic trend in contemporary philosophy.'[10] They were interested in including something on George and his latest work. The reverse side of the coin was that the St Vincent's Press received suggestions relating to off-beat works that it might consider publishing. In November 1975 a letter arrived from a Dr J.G. Thieme (a United Nations consultant in Menton). He had learned of the publication of George's 'controversial and thought-provoking book' and wondered if the press might be 'interested in another controversial and topical subject: the problem of human ideologies and dogmas. I have dealt with it in a just-finished study: *The Ideological Ape. An Inquiry into the Roots of Intolerance.*'[11] George may have found intriguing some of the anatomical details in the summary that Dr Thieme sent him, but there could be no question of the St Vincent's Press blossoming forth as a truly commercial company.

The United States provided a series of interested enquiries about George's work, most of them displaying a flattering appreciation of his ideas. (Indeed, he once remarked that only four people in the whole world understood his work and one of them lived in America. No name was revealed. No matter: George was deliberately selling himself short as a form of inverse intellectual snobbery.) Some of his correspondents seemed to grasp his philosophy as the ultimate haven for the troubled psyche. A Dr K.A. Latchford told him that, having finished his doctorate on the evolution of the wave theory of light, he had run away to a monastery 'to have an "intellectual" collapse'. He explained: 'Many things had come together to prove to me that the logical, rational world (which includes most religious orthodoxies) just isn't the whole story . . . Something was very wrong, and my own research simply showed that it was not only wrong, but very hypocritical and dangerous.'[12] Extensive study of recent New Testament scholarship based more or less on an acceptance of 'the sayings of someone called Jesus' had caused him to review and start rewriting his research, and he informed George: 'I . . . came up with an interpretation that is not entirely different from your own.'[13]

This kind of questing approach with a serious compulsion to fit God into the world of paradox was not untypical of the responses provoked by George. Most who had not read the final (and very explicit) pages of *The Paradoxical Universe* speculated on his own theological position – with amusing results. Only two months before his death, he received a letter from Pennsylvania from the designer and author Charles Wood. The contents were almost predictable and a final PPS posed four biographical questions, among them: 'Are you a priest or a pastor?' and 'What religious implications are there to your philosophy?'[14] George was considerably more charmed, but probably no less amused by the approach of a highly intelligent final-year undergraduate from the University of Sussex. Julie Norman graduated in June 1979 and then went on to Cambridge to tackle a research degree in divinity. But, already inspired by George's work, she had written an article on Nicholas of Cusa and had completed a highly polished extended essay entitled 'Coleridge, Burke and Kant: the Significance of Synthesis as a Metaphor'. With anything literary George was out of his depth. Coleridge was scarcely a familiar author; Burke was not one of his sources of inspiration, and Kant occupied only an 'ancestral' position in respect of the nineteenth-century Hegelian position. But his eye could not fail to be arrested by the exposition of the theme: 'What we have to deal with is an apparent contradiction on the rational level over and against the simple acceptance of an intuitive and imaginative understanding; for reason alone detects paradox and the paradox beyond the paradox is that ultimately there is no paradox.'[15] George was paid the compliment of having the first (lengthy) footnote devoted to himself and his 'concept of a paradoxically energetic state within the matrix of pure change in our experience'.[16]

The irony of the agnostic George as the guide on the road towards theocentric interpretations of life and all its complexities must have amused him, but, by this time, he had himself become highly dependent upon his friend the Benedictine monk, Dom Sylvester Houédard, as a source of dialectical stimulation. His friend Anthony Hill wondered if this were not an attempt at some form of 'Catholic hijacking', but almost the contrary was true. To conventional Catholic eyes it was Dom Sylvester who appeared to stray from the paths of orthodoxy, as his fascination with the monastic ideal as a universal phenomenon led him to explore oriental (and particularly Buddhist) interpretations of the physical and spiritual worlds. But George's reaction to these religious fixations on the part of his various 'disciples' and admirers was one of detachment. He was well on the way to evolving his final philosophical theory, and (to use Lord Weymouth's telling simile) nothing was going to move the favourite doll from the precise position chosen for it by him.

CHAPTER TWENTY-FOUR

THE END OF EMPIRE

Old friendships meant a great deal to George in his declining years and, generally speaking, he expected them to revolve round himself. He seldom visited anybody except his closest neighbours. The one exception was Charmian Deckers. Until the beginning of the 1970s she and her daughter Nina had a base at Bath and he would make the journey to see them. He was invited for Christmas dinner one year. An old school-friend of Nina's, an exotic and relaxed girl called Christine Jones, was staying and, although they had not previously met, George brought her a bottle of champagne as a present. She was delighted, but he was furious when she insisted on drinking it as a cocktail mixed with advocaat. She was just as surprised when, instead of sharing the roast turkey with the rest of them, he produced a jar of chicken breasts in aspic for himself. But once he had overcome his annoyance at her sacrilege and she had recovered from her astonishment, Christine and George became close friends. She thought him charming and, until his death, she kept a soft spot in her heart for him. She was an artist in her own right and was highly appreciative of his artistic work. As second string to her bow she did an occasional modelling job for Bristol artists. His friend George Sweet, President of the Royal West of England Academy, painted her on a number of occasions. But, strangely, George himself never asked her to model for him: their friendship remained very much at the personal level.

George did have at least one striking model around 1973–4, one of his last periods of painting from life. This was Lucy Irvine, who later emerged as the best-selling author of *Castaway*, the story of her experience of spending a year on an uninhabited desert island, which caught the popular imagination in the early 1980s. She had always led an unconventional, Bohemian life, travelling around Europe and the Middle East, often at great risk to life and limb. Nothing deterred her.

She returned to her base in London, but again found herself afflicted with wanderlust – and ended up in Bristol. As she remarked in her second best-seller, *Runaway*, 'if ever I did any "bumming about", it was that year in Bristol. I twirled a finger on the map of Britain and that was where I landed, exchanging the egg-in-a-storm for a cellar in the student quarter.'[1] The cellar was, in fact, in the then less-than-chic Royal York Crescent in Clifton. She went on to explain what happened next: 'I had to come to Bristol to visit friends and stayed on. But money was very scarce so I got a job as a life model with George Melhuish the artist who lived nearby.'[2] His infamous cards in the newsagent's window had borne fruit again. Lucy apparently found the work agreeable and George equally so: 'He was a lovely man, and very kind. He kept me well supplied with tea and biscuits which was very important – I had to eat.'[3] George and the seventeen-year-old girl developed a warm rapport but, predictably, he took fright when she subsequently found herself in police custody for forcibly entering a former boyfriend's flat and, worse, for cutting herself in the process and bleeding all over his exquisite white carpets. Such stories made headlines, but only after her year as a castaway on a tropical island. He was never averse to having his name linked with the famous, but he was not amused by the way in which the *Bristol Evening Post* sensationalized their association by suggesting that she 'used to pose in the nude for tea and biscuits'.[4] Tea and biscuits and in the nude certainly, but not *for* tea and biscuits. The relationship had been conducted on strictly pecuniary lines, even though both preserved fond memories of each other.

Another famous personality (one who was already well established) brightened his existence in the early 1970s. His 'cousin' Cary Grant made periodic visits to Bristol to see his aged mother and he always stayed at the Avon Gorge Hotel directly opposite the Priory. Knowing of his interest in modern art, George invited him over to see his pictures, but the millionaire superstar had not lost any of his West Country carefulness over money matters and showed no inclination to buy any of his works. Nonetheless, George liked to make great play of their relationship and the sight of the painter and the film star waving greetings to each other across Sion Hill certainly impressed friends and neighbours alike.

One of the neighbours, who had lived round the corner in Caledonia Place since her return to Bristol in 1967, was a personality in her own right – his old friend Deborah Jones. Thursday evening was invariably the time when she was expected to call for a glass of wine and a chat – and occasionally he would cook her a simple dinner of fillet steak. Apart from being a fellow artist of similar standing (if radically different in style), she was intellectually on the same wavelength as him and enjoyed nothing more than one of his set-piece discussions on some fundamental question – such as death. But Deborah had another advantage. While preserving memories of their impoverished days during the war, she, like George, was now comfortably rich and extremely shrewd when it came to business matters. He found it invaluable to be able to discuss finances with her (as he could with nobody else except Barbara Thorne). He was well aware that some of his so-called friends in Bristol were nothing but legacy-hunters and, while under the illusion that he was able to keep them at bay, he very much depended upon the advice of real friends like Deborah who had no ulterior financial motives.

She had another enormous advantage. She was an inveterate and adventurous traveller and George, snugly seated in the Duke of Wellington's armchair, loved to listen to tales of her travels without having to set foot out of the Priory himself. One May, Deborah made the journey of a lifetime across the Soviet Union by the Trans-Siberian Railway. On her return George insisted upon a blow-by-blow account of her odyssey. It was snowing in Krasnoyarsk and throughout Siberia. She explained the consequences:[5]

> The Russian train was so dirty that by the time we got to Irkutsk you would have thought you had been down a coal mine. There was snow through Siberia . . . and they lit the heaters on the train. These terribly clever modern Russians, do you know what they had? Stoves fed with logs. We kept taking logs aboard at various stations in Siberia.

But that was all part of the romance of the experience and the rewards were strange and beautiful: the sight of Irkutsk with its delightful carved wooden houses by the side of Lake Baikal. George loved these tales; he shivered with vicarious delight and drew closer to his one-bar electric fire. How easy it would be for him, Deborah explained, to take a car to Heathrow Airport, step on an aeroplane for Japan and there he could be, in Tokyo, in the exotic East, with a minimum amount of fuss and effort.

The faithful Percy Edgell, whom advancing years had also made into an intrepid traveller, tried to tempt George with tales of how simple and convenient it would be to holiday in Mallorca in winter. Seaside hotels with lifts and resident pharmacists, all modern conveniences were to hand and it would do wonders for his bronchitis. But no, George preferred to endure the rigours of an English winter, despite the fact that he was easily rich enough to own a villa in Mallorca if he felt so inclined. The nearest he came to journeying abroad was intermittent talk about returning to Paris. One feels that after such a lapse of time he might have found that the sparkling new Paris of the post-Gaullist period had lost that familiar down-at-the-heel atmosphere that he associated with his youth. He finally contented himself with travellers' tales and postcards. For somebody who, on principle, did not send postcards (and never sent out Christmas cards), he went through the charade of being deeply offended if friends did not send him colourful cards from distant parts. And he even came to expect the charming little gifts that Deborah brought him back from the other side of the globe.

One of the greatest drawbacks to George's life as a traveller was his adamant refusal to fly. He never set foot in an aeroplane in the whole of his life; he was terrified of the thought. In fact, as he grew older, anything that threatened to prise him away from familiar surroundings was avoided. In October 1979 a party from the Irish Georgian Society, headed by the Hon. Desmond Guinness, came by special arrangement to see the Priory. What they thought of the place one cannot tell, but Guinness certainly paid George the compliment of pressing him to come over to the Republic of Ireland to stay with him at Leixlip Castle in County Kildare. He declined as graciously as he could. It was only two months since Earl Mountbatten's murder at Mullaghmore in County Sligo, and he seriously saw himself as next in line for a terrorist bomb.

The furthest he travelled in the latter part of his life was to London. Occasionally Marjorie King's comfortable Jaguar whisked him to Oxford, Weston-super-Mare or Portishead, but only for the day. Alec Hodges used to run him to Prinknash Abbey for lunch with Dom Sylvester. (The taciturn Hodges clearly did not realize that the meal itself would be conducted in silence because he refused to set foot in the abbey.) A trip with John James to Avonmouth to greet the return home to Bristol from the Falkland Islands of Brunel's famous steamship the *Great Britain*, on 4 July 1970, enticed George to brave the high winds and don his top hat in honour of the occasion. His fascination with the sea, inherited from his father, remained with him to the end.

Generally speaking he preferred friends to travel to see him. He would press them to stay at the Priory. Patrick Hughes and his wife Molly Parkin, exotically dressed, behatted and startlingly made-up, made an exciting impression on staid Bristolians, but, as far as George's driver Marjorie King was concerned, it was Patrick who had all the charm. Describing him as 'a poppet', she warmed to his unaffected childlike delight at her Jaguar; he confessed that he had never ridden in one before. Anthony Hill made a regular philosophical pilgrimage to the Priory and latterly came accompanied by his delightful new Japanese wife, Yuriko. Another fascinating couple who got into the habit of visiting George were the Earl of Ilchester's sister Lady Elisabeth and her husband John Livingstone. Their marriage in 1977 had attracted a deal of unpleasant press coverage. Andrew Rogers wrote a sympathetic letter and on George's behalf invited them to visit the Priory. They came, shuddered at the initial impact of the place, but soon settled into a relaxed friendship with George. Although he did most of the talking (since he assumed that new acquaintances had to be introduced to his philosophical ideas), he loved to hear tales of Lady Elisabeth's childhood spent in the South of France with her French grandmother. He had only ever visited the Riviera in his imagination, but he recalled stories of his father's visit. Elisabeth thought of George as Proustian in appearance and manner. One can appreciate the reasons for this impression, although there was no question of him having read even a word of Proust. But George was not above playing Proustian tricks on guests purely in order to observe their reaction. On one occasion he received John and Elisabeth Living-stone in the ground-floor reception room. He carefully seated them in pre-chosen chairs and she found herself staring directly at his astonishing picture of the naked woman with her legs revealingly in the air. From the point at which he was sitting John noticed nothing. 'Oh, my God!' thought Lady Elisabeth, 'I've got to go on making polite conversation here.'[6] Afterwards husband and wife discussed George's possible reasons for exposing a person of refinement to such a dubious sight. But the answer was simple: he liked to shock those whom he considered potentially shockable but, more so, he liked to sit back and observe human reactions to situations contrived by himself. Indeed, in his last years he cared to imagine that he was in control, acting as one of life's puppet-masters.

With his love of music, which grew stronger and more profound towards the end, George was not above testing those whose naivety could be guaranteed to evoke a predictable reaction. He knew that if he played the meditation from Massenet's *Thaïs*, it would evoke sounds of unsophisticated pleasure. One lady was taken to see a performance of Puccini's *La Fanciulla del West*. What did she think of it? She didn't like it. Why? Because of the violence. What violence? Oh, the gun's going off near the end. George might almost have anticipated this reaction and secretly hoped that she might might upset herself from shock. In turn, what was his reaction to the experience of unfamiliar works? How had he appeared to react to Janáček's *Makropulos Affair*? Oh, he found it interesting. Interesting! If only from the point of view of the plot, he, as metaphysician, could not have failed to find it totally fascinating and intellectually stimulating. He was merciless when it came to ignorance and he administered secret acts of retribution. When Wagner's *Parsifal* was broadcast on television on Good Friday 1982, he sat comfortably in his chair relishing every moment of what was the nearest thing to a religious ceremony that he had experienced since his youth. But he knew full well that his Cosima II, despite being cast in such an illustrious role, was sitting on an unyielding Regency *chaise-longue* for almost five hours of painful incomprehension.

Television was a late innovation in George's household. He pretended to believe that it was culturally detrimental; he secretly cavilled at paying the licence fee. But while he went through the motions of rejecting the advice of friends like Barbara Thorne, who assured him that he would get his money's worth of pleasure out of a set, two or three times a week he would secretly slip round the corner to the house of his friends Jack and Esmé White in Caledonia Place. Uninvited, he would be up the stairs like a shot and the colour television would be switched on. He was fascinated by the technical excellence of the machine and particularly liked to watch news and current affairs programmes. The Whites' Sunday afternoons were irritatingly disrupted with predictable regularity. But, equally, they knew that, as evening approached, he would scuttle off to give himself his second injection of the day. But why did he not buy a set of his own? Simple: he wanted to be sure that he would get value for money before taking the risk. He finally took the plunge when he discovered that he could buy a reconditioned set for the knock-down price of £35. It came with a six-month guarantee and obligingly survived for two years. A second one, a massive old-fashioned set, cost him all of £70, but to his annoyance it only lasted six months. A Pye with remote control was then procured. One could not help wondering about the logistical problems of the comings and goings of such massive televisions up and down the Priory's narrow stairs. Marjorie King discovered what happened:[7]

> The men came with the new one, the big one, and George said: 'Right, you can take that one away now.'
>
> And they said: 'Sorry, mate, it's not our job to take the old one away.'
>
> George said, quite abashed: 'Well, I don't want it. What can I do with it?'
>
> They said: 'That's your problem.'
>
> Anyway, he did get a couple of men to bring the old one down – which was very difficult with the stairs.

A music centre was another indulgence of George's old age, though his discs, overworked but cherished over the years, could have done it no good.

Generally he made a point of resisting change and went through the motions of being indifferent to external social and political events. In the period up to the end of his life political tensions distracted most thinking people in the kingdom. He affected an indifference to events such as the major strikes of 1972, 1973–4, 1978–9 and 1984–5 with all their political implications. He ostentatiously refused to register as a voter, but this did not stop him from voicing his preference for certain political personalities. If anything, he was a conservative (with a small 'c') of the Harold Macmillan genre, but in the 1970s he admitted to a sneaking admiration for James Callaghan – why, he never explained. At the same time he was not above wagering the sum of £100 on the outcome of the Conservative leadership contest between Edward Heath and Margaret Thatcher in 1975. He lost. For an inveterate non-gambler, his bet was based upon a calculated consideration of the apparent merits of the case. He simply refused to believe that any British political party would ever be led by a woman, let alone that the country would be ever governed by one. But even before Mrs Thatcher achieved the premiership in 1979, he had converted himself into a devoted admirer of her and her approach to politics. But sentiment was never allowed to cloud his judgment. He would happily attend a local Conservative Party social function if there were personalities, such as William Waldegrave, to be button-holed. The next day he would not think twice about shopping in a 'socialist' organization such as the Co-op, if he thought that they had specifically attractive items 'on offer'.

To be frank, his attitude towards politics was not just non-responsible; it was also irresponsible. To the end he professed to admire the aims and aspirations of the Parti Québécois in Canada because he imagined that this was the Francophile thing to do, little realizing what the French position was on the subject. His attitude, in part, stemmed from an old misconception. In 1942 some French-speaking Canadians had refused to serve the Crown and he, by some fluke of the imagination, saw in their stance something of a parallel with the pacifism that he professed – for very different reasons. The irony is that, on occasions, innate patriotic, even jingoistic, feelings rose to the surface. During the Falklands War of 1982 he was excited by the British refusal to accept the Argentine invasion as a *fait accompli*. But, then again, a lot of his attitude undoubtedly stemmed from a fascination with ships and naval battles cultivated as a child by his father.

His politics often operated, not according to principle, but according to his purse. With his considerable business interests as a landlord, he was not enthusiastic about the type of social legislation designed to extend tenants' rights during the Labour Party's tenure of office in the 1960s and 1970s. Even the fact that he let almost exclusively to students (who tended not to come under the provisions of the Rent Acts) did not mean that he avoided problems. He frankly enjoyed being a landlord. He also rejoiced in the fact that he had made his fortune in the process. However, from the late 1960s onwards, as the student community went through its 'revolutionary' phase, trouble loomed ominously on his horizon. The fabric of his properties had always been a source of concern, but he had often coped with an odd patch-job and the helping hand of an odd unremunerated friend who was not afraid to roll up his sleeves. But when tenants intentionally caused trouble, George lost heart. Students deliberately removed slates from the roof so that rain-water would come in and they could claim that the building was damp and that they should pay only half their rent – or nothing at all. The alternative was a complaint to the local Environmental Health Department with all the concomitant disruptions. This was accompanied by a spate of tenants leaving his properties in a deplorable condition. He had broken his rule to have only female students and had one house full of male medics. The squalor was unbelievable. The ruined furniture and the offensive graffiti on the walls were bad enough, but the pilfering of valuable electrical items began to make the whole operation seem less than worthwhile. Undesirable tenants had to be eased out. Up to June 1977 he had considerable trouble with the occupants of his property at 6 Manor Park in Redland, but as a matter of course they vacated the premises at the end of the academic session. Worse was to come. In October 1979 his property at 7 Rodney Place was infested with squatters, evicted tenants who returned illegally. Given the anomalous state of English law on the subject, George had to go to court to obtain an eviction order, and the respectable inhabitants of Clifton were horrified at the sight of bailiffs descending on the building. By this time the squatters had caught wind of what was about to happen and had vanished into the night – but leaving behind distressingly tangible evidence of their occupation. Less than two years later, on 24 February 1981, the happy news of the Prince of Wales's engagement was spoiled by the discovery of another infestation of squatters, this time in his property at 9 Sydenham Road in Cotham. The police were summoned. Again the tedious business of obtaining a court order had to be endured, an agony for somebody like George who avoided where possible all contact with officialdom. At the end of April bailiffs were still standing guard on the building. The problem with this episode was that he again found himself entangled with the Environmental Health Department. Under the provisions of the Housing Act (1957) the house had to undergo a great deal of basic repair work to make it fit for human habitation again. The total cost came to £9,399.88. He was horrified. And he resolved finally to dispose of his property empire.

He had already begun to sell off his houses. By the mid-1970s new health and safety regulations were beginning to make his life as a landlord difficult. Essential modifications such as fire doors and fire escapes were hideously costly – at least in his eyes. (He did not seem to appreciate how costly in terms of human life existing conditions might prove.) As multi-occupied housing stock was subject, district by district, to new statutory improvements, landlords and local inhabitants held protest meetings. Despite the bitter cold of a winter's night, George was enticed out on 19 January 1977 to attend an angry meeting at St Nathaniel's Church. But nothing could be done about the situation. More than ever convinced, George went on with the sale of his properties. In October 1976 he had gained a settlement from a property in Brighton Street which, with a sitting tenant on a fixed rent of 50p a week, had been more trouble than it was worth. But over the next two years the house at Lower Cotham Road went under the hammer, as did 18 Victoria Walk in Cotham and his property at Ambra Vale. The list continued slowly but steadily.

The moment of decision came when, in December 1978, he contemplated selling 75 Springfield Road, which had belonged to his family since 1915 and was where he had been born. Andrew Rogers asked him if he was sure that he wanted to part with it. George's reply contained a hint of resignation: 'No point in me hanging on to it – not if I have nobody to leave it to.'[8] His more avaricious friends had other suggestions to make. But the list of sales continued, the prices fetched becoming steadily greater as he benefited from the upturn in the property market after the Conservatives' success of May 1979. Houses in Bellevue Crescent, at 12 St John's Road and 6 Manor Park lucratively disappeared. The troublesome 9 Sydenham Road was sold and finally, on 7 November, the sale of the equally troublesome 9 Rodney Place was brought to a satisfactory completion – and George was £39,149.53 the richer for it.

Although he was left with only the dilapidated St Vincent's Priory out of a holding of some sixteen or seventeen properties, he was now sitting on sums of money greater that he would ever have dreamed possible. It was all invested in 'safe' industries: oil, tobacco, drugs and alcohol. His only frivolity was a sizeable block of Premium Bonds, which were a form of fun, but profitable nonetheless. In November 1985, when his estate came to be probated, it was officially estimated as being worth £410,000, a substantial sum for somebody who had started his businesses with virtually nothing. Typically, before his demise, he expressed the regret that he had never managed to become a millionaire. One cannot help feeling that his regret would have been infinitely greater if he had known what was to become of his estate after his death.

CHAPTER TWENTY-FIVE

DEATH AND NOTHINGNESS

In the last decade of his life George's creative existence made its final re-adjustment. Until 1976 he continued to paint, but very sporadically. While summer months lasted he might get out of bed early and paint in the warmth of the morning sunlight. He gained a certain degree of satisfaction from knowing that he was still capable of applying paint to canvas. Even as late as 1977 he accepted a commission from his old friend Dorian Mogg to paint her portrait as a companion to the one painted a quarter of a century earlier. The new work was remarkably full of life and captured the intensity of the sitter. The predominently pale blue tonality was surprising, given his prejudices, but effective since it matched the colours of the first portrait. It was his last completed work of art. Unfortunately there was a misunderstanding between painter and sitter about her supposed reaction to the work, and one suspects that this, more than anything else, discouraged George from taking up his brushes ever again.

Another of George's creative ventures scarcely got off the ground. In May 1977 he started to dictate a sketch outline intended to form the basis for an autobiography. Only a few lines of his rough plan have survived, and they provide no information of substance – just a great deal about his overriding arrogance. Apparently he then devised a scheme, taken from his old friend Sir Francis Rose, who for a decade and more had been working on a sequel to his fantasy memoirs, *Saying Life*, by stitching together essays reminiscing about famous people from his past. Articles on Gertrude Stein and Isadora Duncan appeared in *Vogue* in New York in the late 1960s. George thought that he could imitate Francis, but he was less successful than the eccentric baronet. He began by writing a memoir on Bettina Bergery (whom he had known only slightly in Paris), but the project went no further. The few tentative pages that he did produce mysteriously disappeared after his death. However he did make some provision in his will for the production of a professionally written biography. He had realized that half-recollected memories and emotional fantasies by himself and, worse, by self-appointed hierarchs could never take the place of an objective analysis of his remarkable life and work.

Sensibly he spent his last few years in an attempt to complete his final book of philosophy, *Death and the Double Meaning of Nothingness*, and by his death he had completed a typescript that required only an introduction and a brief summing-up. Most of the work was hammered out in dialogues with Dom Sylvester Houédard. Prinknash Abbey, near Gloucester, was conveniently close to Bristol and, although George attempted that short journey only twice, Sylvester needed no second bidding to seize the opportunity to come and spend a few nights in St Vincent's Priory every two or three months. Together they sorted out George's ideas. Sylvester was an invaluable source of bibliographical information, particularly relating to current trends in philosophy and sub-atomic physics. Otherwise one feels that George's thought would have developed in a dangerous vacuum. Some of his friends were faintly afraid that he was being exposed to too much catholic theology. The truth was almost the opposite. As Sylvester later reflected, the value and uniqueness of George's thought, the result of decades of work, lay in his production of, 'from a non-theistic point of view, the strongest arguments ever made in support of what catholic contemplative writers have always said, only with the benefit of George's insight into the need this created for a second and deeper-level logic that would enable these things to be said without confusion'.[1] Others were worried in case Sylvester's well-known fascination with oriental thought might colour the final formulation of George's philosophy. Sylvester's tentative editing of his surviving manuscript showed little definite influence from either controversial angle.

He began by suggesting that George had taken up from the point at which his mentor, Lupasco, had left off with his logic of contradiction:[2]

Melhuish succeeded in filling that need by erecting a first order antithetical logic, *designed* to cope and *able* to cope with the energy of pure flux: of movement, change and time. Since the flow of reality is the base on which we build our pretence that existence is more like the sequence of stills than the movement of a film has captured and can recreate as its image, he thereby relegated to a second order the old logic designed to cope with things as if they were static and to cope with experience as if mind were a thing.

Sylvester continued by pointing out that George was neither a sub-atomicist nor a theologian:[3]

He designed his work to fill an urgent need exposed by particle physics on finding that problems regarding the origin and nature of the universe make it imperative to speak of anythingness and nothingness and awareness in a new and unexpected way. It was only gradually that he became aware how investigation into the nature of nothingness, having led him to study the eighteen (and sometimes twenty) types of nothingness classified in Buddhist logic, implied the possibility that he was making a systematic contribution to contemplative theology – not, of course, at the pseudo level where even educated people think of God as 'a being' and even imagine God as 'the supreme being' and fail to realize that as being, not a being, God is un-nameable and cannot even be named The Un-nameable.

Just in case this caused confusion about the mystery of the Godhead, Sylvester brought the focus back onto mankind:[4]

Since humans are not beings either, but becomings in a universe of becomings, *beings* are what we encounter nowhere except as fictions of memory or imagination, and *being* (or God) is what we encounter only negatively through the paradoxical energy of becoming and through the paradoxical energy of mind becoming aware of mind as nothing but the possibility of this encounter with the negative infinity of being as exceeding the privative infinity of mind.

In order to back up George's view that 'the division between life and death is equated in the moment of experiential realization' and that 'only his new energetic logic can show innate flux of the conscious moment'[5], Sylvester went on to cite an eye-opening list of authorities with whom he was in accord: Ibn Arabi, St Thomas Aquinas, Eckhart, Rahner, St Gregory of Nyssa, St Benedict, St Gregory Palamas. He explained:[6]

All these writers agree with Melhuish in understanding immortality as guaranteed by the paradox of experiencing now. Like him they all reject the notion of immortality needing any static sort of ego or needing to conserve memories from the past, but unlike the others, George Melhuish and, so far as I know, he alone, has been able to see beyond the logical implications of experiencing now without needing special memories, and into the implications this must have for logic.

And in *Death and the Double Meaning of Nothingness* George displayed this uniqueness by expounding a philosophy that is the product of a singular mind. He asserted:[7]

> Basic Time is isomorphic with sheer disruption of an identity, for it deals not with a specific something as somethingness but with an anything as anythingness. For things apprehended as occurring in specific configurations it is usual to include here memory as identity. Particular Time will permit the measurement of identifiable demarcations but can never be used to meter legitimately the real actualization of the experiential now . . .
>
> Obviously it is at points which are crucial to particular or finite demarcation that the broken or double nature of nothingness will be most effectively revealed, and included here are absolute beginnings and absolute endings, both for experience and for the universe.

George went on to analyse questions of the most fundamental significance to the understanding of the nature of existence:[8]

> In examining the problems of existence *ex nihilo* we are forced to claim an actual union between something and nothing and this must imply active exchange between the one state and the other. Yet, if we agree to any exchange whatsoever between nothing and something, *then by implication there must always have been such an exchange*, and if there has always been an active exchange from nothing to something, then we are barred from conceding a situation where this will not be the case . . . Traditionally, immortality has almost always been maintained because it has been said of a person that he maintains something indestructible, such that, when his physical body suffers terminal corruption, there is an incorruptible aspect, say the soul, by which he will avoid succumbing to mere nothing or mere nothingness.

George was much concerned that[9]

> only when we see the continuum of experience as an antinomy of standard logical laws can we be in a position to realize that immortality is guaranteed in virtue of the nature of the conscious cradle and thereby maintain that the dogmatic division between life and death is fully equated in the moment of experiential actualization.

And he went straight to the heart of the question posed by death:[10]

Although in death, there is effacement of this or that particular thing as may please the diehard materialist, in a central respect, the result is the opposite of what he claims. For although it is correct to say of a so-called deceased person that he is not, the fact that there is no trace of conscious link does not mean that there is only non-entity. In fact, because of the logical ambiguity sanctioned by the non-tautological system, we are in a position to see that the deceased does not leave any gap in the experiential continuum; the resultant immortality comes from the principle of entirely gratuitous non-causal substitution.

He addressed himself to the central point of his thesis:[11]

Standard logic decrees that each particular thing has an alternative or negation where the thing in question is stated not to be. However, contrary to popular opinion, it is necessary to point out that the mere presence of something, even as anything, implies that absolute nothingness never was, or will be the case. In order for absolute nothing or nothingness to be, it must be *without* positive potentiality because, if nothingness *contained* positive potentiality for something, this would deny its absolute negativity which would be isomorphic with absolute nothingness. However, if absolute nothingness is entirely potentialless, then it cannot be a useful feature or tool in the management of existent things used within the standard logical system . . . Users of the traditional conceptual scheme have a great inclination to claim a thing as finite, which is, of course, natural since otherwise they will be precipitated into declaiming everything as infinite. It is here that there is the necessity for the double nature of nothingness, which, although at first sight is bewildering, is a central key for the reality with which we deal. But if the double nature of nothingness holds, then all beginnings and endings appended to a given thing signify only at an interim level.

Received concepts of mortality and immortality continued to exercise George's mind:[12]

Traditionally, we see that on the one side there is the materialist's belief in the exchange of this life for mere nothing, while on the other side there is the immaterialist's belief in the necessity of some identity correspondence between existence here and an existence beyond death, since it has been thought that without the latter claim it is necessary to forego the possibility of immortality. At the level of the present logico-philosophical investigation, all traditional representations in favour of experiential immortality are illegitimate exercises, and yet immortality is the case.

George's problem as an agnostic was that the word 'faith' could never come into his vocabulary, but clearly there is an implicit concept in the background:[13]

> We must be willing to accept that by the advent of terminal death all ingredients and memories of a person are effaced, yet not to concede to the mortality of the conscious continuum. Terminal death of the person appears to imply a total end of his particular situation and memories, yet in fact, it offers an uncompromising anything-elseness . . . Now we are able to see that the plea for experiential immortality, in consequence of special substance, or in consequence of special memory conservation is superfluous, and indeed fallacious.

And, if that were not sufficiently convincing, he added:[14]

> Incredulity may be expressed when it is claimed that the change of experiential ingredients in the afterlife, *vis-à-vis* the present one, occurs at the level of an anythingness, until it is realized that change in experiential realizations, even within the now itself occurs at the level of an anythingness.

Dom Sylvester gave a personal focus to George's point: 'Each of us . . . is never less than the same possibility being made actual through our becoming over this period of twenty-four hours of clock time. God knows us, and all possibilities, by knowing himself and *by* that knowledge we are the human freedoms that we ever remain.' He concluded with the statement that, 'prior to death, we only need this effacement of memory when making the actual inner journey of mind that gives the monastic contemplative life its name of *vita philosophica*'. He added a final compliment that was almost a warning: 'only metaphysicians and the particle-physicists are likely ever to become *aware* of the true extent of what we owe George Melhuish'.[15]

But the confirmation of that conclusion can only come with the publication of his final work.

CHAPTER TWENTY-SIX

ROUNDED WITH A SLEEP

The last decade of George's life was quiet from the social point of view. He did little in the way of formal entertaining and only exceptionally went out to dinner or drinks with friends. But he liked to maintain contact with friends of the past. Brian Jenkins and his new wife Carole, Peter Tiley and his wife Norma entertained him. Dorothy Irving-Bell did not attempt to entice him to visit her because her flat was at the top of an impossible flight of stairs, but she would drop into the Priory for a chat or just bump into him while shopping in Clifton Village. Percy Edgell continued to call on Wednesday evenings. George appreciated his coming because he could discuss in confidence a lot of the general business questions that vexed him latterly. Indeed, Percy became one of his closest confidants and George acknowledged this by making the effort to attend the wedding of his daughter Rosemary to David King on 31 July 1982. He stayed only briefly for the reception at Ashton Court Mansion because he was not well, but long enough to meet again Mrs Margaret (Carl) Hibbs. He had not seen her since the 1930s when he had patted her head and suggested to her horrified mother that he should paint her. Barbara and Barrie Thorne were much more successful in tempting him out for dinner. They made a habit of inviting him to their Christmas celebrations. They would suppress their mirth as the turkey was brought in because, without fail, he would say: 'Only white meat for me!' The first Christmas after his death was poignant because on the turkey's arrival they could almost hear him grinding out the predictable request.

George had not kept up close contacts with his family, but during this period he saw more of his Seymour cousin Kay Burnett. She and her husband Brian lived in a delightful house at Failand in the countryside outside Bristol. George enjoyed it when Kay's daughter Heather joined them with her own three boys, Chris, Andrew and Tim. Kay's younger sister, Tenny Jones, who as a child had been closer to George than the rest of his cousins, induced him to visit her at her home in Stadium Road. He was deeply saddened by her death in 1980. It gave him pause for thought since she was younger than both Kay and himself.

Others from his past were survivors. Charmian Deckers had moved to Richmond and coped bravely with treatment for a severe heart condition, but she always found time to keep in touch by letter or telephone. Vicky Malins never lost contact and made a special visit to the Priory in August 1981 with her husband John Ayling. George must have been happy for her for having married so gentle and protective a man with a fine artistic temperament to match her own. And Rita McKerrow re-encountered George after more than forty years because, by an odd coincidence, she was Andrew Rogers' singing teacher and close friend. She, Andrew and George made a trip to the Royal West of England Academy for the 1984 exhibition of students' drawings. (Andrew, in his full natural glory, had been the model for many of the studies.) The trio did not stay long but repaired to the Priory by taxi – for which, to Andrew's horror, George allowed Rita to pay. However, with a glass of wine and George's sudden discovery of her connection with the creator of his beloved Railton motor car, all else was forgotten. Rita explained:[1]

> My father was in the navy with Railton at the end of the 1914–18 war. They were both engineers and, when I was a child of about four, Reid Railton – I called him 'Uncle John' – came to live in our house in Birmingham and my father was working for him and between them they designed a racing car, which they built in a funny sort of shed in the artisan area of Birmingham. We lived in Moseley and they converted the top two attic rooms into offices – for drawing . . . John stayed with us for at least six months. And during that time we had visits from Kaye Don and Sir Henry Segrave and all the old racing drivers.

George loved talking about motor cars and this revived memories of the Railton in which he had taken particular pride. Strangely he did not mention that he had once been in the second-hand car 'trade'. Perhaps the successful businessman was just a little ashamed of this slightly shady aspect of his past.

About other things he was less sensitive. Except during the final year of his life he retained a certain amount of mobility. He made a point of getting out of the Priory on regular days to be driven by Marjorie King, often simply in order to do shopping, or he was to be seen pottering around Clifton Village, browsing round what Oddbins had on offer. He had always been a figure of eye-catching eccentricity, but even he managed to surpass himself. All his friends were speechless with astonishment, but Marjorie King did manage to capture the image that he presented:[2]

> George always wore rather flamboyant clothes, a beautiful red velvet suit. He had a bright yellow velvet suit – or very heavy tweed clothes. Always overdressed . . . I could be sitting wringing in the car and George would be sitting there as cool as a cucumber. But there was one year [1981] I called for him during the day and I just could not believe my eyes. He had an extraordinary pair of brogue shoes on with long socks and he had some bathing trunks on and a striped shirt and a bow tie. You never saw anything so extraordinary. It wasn't even Bermuda shorts or anything; it was real bathing trunks . . . I didn't bat an eyelid . . . He had no idea how extraordinary he looked. And everybody looked at him, everywhere he went. He didn't turn a hair. He couldn't think why everybody else wasn't dressed in the same way in that terribly hot summer.

What made this arresting vision even worse was that in old age he had become a little portly and his spindly legs issuing from this old-fashioned swimming costume made him look like Tweedledum – or was it Tweedledee? What his stockbroker thought when George appeared, so attired, in his office nobody knows since he was unaware of any reaction of surprise and so did not comment on it.

His appearances in public were also unpredictable. He had never enjoyed good health and all his old diseases continued to afflict him and periodically lay him low. In the years before his death he suffered from at least two coronaries. Periodically he would develop stones in his bladder. Usually he was able to pass them. This was not pleasant, but at least it obviated the need for surgery. However, in August 1976, he developed an intractable stone and had to be admitted to the Chesterfield Nursing Home to have it removed. He was said to hate hospitals, but this was largely psychological. In the Chesterfield he loved being pampered by the nurses and by friends who visited him. Although she should have been used to his idiosyncratic ways, Barbara Thorne was surprised at the post-operative George's off-hand request for some of his favourite chicken breasts – duly preserved in aspic by Messrs Shipham.

After this George's health revived, but it always remained precarious and it could deteriorate suddenly. In April 1979 he was deemed so ill that he was paid a sickness and disability payment until March 1980. However, he was not so ill that he was unconcerned about the effect on his pension rights. He wrote to the Department of Health and Social Security on 23 September 1980 explaining the situation:[3]

> In March 1980 I was said to be medically fair, although in fact, since this date I have had to give up any form of business. I have been told that for the year or so that I received sickness benefit I am exempt from paying contributions. May I take this opportunity, since I am sixty-five on 26 August 1981, to enquire if I have to pay contributions from April 1980 until August 1981? I am naturally anxious to receive my old age pension from my sixty-fifth birthday.

He ceased to be sensitive about admitting to his age when money was involved. However, he was endlessly conscious of the fragility of human life. He had reached the age when one might expect contemporaries to begin to die but, in this respect, he was remarkably fortunate, and in the case of those who did die before him, he was self-orientated enough to see this as a personal success in cheating the Grim Reaper. The death of his cousin Tenny, however, was a sad event, and his friend from pacifist and Torch days, Norman, also went the way of all flesh. For many years Norman had existed well beyond the bounds of mere eccentricity. He used to buy a gross of ball-point pens and sell them on the streets in the centre of Bristol – ostensibly in aid of charity. He always refused to walk on the pavement out of a neurotic fear of treading on something that a pampered Clifton canine had left behind. However, he had remained a faithful friend and, without any apparent ulterior motive, had visited George in the Priory regularly once a week to keep him amused. (George was slightly annoyed that he left an estate of £20,000 but nothing to himself.)

More disturbing was the death of Sir Francis Rose on 19 November 1979. He had died in Charing Cross Road quite painlessly (two months after his seventieth birthday) following a highly liquid lunch in a Greek restaurant in Soho. The problem for George was that he looked back over his long association with his wayward friend and relived all the problems and crises. In the latter years of Francis' life they had kept in touch and Francis even pressed him to come to stay at his little pensioner's flat in Walton-on-Thames. George, needless to say, 'postponed' accepting the invitation and was vague about a reciprocal offer of hospitality at the Priory. Despite all that he had endured at Francis' hands, he had, in fact, loved him and remained extremely fond of him. But with George there was always an ambiguity of motive. The farcical episode of Francis making a will entirely in his favour lingered on in his mind and he was genuinely surprised when Francis' solicitors could find no trace of the document. However, since he left a bankrupt estate and an outstanding solicitors' bill, they suggested that George might care to buy the residue of Francis' paintings, held by them as surety. He made the journey with Marjorie King, a long round trip to Camberley in a Jaguar that was never allowed to top forty miles per hour. The sum demanded was paltry, but he clearly thought that he was being cheated out his 'rightful inheritance' and demurred.

He had just as mixed feelings about the death of George Ward-Jackson in October 1982. Although he had not ceased to be offended at his abrupt termination of their friendship, he had retained an admiration and even affection for him. Ward-Jackson clearly had similar feelings and, when he fell seriously ill with a brain tumour, he told his wife (and devoted nurse) Muriel that he wanted to speak to George on the telephone. Alas, the disease was so advanced that his powers of speech often deserted him in mid-sentence. Every time she tried the number he indicated that she should ring off before speaking to George. But after her husband's death, Muriel Ward-Jackson made a point of telephoning to inform him of what had happened. His response was touching, as she later recalled:[4]

> 'Well it's a funny thing. These last few days I've been thinking about him the whole time. I'm so glad you rang me up because I was terrified that he would die and I wouldn't even ever know about it.' So, after that, I used to ring him up perhaps every six months or so, just for a chat about how things were going.

For somebody whose philosophy was veering more and more towards concepts in which death played a decreasingly significant role, George was acutely anxious that, when physical death came, he and his work would not be forgotten. One way in which he took steps to ensure his own immortality was to draw up a will that left a number of token legacies to friends, but otherwise was entirely angled towards maintaining a high awareness of his own achievements. He was always talking in grand but vague terms about his will. Alas, some took him seriously and let their expectations soar. Barbara Thorne took the matter with a pinch of salt and used to play the 'will game' with him. She recalled it with amusement:[5]

> He was always talking to me about his will. We had great conversations about our various wills. From time to time he would inform me that he'd left me a house. And I'd say to him: 'Well, I've left you a choice of furniture.' But the point is that George was perpetually altering his will because of these girls. Every time a girl went he had to

alter his will. I said to him one day: 'Now look, George, if you want to perpetuate your memory in some sort of memorial, the best thing for you to do would be to found some sort of scholarship or some such thing, say for the Royal Western Academy or for something to do with philosophy. And in that way your memory would be perpetuated.' And he thought that was a very good idea.

He turned for advice to Anthony Hill, who not only shared his interest in art and philosophy but also had his finger on the pulse of what was currently happening in these areas in the capital. He suggested that they should consult a mutual acquaintance of long standing, the Freud expert Richard Wollheim of University College, London. In fact, during a visit to Bristol on 24 November 1978, the professor even called at the Priory to discuss the matter. And then he took the question up with the university authorities so that George could be absolutely clear about how endowment trust funds operated.

Unfortunately George had such high-flown ideas about what he wanted to happen to his estate that either he had to be told that they were impracticable or, after his death, they proved to be so. In the will that he signed on 20 August 1981, a week before his sixty-fifth birthday, he wanted his house, St Vincent's Priory, to be taken over by the Bristol City Art Gallery and opened to the public as a gallery, displaying his furniture and paintings. Unfortunately he left an endowment of only forty thousand pounds and, given the state of the building's fabric, this would have scarcely paid for basic repairs, let alone for alterations required by law for safety in a public building. He also seems to have been unaware of how much the annual salary and maintenance bill would be for such an impossible building. This memorial plan had to be abandoned and the Priory was sold at auction on 20 March 1986 for the substantial sum of £64,000. (It cost almost as much to do the fundamental repairs to the fabric before it became habitable as a conventional dwelling.)

He made provision for the completion and publication of his philosophical writings extant at the time of his death. A sum was left for the writing of 'a philosophical essay of book length' and a similar provision was made for an author deemed to have 'the capabilities of writing a biography of my life'.[6] But, apart from the handful of small legacies, the bulk of the estate was destined to be devoted to the creation of 'a Trust to carry my name and to provide for prizes and scholarships for artists and sculptors' and a similar 'Trust to carry my name to provide for postgraduate study of philosophy culminating in the writing of a suitably extensive essay or book every Five or Ten years.'[7] None of the sums of money involved were excessive, but he clearly wanted to avoid having the estate that he had so meticulously built up and nurtured frittered away as legacies to friends. One cannot but admire him for devoting its bulk to such laudable and useful ends. Unfortunately, after his death one legatee expressed dissatisfaction with what he had left her, and the legal complications indefinitely halted the implementation of George's worthy schemes. He had left selected friends sums that were not a penny more and not a penny less than he wanted them to have.

Despite the fact that all his friends knew that he had long suffered from a number of more or less serious ailments, when death finally came on 13 July 1985, they were taken by surprise. During the previous winter he had avoided going out as much as possible, but this was seen as an overcautious concern for his health. His cousin Kay Burnett saw him some months before his death and thought that he looked fine. Marjorie King (now Comfort) continued to work for him as a driver and, when he would not venture out, did the shopping for him. She did not believe that he was on the point of death – nor did he. As she remarked,[8]

> I don't think for a minute that he realized how ill he was. I didn't, although over the years he had taken very good care of himself. He really was a hypochondriac with the potions and medicines that he had and was very, very careful with his health – I don't really think that he thought for a moment that he was very bad. I mean he had been saying so long, 'If I'm here next year', it was almost like crying wolf.

A week before George died Brian Jenkins bumped into him outside a supermarket in Whiteladies Road. Brian recalled that 'he said that he hadn't been too well, but he didn't look too bad'.[9] And he invited the Jenkinses to call and see him at the Priory. Deborah Jones called on George one evening a few days before his death and they had a lively time together. She later could not believe that he could have died so suddenly and was curiously upset by what, by comparison, was a trivial incident: 'I had my camera with me but the thing wouldn't work. The lights had just come on on the bridge and George was sitting there looking very royal in his big chair. And the thing didn't work. I was so angry.'[10] Dom Sylvester Houédard arrived at George's invitation late on the evening of 8 July, around ten o'clock. The George who greeted him was quite bright and cheerful and was clutching in his hands the final pages of his manuscript of *Death and the Double Meaning of Nothingness*. Sylvester did not think that the strain of his staying for two nights was too much for his host, although he did leave on 10 July with his plea to be given a few more days to work on the manuscript before sending it to him at Prinknash Abbey.

Since the beginning of the year George had been having problems with his medication. The National Health Service clamped down on cases of over-prescription of drugs and, with his unusually high consumption of sleeping pills and tranquillizers, he was hit badly. He even offered to pay for them privately, but arguments about health safety rather than cost had to be considered. It was clear, however, that somehow he managed to obtain a supply of the damaging drugs upon which he imagined himself dependent. Then the insulin medication for his diabetic condition had to be re-adjusted and, not only did he have considerable difficulty in adapting to the new regime, but it was clear to others that it put him in a vulnerable position. All this, in addition to minor angina attacks, upset his metabolism and by Friday, 12 July, he was in a fairly confused state. He spent a night of lone anxiety. He could not sleep and in the middle of the night he dragged himself into the study where he sat in the Wellington chair, alone, in distress, longing for dawn to break once again.

Later that day a friend arrived to check on him, but soon had to leave. She did not return until late that afternoon. In the meantime he had managed to climb up the stairs to the drawing-room, where he sat for hours confused and ill. Eventually at about 5 p.m. he had to be assisted down the difficult flight of stairs to his bedroom. It was only after further delays (and after fully twenty-four hours in which he was manifestly seriously unwell) that a doctor was called. Peter Featherstone, the doctor on call that Saturday evening, came immediately, arriving about seven o'clock. He did his best to stabilize George's condition, giving him an injection to inhibit his nausea, and then started to make arrangements for him to be taken to an hospital equipped to cope with emergency situations – a public one, needless to say. This met with a degree of resistance, but, in effect, it was too late. George had been settled with difficulty in the bed in his little ground-floor room and, still watched over by his favourite portrait of the young Edna Orchard, his eyelids fluttered suddenly and he died.

Dr Featherstone's arrival was most opportune because, not only was he able to make George's last moments comfortable, but also his presence obviated the unpleasant statutory need for a post-mortem. Given his medical history, the primary cause of death was recorded as 'congestive heart failure' and 'ischaemic heart disease', which was predictable enough with his diabetic condition and the consequent state of his heart. By nine o'clock, on that fateful 13 July, the undertakers removed his body from the Priory which he had so inexplicably loved, just as the sun was beginning to fade across the Avon Gorge and the great bridge that he had also loved.

He left no specific instructions as to the disposal of his remains and so, for some reason, it was considered more convenient for him to be cremated rather than interred. Nonetheless, it took an unaccountably long six days before the ceremony could go ahead. Given the time of year, many friends were away and not able to be contacted. Friends and family who did learn the news, genuinely shocked and surprised at the suddenness of his death, gathered, still confused, at the Canford Crematorium on Friday, 19 July 1985, at 2.20 p.m.

Dom Sylvester hurried down from Prinknash Abbey to conduct what purported to be a religious ceremony in honour of an old friend who, he knew, had not set foot in a church since his mid-teens and who disapproved of organized religion. But he could only have been amused (as some staid Bristolians were taken aback) by Sylvester's words greeting the arrival of the coffin. The *In Paradisum* was colourfully adapted for the occasion:[11]

> May Michael and all the angels lead you into Paradise. May George and Vincent with all the martyrs bring you to the heavenly city of Sion. May William and Maurus and all the saints present you to God. May Abraham welcome you to sit with all the prophets, martyrs and saints at the banquet prepared for those who hear the word and live in the way of truth.

The ceremony itself was simple. This meant that attention was focused primarily upon what Dom Sylvester had to say about his old friend. The congregation had the sensation of somebody speaking from the heart, somebody who had known and cared for the deceased. But some, who were unused to his particular brand of metaphysical preoccupation, thought it incongruous of him to digress into Eastern philosophy. He told them that one of the last pieces of material that he had prepared for George (but had forgotten to give him) was a quotation from the present Dalai Lama:[12]

> How mistaken are those who think that, while the body at death reverts to the elements, mind disappears as a rainbow in the sky – how limited their view. They see the dependence of mental continuity on the physical body and fail to understand that mind can also be independent of a gross physical base.

Sylvester felt that he had to explain:[13]

> For this is the point where George's investigations find their harmony with the teachings of Tibet and with the catholic and orthodox teaching

of the church on the creation of immortal mind or soul in the image of God – on the resurrection of what – 'sown [on] a gross physical base' – rises spiritual and glorified.

The problem of what to do with George's ashes remained unsolved for two years. Then, on 26 August 1987, after a controversial memorial service of dubious taste (the only virtue of which was to give Dom Sylvester the opportunity to introduce George's final work to the public) the ashes were buried in a peaceful, southward-facing angle of the churchyard of Bristol Cathedral. This was a lot less of a tribute than one of the city's more remarkable sons deserved, and certainly a less than appropriate memorial for one of his cast of mind. With restrained irony Dom Sylvester was able to make the point graphically:[14]

> The annals of Bristol have been frequently distinguished by citizens who sail away, change the course of history and make their birthplace famous: now the city is able to take an equal pride in George Melhuish as yet one more explorer and adventurer whose voyages, however, were into the unvisited regions of the mind.

SOURCE NOTES

This study is based on some material located in published monographs. Rather than list such works in a separate bibliography, all references to books and articles are incorporated into the following source notes. Unpublished material, either in the form of letters or written reminiscences, is referred to by the name of the author and the recipient and by date. Material derived from recorded interviews with individuals is referred to simply by the name of the source in question and by the date upon which they took place.

In the notes some abbreviations are employed; the name of the subject of the biography is usually abbreviated, as are the titles of his major monographs published to date:

> GM   George Melhuish
> *PNR*   *The Paradoxical Nature of Reality*, St Vincent's Press, Bristol, 1973.
> *PU*   *The Paradoxical Universe*, Rankin, Bristol, 1959.

CHAPTER ONE
1.   Frank Evans to George Barnett Melhuish, 11 Oct. 1898.

CHAPTER TWO
1.   Barbara Thorne, 13 July 1986.
2.   GM, *PU*, p. 114.
3.   Marcel Proust, *Du côté de chez Swann*, Gallimard, Paris, 1954, pp. 195–6.
4.   Anthony Hill, 19 Aug. 1986.

CHAPTER THREE
1.   W.R. Hutton, *George Melhuish*, Writers' and Artists' Association, Bristol, 1946, pp. 7–8.

2. R.H. Sawkins, 'Artists of Note. George Melhuish', *The Artist*, May 1948, p. 59.
3. Ibid.
4. Margaret Carl Hibbs to author, July 1986.
5. Barbara Thorne, 13 July 1986.
6. Ibid.
7. GM, *PU*, pp. 156–7.

CHAPTER FOUR
1. Peter Tiley, 15 July 1986.
2. Patricia Brennan, 25 Sept. 1986.

CHAPTER FIVE
1. Max Barnes, 'George Melhuish – Bristol Artist', *Bristol Week-End*, 13 Oct. 1961, p. 9.
2. R.H. Sawkins, op. cit., p. 60.
3. Barbara Thorne, 13 July 1986.
4. Deborah Jones, 14 July 1986.
5. Jean Glen to author, 29 Apr. 1987.

CHAPTER SIX
1. Barbara Thorne, 13 July 1986.
2. Patricia Brennan, 25 Sept. 1986.
3. Ibid.
4. Deborah Jones, 14 July 1986.
5. Dorothy Irving-Bell, 31 Oct. 1986.
6. Ibid.
7. Ibid.
8. Patricia Brennan, 25 Sept. 1986.
9. Deborah Jones, 14 July 1986.
10. Barbara Thorne, 13 July 1986.
11. Percy Edgell, 14 July 1986.
12. Barbara Thorne, 13 July 1986.
13. W.R. Hutton, op. cit., p. 6.
14. R.H. Sawkins, op. cit., p. 60.
15. Ibid.
16. Barbara Addison, 'An Exhibition of Paintings by George Melhuish. Catalogue', Foyle's Art Gallery, London, 1944, p. 1.
17. H. Granville Fell, 'The Connoisseur Divan', *The Connoisseur*, June 1943, p. 145.
18. Ibid., pp. 145–6.
19. Patricia Brennan, 25 Sept. 1986.
20. Quoted W.R. Hutton, op. cit., back cover.

CHAPTER SEVEN

1. GM, 'Painting Townscapes in Oils', *The Artist*, pt 1, March 1944, p. 3.
2. Ibid.
3. Ibid.
4. Ibid., pp. 3–4.
5. Ibid., p. 4.
6. Ibid., pt 2, Apr. 1944, p. 27.
7. Ibid., p. 28.
8. Ibid., pt 3, May 1944, p. 52.
9. Ibid., pt 5, July 1944, p. 99.
10. Ibid.
11. Ibid.
12. Ibid., pt 6, Aug. 1944, p. 123.
13. Barbara Thorne, 13 July 1986.
14. Barbara Addison, 'George Melhuish', *The Studio*, vol. 128, July 1944, pp. 19, 21.
15. Ibid., p. 21.

CHAPTER EIGHT

1. Victoria Ayling to author, 14 Aug. 1986.
2. GM, *PU*, p. 9.
3. Ibid.
4. Ibid., p. 13.
5. Ibid., p. 12.
6. Ibid.
7. Ibid., p. 21.
8. Barbara Thorne, 13 July 1986.
9. Barbara Addison to Patricia Daly, 5 Feb. 1945.
10. Patricia Brennan to author, 24 Oct. 1986.
11. Barbara Addison to Patricia Daly, 5 Feb. 1945.
12. Ibid., 27 Feb. 1945.
13. Ibid.
14. Barbara Thorne, 13 July 1986.

CHAPTER NINE

1. Barbara Addison to Patricia Daly, 5 Feb. 1945.
2. Ibid., 31 July 1945.
3. Ibid., 27 Feb. 1945.
4. Ibid.
5. Barbara Addison to Patricia Daly, 19 July 1945.

6. Ibid., 31 July 1945.
7. Ibid., 21 Aug. 1945.
8. Ibid., 19 July 1945.
9. Ibid.
10. Ibid., 21 Aug. 1945.
11. Ibid., 31 July 1945.
12. W.R. Hutton, 'The Paintings of George Melhuish, 1934–1945. Leaflet', Writers' and Artists' Association, Bristol, 1945, p. 2.
13. Ibid., p. 3.

CHAPTER TEN
1. Barbara Addison to Patricia Daly, 10 Jan. 1946.
2. Barbara Addison, 'An Exhibition of Paintings of George Melhuish. Catalogue', Alpine Gallery, London, 4 June 1946, p. 2.
3. Barbara Addison to Patricia Daly, 10 Jan. 1946.
4. Ibid., 28 June 1946.
5. Ibid.
6. George Melhuish, 30 Aug. 1984.
7. Ibid.
8. R.H. Sawkins, op. cit., p. 60.
9. J.B., 'George Melhuish at the Irving Galleries', *New Statesman and Nation*, 1 Dec. 1951.
10. Anon., *The Scotsman*, Nov. 1951.
11. George Melhuish, 30 Aug. 1984.
12. Ibid.
13. Ibid.
14. Sir Francis Rose, *Saying Life*, Cassell, London, 1961, p. 111.
15. P.S., *Cette Semaine*, Jan. 1947.
16. Anon., *Nouvelles Littéraires*, Jan. 1947.
17. Guy Dornand, 'George Melhuish', *Le Spectateur*, Jan. 1947.
18. Anon., *New York Herald Tribune*, Jan. 1947.

CHAPTER ELEVEN
1. Elsie Melhuish to Patricia Daly, 3 Sept. 1952.
2. Deborah Jones, 14 July 1986.
3. Ibid.
4. Anne Hewer to author, 15 Apr. 1987.
5. Ibid.
6. Kenneth Smith, 23 Sept. 1986.
7. Ibid.
8. Ibid.
9. Vera Apter Smith, 23 Sept. 1986.

10. Ibid.
11. Dorian Mogg, 18 July 1986.

CHAPTER TWELVE
1. Percy Edgell, 14 July 1986.
2. Brian Jenkins, 16 July 1986.
3. Percy Edgell, 14 July 1986.
4. Charmian Deckers, 15 Aug. 1986.
5. Ibid.
6. Rosemary King to author, 12 July 1986.
7. Ibid.
8. F.W. Brown, 'Modern Style. Bristol Art Exhibition', *Bristol Evening Post*, 25 Feb. 1949.
9. GM, 'Exhibition of Works by Contemporary Painters. Catalogue', Bristol City Art Gallery, 26 Feb. 1949, p. 2.
10. Anon., 'Painting People', *Bristol Evening Post*, 12 Apr. 1949.
11. Ibid.
12. A. de Falgairolle, 'Melhuish', *Le Monde*, 17 Apr. 1950.
13. P.D., 'George Melhuish', *Le Figaro*, 17 Apr. 1950.
14. Barnett D. Conlan, 'Art in Paris. His Painting is almost "Explosive"', *New York Herald Tribune*, 17 Apr. 1950.
15. Geoffrey Fraser, 'Bristol Artist's Paris Exhibition. Distinct Success', *Bristol Evening Post*, 22 Apr. 1950.
16. Ibid.
17. Ibid.
18. C.B., 'Georges Melhuish, peintures. Catalogue', Galerie Parenthou, Roubaix, 15 May 1950, p. 3.
19. Ibid.
20. Ibid., p. 4.

CHAPTER THIRTEEN
1. Anon., 'Melhuish in Paris', *Bristol Evening Post*, May 1951.
2. Louise Andrée Coury to GM, 28 Nov. 1951.
3. Mervyn Levy, 'A Pre-View of the Future?' *Bristol Evening Post*, 10 Apr. 1951, p. 2.
4. Anon., 'Art Secrets', *Bristol Evening Post*, Apr. 1951.
5. Anon., '"Expressionist". Bristol Artist Praised', *Western Daily Press*, Apr. 1951.
6. Anon., 'The Progress of a Bristol Painter', *Bristol Evening Post*, Apr. 1951.
7. Anon., 'Two Opinions on Two Bristol Figures', *Western Daily Press*, May 1951.

8. Ibid.
9. Anon., 'Controversial Bristol Artist is defended', *Bristol Evening Post*, May 1951.
10. F.C.J., 'Questions They'll Ask at City Art Exhibition. Profound or Funny?' *Bristol Evening Post*, 10 May 1951.
11. Anon., 'Art Exhibition. Bristolian's New Works', *Bristol Evening Post*, 30 Apr. 1951.
12. Lord Methuen, 'George Melhuish. Exhibition of Recent Paintings. Catalogue', Irving Galleries, London, 7 Nov. 1951, p. 2.
13. Anon., 'One Man Shows', *Manchester Guardian*, 7 Nov. 1951.
14. Anon., *Art News and Review*, Dec. 1951.
15. J.B., 'George Melhuish at the Irving Galleries', *New Statesman and Nation*, 1 Dec. 1951.
16. Anon., 'George Melhuish', *The Scotsman*, Nov. 1951.
17. Patrick Hughes, 'George Melhuish, recent paintings. Catalogue', Royal West of England Academy, Bristol, 1971, p. 1.
18. Max Barnes, 'George Melhuish – Bristol Artist', *Bristol Week-End*, 13 Oct. 1961, p. 9.
19. Charmian Deckers, 15 Aug. 1986.
20. Ibid.

CHAPTER FOURTEEN

1. Alison Settle, 'A Woman's Viewpoint', *Manchester Guardian*, Apr. 1953.
2. Anon., *The Studio*, May 1953, p. 60.
3. Anon., 'Other-worldly', *Bristol Evening Post*, 12 May 1953.
4. Patrick Hughes, op. cit., p. 2.
5. Anon., *Manchester Guardian*, 13 May 1953.
6. Anon., 'A Stimulating 101st Show', *Bristol Evening Post*, 6 Nov. 1953.
7. Ibid.
8. Anon., 'What they think of the £765 bronze', *Bristol Evening Post*, 29 Apr. 1954.
9. Ibid.
10. Anon., 'Picture Fair. Catalogue', Institute of Contemporary Arts, London, 1 Dec. 1954, p. 2.
11. Anthony Hill, 19 Aug. 1986.
12. Effie Damoglou, 16 Aug. 1986.
13. Effie Damoglou, 'Aspects of Contemporary English Painting. Catalogue', Parsons Gallery, London, 2 Jan. 1956, p. 1.
14. Ibid.

CHAPTER FIFTEEN
1. George Melhuish, 30 Aug. 1984.
2. Ibid.
3. Charmian Deckers, 15 Aug. 1986.
4. F.W. Brown, 'Melhuish Paintings in Paris Show', *Bristol Evening Post*, Nov. 1954.
5. Anon., 'George Melhuish', *Peinture*, Apr. 1956.
6. Yvonne Hagen, 'Art and Artists. Some non-figurative approaches', *New York Herald Tribune*, Apr. 1956.
7. Ibid.
8. R.C. 'Les Galeries de Paris. Melhuish', *Arts*, Apr. 1956.
9. Ibid.
10. Ibid.
11. GM, 'Paris Exhibition', *Bristol Evening Post*, Apr. 1956.
12. George Melhuish, 30 Aug. 1984.
13. Charmian Deckers to Elsie Melhuish, June 1956.
14. Charmian Deckers, 15 Aug. 1986.
15. Ibid.

CHAPTER SIXTEEN
1. Charmian Deckers, 15 Aug. 1986.
2. Ibid.
3. Dorian Mogg, 18 July 1986.
4. Rosemary King to author, 12 July 1986.
5. Charmian Deckers, 15 Aug. 1986.
6. Percy Edgell, 14 July 1986.
7. Brian Jenkins, 16 July 1986.
8. Ibid.
9. Barbara Thorne, 13 July 1986.
10. Barnes, op. cit., p. 9.
11. Sylvester Houédard to author, 8 Oct. 1987.
12. Eugène Ionesco, *Victimes du devoir*, in *Théâtre*, vol. 1., Gallimard, Paris, 1954, pp. 219–20; and tr. Donald Watson, *Plays*, John Calder, London, 1958, p. 308.
13. Patrick Hughes, op. cit., pp. 2–3.
14. Stéphane Lupasco, *L'Expérience microphysique et la pensée humaine*, Presses Universitaires de France, Paris, 1941, p. 286.
15. Ibid.
16. Erik Lund, Mogens Pihl and Johannes Sløk, *A History of European Ideas*, Hurst, London, 1962, p. 293.
17. Sylvester Houédard to GM, 19 June 1985.

18. Lund, Pihl and Sløk, op. cit., pp. 293–4.
19. Ibid., pp. 295–6.
20. Sylvester Houédard to GM, 19 June 1985.
21. GM, *PNR*, p. xvii.
22. Ibid.
23. GM, *PU*, pp. 9–10.
24. Effie Damoglou, 16 Aug. 1986.
25. GM, '*The Paradoxical Universe*. Blurb', Rankin, Bristol, 1959.
26. Ibid.
27. GM, '*The Paradoxical Universe*. Advertisement', *Times Literary Supplement*, 24 Apr. 1959.

CHAPTER SEVENTEEN

1. Anthony Hill, '*The Paradoxical Universe*', *Art News and Review*, 4 July 1959, p. 7.
2. Ibid.
3. Mike Smith, 'Paradoxically', *Encounter*, Aug. 1959.
4. Ibid.
5. Ibid.
6. Margaret Bean and M. Seton-Karr, 'An Artist-Philosopher's One-Man Show at the Paris Gallery', *To-Morrow's News*, Oct. 1959.
7. GM, *PU*, pp. 114–15.
8. Bean and Seton-Karr, op. cit., Oct. 1959.
9. Jasia Reichardt, 'George Melhuish', *Art News and Review*, 7 Nov. 1959, p. 8.
10. N. Sri Ram, '*The Paradoxical Universe*', *Theosophical News and Notes*, Nov.–Dec. 1959, p. 21.
11. Ibid.
12. GM, *PU*, pp. 142–3.
13. Ibid., pp. 144–5.
14. N. Sri Ram, op. cit., p. 21.
15. Helen Anderson to GM, 29 April 1959.
16. I.J. Good to GM, 28 Apr. 1959.
17. Revd R. Woolley to GM, 6 Apr. 1959.
18. J.O. Wisdom to GM, Jan. 1960.
19. Ian Ramsey to GM, 13 May 1959.
20. Karl Popper to GM, 15 Apr. 1959.
21. Sir Russell Brain to GM, 29 June 1959.
22. Richard Wollheim to GM, 20 Mar. 1959.
23. Stéphane Lupasco to GM, 6 Apr. 1959.
24. Frank Avray Wilson to GM, 23 Apr. 1959.
25. Ibid.

26. James Bomford to GM, 15 Apr. 1959.
27. Ibid., May 1959.
28. Colin Wilson to GM, 13 July 1959, fol. 2.
29. Ibid., fols 2–3.
30. Patrick Hughes, 20 Aug. 1986.
31. Ibid.
32. Patrick Hughes to GM, 24 Sept. 1959.
33. Ibid.
34. Ibid.

CHAPTER EIGHTEEN

1. Anon., 'Bristol Painter's one-man show in London', *Bristol Evening Post*, 19 Oct. 1959.
2. Jasia Reichardt, op. cit., 7 Nov. 1959, p. 8.
3. Ibid.
4. Maurice Carpenter to GM, 1 Nov. 1959.
5. Effie Damoglou, 16 Aug. 1986.
6. Effie Damoglou, *Art and Ideas and their Relation to Life*, Paris Press, London, 1963, p. 1.
7. Brian Jenkins, 16 July 1986.
8. Patrick Hughes, op. cit., p. 2.
9. Max Barnes, op. cit., p. 9.
10. Ibid.
11. Ibid.
12. Ibid.
13. Anon., 'George Melhuish. Paintings, 1941–1962. Catalogue', Royal West of England Academy, Bristol, 10–30 May 1962, p. 2.
14. Vivian Ogilvie, 'George Melhuish. Exhibition', *Round-Up*, BBC Radio, 10 May 1962.
15. Ibid.
16. Valerie Roach, 'Art', *Nonesuch News*, 11 May 1962, p. 7.
17. Ibid.
18. F.W. Brown, 'George Melhuish: a personal memoir', *Western Daily Press*, 14 May 1962.
19. Ibid.
20. Ibid.
21. Richard Blake Brown to GM, 20 May 1962.
22. Anon., 'An Artist's Home', *Bristol Week-End*, 22 Aug. 1962, p. 5.
23. Ibid.
24. 'Blackboy', 'Mood Pictures', *Bristol Evening Post*, 12 Nov. 1963, p. 4.
25. Ibid.

CHAPTER NINETEEN

1. Victoria Ayling to author, 14 Aug. 1986.
2. Ibid.
3. Ibid. to author, 12 Aug. 1987; and to author, 14 Aug. 1986.
4. Ibid., 17 Aug. 1986.
5. Ibid. to author, 14 Aug. 1986.
6. Ibid.
7. Ibid. to author, 12 Aug. 1987.
8. Muriel Ward-Jackson, 7 Jan. 1987.
9. Ibid.
10. GM, *PU*, p. 130.
11. Muriel Ward-Jackson to author, 14 March 1987.
12. George Ward-Jackson to GM, 24 Apr. 1963.
13. GM, *PU*, p. 24.
14. George Ward-Jackson to GM, 24 Apr. 1963.
15. Ibid., ? May 1964.
16. Muriel Ward-Jackson, 7 Jan. 1987.
17. George Ward-Jackson to GM, 21 May 1968.

CHAPTER TWENTY

1. Victoria Ayling to author, 14 Aug. 1986.
2. Eric Toms to GM, 26 July 1964.
3. Eric Toms, 3 Aug. 1986.
4. Ibid.
5. Ibid.
6. Ibid.
7. Anthony Hill, 19 Aug. 1986.
8. George Melhuish, 30 Aug. 1984.
9. Ibid.

CHAPTER TWENTY-ONE

1. Barbara Thorne, 13 July 1986.
2. GM, *St Vincent's Priory. Guide*, Taylor Brothers, Bristol, 1973, p. 1.
3. Ibid., pp. 2–3, 5.
4. Anthony Hill, 19 Aug. 1986.
5. George Melhuish, 30 Aug. 1984.

CHAPTER TWENTY-TWO

1. David Cross, 30 Oct. 1986.
2. James Belsey, 'The Artist who owes a lot to a table knife', *Bristol Evening Post*, 17 Apr. 1971, p. 19.

3. Ibid.
4. Ibid.
5. 'Blackboy', 'Art by the acre', *Bristol Evening Post*, 2 Feb. 1972, p. 4.
6. Anon., 'Bristol Artist's exhibits at City Gallery', *The Citizen*, 4 Feb. 1972.
7. Ibid.
8. Patrick Hughes to GM, 20 Jan. 1969.
9. GM, *PNR*, p. 2 (cover) and cf. p. 82.
10. Ibid.
11. Ibid., p. xviii.
12. Ibid.
13. Ibid., p. 3 (cover).
14. Ibid., pp. xvi, 81.
15. Ibid., p. 27.
16. John Walker, 'Hard Edges', *Studio International*, vol. 187, no. 964, March 1974, pp. 150–1.
17. Ibid., p. 151.
18. Ibid.
19. Ibid.
20. Ibid.
21. GM, *PNR*, p. 52.
22. Ibid., p. 20.
23. Robert Blanché, '*The Paradoxical Nature of Reality*', *Revue Philosophique*, vol. 165, June 1975, p. 180.
24. Eric Toms, '*The Paradoxical Nature of Reality*', *Leonardo*, vol. 8, no. 2, 1975, p. 167.
25. Ibid.
26. Ibid.
27. Ibid.
28. William McRea to GM, 13 Apr. 1974.
29. Ibid.
30. Philip Toynbee to GM, 9 Apr. 1974.
31. Ibid.

CHAPTER TWENTY-THREE

1. Charles Lines, 'Clifton's "Upstairs-Downstairs" House', *Gloucestershire and Avon Life*, July 1975, p. 62.
2. Harry Smith, 'A Stately Semi?', *Western Daily Press*, 30 July 1975, p. 6.
3. George Melhuish and Patrick Hughes, 'Interview', ms., 1974, fol. 3.
4. Ibid., fol. 6.
5. Patrick Hughes and George Brecht, *Vicious Circles and Infinity. A Panoply of Paradoxes*, Cape, London, 1976, p. vii.

6. Ibid., p. 14.
7. Ibid., pp. 84, 86.
8. George Brecht to GM, 12 June 1975.
9. Ibid, 14 Feb. 1976.
10. Lawrence Shaffer to GM, 4 Dec. 1973.
11. J.G. Thieme to GM, 4 Nov. 1975.
12. K.A. Latchford to GM, 10 Feb. 1981.
13. Ibid.
14. Charles Woods to GM, 4 May 1985.
15. Julie Norman, 'Coleridge, Burke and Kant: the Significance of Synthesis as a Metaphor', ms., 1979, fol. 1.
16. Ibid., fol. 12.

CHAPTER TWENTY-FOUR
1. Lucy Irvine, *Runaway*, Penguin, Harmondsworth, 1987, p. 303.
2. Alston Thorne, 'Lucy bared all for her tea and biscuits', *Bristol Evening Post*, 10 Oct. 1983, p. 6.
3. Ibid.
4. Ibid.
5. Deborah Jones, 14 July 1986.
6. Lady Elisabeth Livingstone, 28 Sept. 1986.
7. Marjorie Comfort, 17 July 1986.
8. Andrew Rogers to author, 31 Oct. 1986.

CHAPTER TWENTY-FIVE
1. Sylvester Houédard to Andrew Rogers, 3 Aug. 1987.
2. Sylvester Houédard, 'Oration', 3 Aug. 1987, fol. 1.
3. Ibid., fols 3–4.
4. Ibid., fol. 4.
5. Ibid., fol. 5.
6. Ibid., fols 5–6.
7. GM, 'Death and the Double Meaning of Nothingness', ms., fols 13, 24.
8. Ibid., fols 47, 102.
9. Ibid., fol. 89.
10. Ibid., fol. 92.
11. Ibid., fols 95c, 95f.
12. Ibid., fol. 120.
13. Ibid., fols 122–3.
14. Ibid., fol. 127.
15. Sylvester Houédard, 'Oration', 3 Aug. 1987, fol. 6.

CHAPTER TWENTY-SIX

1. Rita McKerrow, 26 Sept. 1986.
2. Marjorie Comfort, 17 July 1986.
3. GM to the DHSS, 23 Sept. 1980.
4. Muriel Ward-Jackson, 7 Jan. 1987.
5. Barbara Thorne, 13 July 1986.
6. GM, 'Will', 20 Aug. 1981, fol. 4.
7. Ibid.
8. Marjorie Comfort, 17 July 1986.
9. Brian Jenkins, 16 July 1986.
10. Deborah Jones, 14 July 1986.
11. Sylvester Houédard, 'Funeral Service for GM', 19 July 1985, fol. 2.
12. Quoted ibid., fol. 6.
13. Ibid.
14. Sylvester Houédard, 'Oration', 3 Aug. 1987, fol. 1.

INDEX